ULTIMATE GUIDE TO DEFEND YOUR FAITH

ULTIMATE GUIDE SERIES

ULTIMATE GUIDE TO DEFEND YOUR FAITH

DOUG POWELL

HOLMAN®
REFERENCE

BRENTWOOD TENNESSEE

Formerly published as and updated from the *Holman QuickSource Guide to Christian Apologetics* (copyright © 2006 by Doug Powell).

Back matter charts originally published in the CSB Apologetics Study Bible (Copyright © 2017).

Maps © 1998 by Holman Bible Publishers Brentwood, Tennessee
All rights reserved

Typesetting and design by 2K DENMARK, Højbjerg, Denmark

Dewey Decimal Classification: 239
Subject Heading: APOLOGETICS \ CHRISTIANITY--APOLOGETIC WORKS

ISBN: 978-1-5359-5328-3

Printed in China
2 3 4 5 6 7 8 9 • 27 26 25 24 23
RRD

CONTENTS

Introductory Articles
What Is Apologetics? VII
How Apologetics Changed My Life IX

CHAPTER 1: What Is Apologetics? 1
CHAPTER 2: Does God Exist? The Cosmological Argument 13
CHAPTER 3: Does God Exist? The Design Argument 23
CHAPTER 4: Does God Exist? The Moral Argument 34
CHAPTER 5: Which God Exists? 46
CHAPTER 6: Where Did the New Testament Come From? 58
CHAPTER 7: Is the New Testament Reliable? 75
CHAPTER 8: Is the Old Testament Reliable? 88
CHAPTER 9: Do Miracles Happen? 102
CHAPTER 10: What about Prophecy? 119
CHAPTER 11: The Resurrection? 132
CHAPTER 12: Did Jesus Claim to Be God? Is Jesus the Only Way? 151
CHAPTER 13: How Could God Allow Evil? 164
CHAPTER 14: Methodology 175

Back Matter Content
Timeline of Apologists and Notable Works 185
Selected Important Old Testament Archaeological Finds 189
Selected Important New Testament Archaeological Finds 190
Manuscript Authority of the New Testament 191
Naturalism vs. Theism 192
Comparisons of World Religions 193
Comparisons of New Religious Movements 195
Hebrew Kings Chronology 197
Maps 199
Art Credits 204

WHAT IS APOLOGETICS?

BY KENNETH D. BOA

Apologetics may be simply defined as the defense of the Christian faith. The simplicity of this definition, however, masks the complexity of the problem of defining apologetics. It turns out that a diversity of approaches has been taken in defining the meaning, scope, and purpose of apologetics.

The word "apologetics" derives from the Greek word *apologia*, which was originally used as a speech of defense. In ancient Athens it referred to a defense made in the courtroom as part of the normal judicial procedure. After the accusation, the defendant was allowed to refute the charges with a defense (*apologia*). The classic example of an *apologia* was Socrates's defense against the charge of preaching strange gods, a defense retold by his most famous pupil, Plato, in a dialogue called *The Apology*.

The word *apologia* appears 17 times in noun or verb form in the New Testament, and can be translated "defense" or "vindication" in every case. The idea of offering a reasoned defense of the faith is evident in Philippians 1:7,16; and especially 1 Peter 3:15, but no specific theory of apologetics is outlined in the New Testament.

In the second century this general word for "defense" began taking on a narrower sense to refer to a group of writers who defended the beliefs and practices of Christianity against various attacks. These men were known as the *apologists* because of the titles of some of their treatises, but apparently not until 1794 was *apologetics* used to designate a specific theological discipline.

It has become customary to use the term *apology* to refer to a specific effort or work in defense of the faith. An apology might be a written document, a speech, or even a film. Apologists develop their defenses of the Christian faith in relation to scientific, historical, philosophical, ethical, religious, theological, or cultural issues.

We may distinguish four functions of apologetics, though not everyone agrees that apologetics involves all four. Such opinions notwithstanding, all four functions have historically been important in apologetics, and each has been championed by great Christian apologists throughout church history.

The first function may be called *vindication* or *proof*, and involves marshaling philosophical arguments as well as scientific and historical evidences for the Christian faith. The goal of this function is to develop a positive case for Christianity as a belief system that should be accepted. Philosophically, this means drawing out the logical implications of the Christian worldview so that they can be clearly seen and contrasted with alternate worldviews.

The second function is *defense*. This function is closest to the New Testament and early Christian use of the word *apologia*, defending Christianity against the plethora of attacks made against it in every generation by critics of varying belief systems. This function involves clarifying the Christian position in light of misunderstandings and misrepresentations; answering objections, criticisms, or questions from non-Christians; and in general clearing away any intellectual difficulties that nonbelievers claim stand in the way of their coming to faith.

The third function is *refutation* of opposing beliefs. This function focuses on answering the arguments non-Christians give in support of their own beliefs. Most apologists agree that refutation cannot stand alone, since proving a non-Christian religion or philosophy to be false does not prove that Christianity is true. Nevertheless, it is an essential function of apologetics.

The fourth function is *persuasion*. By this we do not mean merely convincing people that Christianity is true, but persuading them to apply its truth to their life. This function focuses on bringing non-Christians to the point of commitment. The apologist's intent is not merely to win an intellectual argument, but to persuade people to commit their lives and eternal futures into the trust of the Son of God who died for them.

HOW APOLOGETICS CHANGED MY LIFE!

BY LEE STROBEL

AUTHOR, THE CASE FOR CHRIST *AND* THE CASE FOR THE REAL JESUS

Skepticism is part of my DNA. That's probably why I ended up combining the study of law and journalism to become the legal editor of The Chicago Tribune—a career in which I relentlessly pursued hard facts in my investigations. And that's undoubtedly why I was later attracted to a thorough examination of the evidence—whether it proved to be positive or negative—as a way to probe the legitimacy of the Christian faith.

A spiritual cynic, I became an atheist in high school. To me the mere concept of an all-loving, all-knowing, all-powerful creator of the universe was so absurd on the surface that it didn't even warrant serious consideration. I believed that God didn't create people, but that people created God out of their fear of death and their desire to live forever in a utopia they called heaven.

I married an agnostic named Leslie. Several years later she came to me with the worst news I thought I could ever get: She had decided to become a follower of Jesus. My initial thought was that she was going to turn into an irrational holy roller who would waste all of her time serving the poor in a soup kitchen somewhere. Divorce, I figured, was inevitable.

Then something amazing occurred. During the ensuing months, I began to see positive changes in her character, her values, and the way she related to me and to the children. The transformation was winsome and attractive. So one day when she invited me to go to church with her, I decided to comply.

The pastor gave a talk called "Basic Christianity" in which he clearly spelled out the essentials of the faith. Did he shake me out of my atheism that day? No, not by a long shot. Still, I concluded that if what he was saying was true, it would have huge implications for my life.

That's when I decided to apply my experience as a journalist to investigating whether there is any credibility to Christianity or any other faith system. I resolved to keep an open mind and follow the evidence wherever it pointed—even if it took me to some uncomfortable conclusions. In a sense, I was checking out the biggest story of my career.

At first, I thought my investigation would be short-lived. In my opinion, having "faith" meant you believed something even though you knew in your heart that it couldn't be true. I anticipated that I would very quickly uncover facts that would devastate Christianity. Yet as I devoured books by atheists and Christians, interviewed scientists and theologians, and studied archaeology, ancient history, and world religions, I was stunned to find that Christianity's factual foundation was a lot firmer than I had once believed.

Much of my investigation focused on science, where more recent discoveries have only further cemented the conclusions that I drew in those studies. For instance, cosmologists now agree that the universe and time itself came into existence at some point in the finite past. The logic is inexorable: Whatever begins to exist has a cause, the universe began to exist, and therefore the universe has a cause. It makes sense that this cause must be immaterial, timeless, powerful, and intelligent.

What's more, physicists have discovered over the last 50 years that many of the laws and constants of the universe—such as the force of gravity and the cosmological constant—are finely tuned to an incomprehensible precision in order for life to exist. This exactitude is so incredible that it defies the explanation of mere chance.

The existence of biological information in DNA also points toward a Creator. Each of our cells contains the precise assembly instructions for every protein out of which our bodies are made, all spelled out in a four-letter chemical alphabet. Nature can produce patterns, but whenever we see information—whether it's in a book or a computer program—we know there's intelligence behind it. Furthermore, scientists are finding complex biological machines on the cellular level that defy a Darwinian explanation and instead are better explained as the work of an Intelligent Designer.

To my great astonishment, I became convinced by the evidence that science supports the belief in a Creator who looks suspiciously like the God of the Bible. Spurred on by my discoveries, I then turned my attention to history.

I found that Jesus, and Jesus alone, fulfilled ancient messianic prophecies against all mathematical odds. I concluded that the New Testament is rooted in eyewitness testimony and that it passes the tests that historians routinely use to determine reliability. I learned that the Bible has been passed down through the ages with remarkable fidelity.

However, the pivotal issue for me was the resurrection of Jesus. Anyone can claim to be the Son of God, as Jesus clearly did. The question was whether Jesus could back up that assertion by miraculously returning from the dead.

One by one, the facts built a convincing and compelling case. Jesus's death by crucifixion is as certain as anything in the ancient world. The accounts of his resurrection are too early to be the product of legendary development. Even the enemies of Jesus conceded that his tomb was empty on Easter morning. And the eyewitness encounters with the risen Jesus cannot be explained away as mere hallucinations or wishful thinking.

All of this just scratches the surface of what I uncovered in my nearly two-year investigation. Frankly, I was completely surprised by the depth and breadth of the case for Christianity. And as someone trained in journalism and law, I felt I had no choice but to respond to the facts.

So on November 8, 1981, I took a step of faith in the same direction that the evidence was pointing—which is utterly rational to do—and became a follower of Jesus. And just like the experience of my wife, over time my character, values, and priorities began to change—for the good.

For me, apologetics proved to be the running point of my life and eternity. I'm thankful for the scholars who so passionately and effectively defend the truth of Christianity—and today my life's goal is to do my part in helping others get answers to the questions that are blocking them in their spiritual journey toward Christ.

CHAPTER 1
WHAT IS APOLOGETICS?

Supermarket or Antidote?

Picture yourself in a vast supermarket that is fully stocked. Yet instead of selling food, this supermarket sells religions. The departments are all the same but have taken on symbolic meaning. For example, the meat department sells Judaism, representing the animal sacrifice needed for blood atonement. The cereal aisle is where Hinduism is found. "A different God in each box! Collect all 330,000,000!" In the baking goods aisle, Islam is for sale since all the other foods started with this stuff but became corrupted when it was baked. New Age religion is found in the candy section; the power behind both is in how appealing they are. Dead religions, beliefs no one holds anymore, such as Greek mythology, Molech worship, and golden calves, are found in the frozen food section. Christianity, with all its scenes in gardens and agricultural parables, is in the produce department. Mind sciences

In charge of the checkout counter is death itself. After your selection is made, you pay with your life. Whether there is anything outside the exit door and what happens there are the big questions.

are available in the magazine aisle. There is a person sitting in an empty shopping cart, pushing him- or herself around the store—a Buddhist.

There is another person who can't find anything in the store at all—an atheist. Some shoppers are strictly vegetarian, some eat only meat, but all the diets are of equal value. They all basically do the same thing—feed you. In charge of the checkout counter is death itself. After your selection is made, you pay with your life. Whether there is anything outside the exit door and what happens there are the big questions.

Is religion really like this, an act of preference where different elements can be mixed and matched at will? Or is religion something entirely different, like an antidote?

Instead of a supermarket, picture yourself in an emergency room with a serious illness. The doctor explains that the illness is 100-percent fatal unless one particular antidote is administered. The doctor then goes on to say that recovery from the illness after taking the antidote has a 100-percent success rate. By this, the doctor is proclaiming that your preferences do not matter at all; they are not a part of the conversation. Whether you like or don't like to get shots or take pills is irrelevant. This particular ailment has a particular remedy that needs to be administered in a particular way. Do it or die.

Given this illness and the necessary treatment, a misdiagnosis is dangerous. No one having a heart attack wants to go to a doctor who thinks the proper response is to put a leg in a cast. Proper treatment is necessary no matter how distasteful, inconvenient, painful, or even offensive. There is no going shopping for the treatment you like best. The remedy is the remedy—period. As the patient, you must conform your thinking to accept the remedy or face the alternative.

The remedy is the remedy—period. As the patient, you must conform your thinking to accept the remedy or face the alternative.

Christianity properly understood is an antidote, not a lifestyle choice or part of a well-balanced religious view. Like an antidote, it can be painful and inconvenient. It can be socially unacceptable. But most of all, it can be offensive. Most of us would much rather take the supermarket approach where we always ended up with a religion tailored to our lifestyles and preferences and could change as we changed.

But we cannot seriously believe like this. As human beings capable of rational thought, we are obliged to conform our beliefs to reality, not the other way around. Not to approach the world in this way is to create dangerous situations. Before attempting to cross a street we must conform our beliefs about current traffic conditions to what we see around us. If we begin crossing the street because we prefer the street to be free of traffic and because it is more

convenient to us, we risk being flattened by a bus. The bus doesn't care what we prefer or what is convenient. It is our responsibility to respond to the facts of the matter, to conform ourselves to them.

To do this, to form beliefs, we must investigate the world and its issues to discover facts and truths about them. This process, which we all employ, is useful for one simple reason: truth is true whether you believe it or don't. Truth does not require belief in order to be true, but it does deserve to be believed.

Spiritually speaking, we must gain an understanding of our situation to be able to understand why an antidote is necessary. It is the goal of the law of God to give us that understanding, that diagnosis, and the goal of the gospel of Jesus Christ to provide the antidote. Jesus is not just a cherry-flavored cough syrup that works just as well as the lemon-flavored Buddha. Belief in Jesus is an extremely invasive heart procedure that brings people to life. And it is the only procedure that will work.

But as human beings who would rather be in the supermarket, we must be persuaded to go to the emergency room. We have many objections, barriers, biases, acculturations, conditions, misconceptions, presuppositions, distortions of facts, and any number of excuses. It is the goal of Christian apologetics to remove these hindrances that stand between a person and the cross of Christ.

Truth is true whether you believe it or don't. Truth does not require belief in order to be true, but it does deserve to be believed.

As a result, some Christians see apologetics as pre-evangelism; it is not the gospel, but it prepares the soil for the gospel.[1] Others make no such distinction, seeing apologetics, theology, philosophy, and evangelism as deeply entwined facets of the gospel.[2] Whatever its relation to the gospel, apologetics is an extremely important enterprise that can profoundly impact unbelievers and be used as the tool that clears the way to faith in Jesus Christ.

Whatever its relation to the gospel, apologetics is an extremely important enterprise that can profoundly impact unbelievers and be used as the tool that clears the way to faith in Jesus Christ.

Apologetics Is for Believers as Well

For some, though, apologetics is not discovered until after making a profession of faith. Many Christians did not come to believe as a result of investigating the authority of the Bible, the evidence for the resurrection, or as a response to the philosophical arguments for God's existence. They simply responded to the proclamation of the gospel. Although these people have reasons for their belief, they are deeply personal reasons that often do not make sense to unbelievers. They know the truth but are not necessarily equipped to share or articulate the truth in a way that is understandable to those who

have questions about their faith. It is quite possible to believe something is true without having a proper understanding of it or the ability to articulate it.

Christians who believe but don't know why are often insecure and comfortable only around other Christians. Defensiveness can quickly surface when challenges arise on issues of faith, morality, and truth because of a lack of information regarding the rational grounds for Christianity. At its worst this can lead to either a fortress mentality or a belligerent faith, precisely the opposite of the Great Commission Jesus gave in Matt. 28:19-20. The charge of the Christian is not to withdraw from the world and lead an insular life. Rather, we are to be engaged in the culture, to be salt and light.

The solution to this problem is for believers to become informed in doctrine, the history of their faith, philosophy, logic, and other disciplines as they relate to Christianity. They need to know the facts, arguments, and theology and understand how to employ them in a way that will effectively engage the culture. In short, the answer is Christian apologetics.

The solution to this problem is for believers to become informed in doctrine, the history of their faith, philosophy, logic, and other disciplines as they relate to Christianity.

One of the first tasks of Christian apologetics is to provide information. A number of widely held assumptions about Christianity can be easily challenged with a little information. This is even true for persons who are generally well educated. C. S. Lewis had always believed the Gospels were collections of myths like those of Balder, Adonis, and Bacchus. Lewis held this view until he first read the Gospels at age thirty-one. Having read as many myths and legends as he had, Lewis recognized that what was in the Gospels did not fit this literary genre. The Gospels were simple eyewitness accounts of historical events, lacking the artistry of ancient myths.

Other assumptions widely held in our culture can be challenged by both information and argument:

- Jesus never lived.
- You can't prove God exists.
- There are no such things as miracles.
- There is no evidence that Jesus rose from the dead.
- The Bible wasn't written until hundreds of years after the life of Jesus.
- What about the books that got left out of the Bible?
- All religions basically teach the same thing.
- If the God of the Bible is real, how could he allow evil to exist?
- What's true for you is true for you; what's true for me is true for me.
- Christianity is unreasonable.

This is just a sample of the challenges and questions that apologetics training equips believers to answer. And it does so in three ways. First, it shows that while Christian faith cannot be proven by reason, Christian faith isn't irrational—contrary to reason. This is important because it demonstrates that Christianity is not simply personal preference, a function of how one was raised, or a worldview supported only by emotional considerations. Second, it answers objections against the faith and seeks to remove misconceptions. Third, Christian apologetics not only provides evidence and arguments for Christianity but demonstrates the weaknesses of atheism and other belief systems logically incompatible with historic Christian faith. It offers something far better to replace these worldviews.

The results of training in apologetics are boldness, security, and a lack of defensiveness.

The results of training in apologetics are boldness, security, and a lack of defensiveness. Apologetics enables the believer to engage the world without acquiescing to it and without compromise. Much as the antidote mentioned above that one must understand a virus or poison in order to counteract it, so must Christians understand and recognize the fatal flaws of unbelieving thought, be able to expose them, and provide a more adequate worldview. These are the tasks of apologetics.

Apologetics in the Bible

Some believers are suspicious of and opposed to apologetics. They view it as being contrary to faith. They fear that if Christianity can be shown to be reasonable, then there is no place for faith. This anti-intellectual approach to Christianity is rooted in a misunderstanding of the word "faith" itself.

The word translated as "faith" and "belief" in the New Testament is *pistis*. Pistis encompasses a number of ideas, all of them revolving around an intentional, engaged trust.

Definitions include "firm persuasion, the conviction . . . a firmly relying confidence."[3] Lawrence O. Richards notes, "*Pistis* and related words deal with relationships established by trust and maintained by trustworthiness."[4] When we trust something, we have reasons for it, evidence that justifies and supports it.

A claim is not true just because we believe it or untrue because we don't believe it. First, we assess the evidence and reasons for its truth. Next, we weigh the evidence to determine how well supported these claims are. Finally, we trust; we exercise faith based on the weight of the evidence. Faith is not Christian-branded hoping or wishing. Those who embrace other belief systems incompatible with Christianity will often follow this same process. The difference comes down to how each assesses the evidence for its position as well as others. Faith is the product of investigation and deliberation, and reason is its grounding and its backbone, not its enemy.[5]

On the other hand, to believe in something without first seriously reflecting on it or looking into it is not an act of faith; it is an act of foolishness. It is not, as some have held, a virtue to believe something without evidence or reason. Those who say, "You just have to have faith," are really proclaiming they have no idea what faith is. The whole point of Christianity is not that we have faith; that is no different from any other religion or worldview. If having faith were the goal, all would be saved since everyone believes something. No, faith itself is not the object. In fact, what differentiates religions is the object of each faith. The content of faith ultimately is what matters. And the content of a faith is what must be investigated and then embraced or rejected.

Christian apologetics is neither a new practice nor unbiblical. In fact, it is not only modeled in the New Testament, but it is also commanded. The Greek word *apologia*, which is where we get our word "apologetics," is used to describe a defense, as in a legal defense or making a case.[6] In the New Testament, it is translated as "defense" or "vindication" as in the following verses:

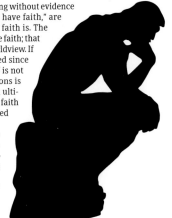

"Brothers and fathers, listen now to my defense before you." —Paul before a Jewish crowd as he was arrested in the temple, Acts 22:1

"It is right for me to think this way about all of you, because I have you in my heart, and you are all partners with me in grace, both in my imprisonment and in the defense and confirmation of the gospel. —Paul, Phil. 1:7

"I am appointed for the defense of the gospel." —Paul, Phil. 1:16b

"But in your hearts regard Christ the Lord as holy, ready at any time to give a defense to anyone who asks you for a reason for the hope that is in you. Yet do this with gentleness and respect, keeping a clear conscience, so that when you are accused, those who disparage your good conduct in Christ will be put to shame." —Peter to suffering Christians in what is modern-day Turkey, 1 Pet. 3:15-16

The idea of apologetics is assumed in the exhortation of Jude 3 when he tells believers to "contend for the faith."

In Acts 17:22-34, we see a picture of Paul practicing apologetics in Athens on Mars Hill.

> Paul stood in the middle of the Areopagus and said: "People of Athens! I see that you are extremely religious in every respect. For as I was passing through and observing the objects of your worship, I even found an altar on which was inscribed: 'TO AN UNKNOWN GOD.'
>
> "Therefore, what you worship in ignorance, this I proclaim to you. The God who made the world and everything in it— he is Lord of heaven and earth—does not live in shrines made by hands. Neither is he served by human hands, as though he needed anything, since he himself gives everyone life and breath and all things. From one man he has made every nationality to live over the whole earth and has determined their appointed times and the boundaries of where they live. He did this so that they might seek God, and perhaps they might reach out and find him, though he is not far from each one of us. For in him we live and move and have our being, as even some of your own poets have said, 'For we are also his offspring.' Since we are God's offspring then, we shouldn't think that the divine nature is like gold or silver or stone, an image fashioned by human art and imagination.
>
> "Therefore, having overlooked the times of ignorance, God now commands all people everywhere to repent, because he has set a day when he is going to judge the world in righteousness by the man he has appointed.
>
> "He has provided proof of this to everyone by raising him from the dead."
>
> When they heard about the resurrection of the dead, some began to ridicule him, but others said, "We'd like to hear from you again about this." So Paul left their presence. However, some people joined him and believed, including Dionysius the Areopagite, a woman named Damaris, and others with them.

This led him to argue for the faith in two ways. First, Paul found common ground in the fact that his audience believed in some form of religion. The problem, according to Paul, was

that they believed in something false, not that they believed in nothing. They had a religious worldview, but it was full of holes. Knowing the egregious flaws in their religious systems, he made a case for Christianity as a belief system in which there is coherence between the Power that created and sustains the universe and the sense of justice widely prevalent in Greek society.

Second, Paul argued based on facts that could be investigated by anyone who was interested. He recognized that if Christianity were true, it must be rooted in facts. Paul saw the contact point in the historical, physical, and temporal aspects of the life of Jesus. Jesus was a real person who did and said certain things in certain places at certain times. Witnesses to Jesus's life and teaching could be found and questioned regarding these things.

Jesus's reality—his historicity—is the foundation of Christianity. Without it, there is no Christianity. Paul was so sure of this foundation that he went so far as to point out the most vulnerable claim of the Christian faith:

> Now if Christ is proclaimed as raised from the dead, how can some of you say, "There is no resurrection of the dead"? If there is no resurrection of the dead, then not even Christ has been raised; and if Christ has not been raised, then our proclamation is in vain, and so is your faith. Moreover, we are found to be false witnesses about God, because we have testified wrongly about God that he raised up Christ—whom he did not raise up, if in fact the dead are not raised. For if the dead are not raised, not even Christ has been raised. And if Christ has not been raised, your faith is worthless; you are still in your sins. Those, then, who have fallen asleep in Christ have also perished. If we have put our hope in Christ for this life only, we should be pitied more than anyone. (1 Cor. 15:12-19)

If Jesus did not live, do, and say the things claimed by the apostles, then Christianity is false. If there is a better explanation for the resurrection, then Christians are simply wasting their time.

By pointing out this vulnerability, Paul was really pointing out the strength of Christianity. So convinced was he of the historicity and verifiability of the resurrection, the event that confirmed the claims of Jesus, that he pointed out how to prove it false—almost as a challenge. Christian claims can be investigated and tested. This challenge has no parallel in other religions. No other sacred text shows how to destroy its own claims.

The church fathers showed they understood the importance of Jesus's historicity when they crafted the Nicene Creed, the universally accepted creed of the church. The creed says, "For our sake he was crucified under Pontius Pilate; he suffered death and was buried." Why mention Pontius Pilate? What doctrine is based on him? The answer is none; there is no doctrine based on Pilate. He is mentioned to remind us that these were real events happening to a real person at a particular point in history.

Many critics of the New Testament understood this and used it as a point of attack, saying that Pilate never even existed, that there was no evidence of Pilate outside the New Testament. That changed in 1961 because of an archaeological find at Caesarea Maritima. A team of Italian archaeologists were excavating the theater there and found an inscribed stone that

Inscription on the Pilate Stone

had been repurposed to be used in a repair. Some of the inscription was still legible and gave the names of Tiberius and Pontius Pilate, as well as the title Prefect of Judea.[7] As a result, the historicity of Pontius Pilate is no longer questioned.

Behind Paul's bold approach is a logic and coherence that empowered him because he understood the importance of the intellect as it relates to faith. The importance of the life of the mind was directly addressed by Jesus himself when he quoted the greatest commandment, which is found in Deuteronomy. In Matt. 22:37, Jesus said, "Love the Lord your God with all your heart, with all your soul, and with all your mind." The Christian life is a balance of the intellect, emotions, and experience. God is the object on which they should all be focused, in which reason is grounded, and that which gives the world coherency and meaning.

The importance of the life of the mind was directly addressed by Jesus himself when he quoted the greatest commandment, which is found in Deuteronomy. In Matt. 22:37, Jesus said, "Love the Lord your God with all your heart, with all your soul, and with all your mind."

Use and Abuse

Two things need to be made clear at this point regarding the use of apologetics. First, the goal of Christian apologetics is not to win an argument at all costs. It is quite possible to win an argument but do it in such a way that it reflects badly on the gracious love of Jesus Christ. Christians are to speak truth in this world, and apologetics is one way believers do that. God could choose to make himself known by knocking everyone to the ground for a few days, as he did Paul. Instead God uses his people as his agents. And as his agents, Christians need to speak the truth in love. Sometimes this calls for using well-formed argument.

Second, it is the work of the Holy Spirit to save people; it is the work of the Christian to bear witness to the truth. The Holy Spirit takes such witness and uses it to open the minds

and hearts of those who listen. An apologist is never going to argue someone into the kingdom. Christians need to do their job in an informed and gracious way and try not to add any offense or stumbling block to the gospel.

The vast majority of Christian apologetics is done every day through casual conversation, not in classrooms or debates that can seem to be detached from any personal relevance. It is here that we discuss and attempt to make sense of the issues of life. And it is for such spontaneous conversations that Christians need to be prepared.

> The Christian worldview is not proven in one or two strokes, but is rather verified by appealing to a wide and compelling variety of converging arguments. Christianity is shown to be the best explanation for origin and nature of the universe as well as the human condition and the facts of history. Moreover, Christians must be pastoral in their apologetic practices. We must care deeply for the lost, not simply desire to defeat their arguments. The stakes are too high for apologetic one-upmanship.[8]
> —*Douglas Groothius*

Tollers and Jack

A good example of an informed, gracious Christian's participation in the salvation of another took place on September 19, 1931, at Magdalen College, Oxford. That evening three men were strolling along Addison's Walk. One man, Jack, was a longtime atheist who had recently embraced theism but had many objections to Christianity. The other two men were Christians. They shared a common interest in mythology and that night were discussing what gave myths their truth. "Tollers," one of the Christians, argued that the truth of myth is the degree to which it reflects the story of Jesus. He then went on to explain and argue for the truthfulness of Christianity. The conversation continued into the early morning back in Jack's room.

The arguments and manner of Tollers and Hugo Dyson, the third friend, had a profound impact on Jack. Twelve days later, Jack wrote in a letter, "I have just passed on from believing in God to definitely believing in Christ—in Christianity. . . . My long night talk with Dyson and Tolkien had a good deal to do with it."[9]

Jack had committed himself intellectually and spiritually to Jesus. Over the next thirty years Jack grew to become the most popular Christian apologist of the twentieth century. Jack was the nickname of C. S. Lewis, author of not only apologetics works, but also of novels for both children and adults as well as works in his academic specialty—medieval and renaissance literature.

C.S. Lewis

J. R. R. Tolkien

Tollers went on to incorporate his ideas about myth into his own elaborate mythology. His works of fantasy are now widely regarded as the greatest works of the fantasy genre. Tollers was the nickname of J. R. R. Tolkien, the author of *The Lord of the Rings* trilogy as well as *The Hobbit*.

Tolkien and Dyson had no way of knowing, of course, what impact that conversation would have, or even that the conversation on their walk would turn to that subject. But they were prepared to respond when the subject did arise. And who knows how many others they helped in the same way.

> I have just passed on from believing in God to definitely believing in Christ—in Christianity. . . . My long night talk with Dyson and Tolkien had a good deal to do with it.[10]
> —C. S. Lewis

Conclusion

In light of the command to be able to give a defense for the truth that is within us and to love God with all our minds, we must equip ourselves with the facts, evidence, and arguments for Christianity. We must equip ourselves with a knowledge of the culture we live in and a will to engage it. And we must equip ourselves with a manner that can administer an antidote effectively. We are not to be clanging gongs but as the most beautiful music—welcoming, infectious, and irresistible.

To begin this training, we will start by assuming nothing. Before we can talk about Christianity, we must be able to show that

In light of the command to be able to give a defense for the truth that is within us and to love God with all our minds, we must equip ourselves with the facts, evidence, and arguments for Christianity.

Addison's Walk at Oxford—one of C. S. Lewis's favorite paths

God exists, period. But can we reasonably believe that God exists? And if God does exist, which religion describes him most accurately? The next section looks at several arguments for God's existence and his attributes. We will then compare our discoveries with how God is viewed by a variety of religions.

Notable Quote

When people see this—our love for one another and our unity through love—then they will in turn be drawn by this to Christ and will respond to the gospel's offer of salvation. More often than not, it is what you are rather than what you say that will bring an unbeliever to Christ.

This, then, is the ultimate apologetic. For the ultimate apologetic is: your life.[11]
—*William Lane Craig*

Notes

1. Norman Geisler and Ron Brooks, *When Skeptics Ask* (Grand Rapids: Baker Books, 1996), 11.
2. Greg Bahnsen, *Van Til's Apologetic* (Phillipsburg, NJ: Presbyterian & Reformed, 1998), 43.
3. Ethelbert W. Bullinger, *A Critical Lexicon and Concordance to the English and Greek New Testament* (Grand Rapids: Zondervan, 1975, 1978), 271.
4. Lawrence O. Richards, *Expository Dictionary of Bible Words* (Grand Rapids: Zondervan, 1985), 116.
5. The issue of where reason comes from or why it has force is mentioned in chap. 14.
6. Cp. Bullinger, *Critical Lexicon,* 212.
7. Josh McDowell, *A Ready Defense* (Nashville: Thomas Nelson, 1993), 111–12.
8. Douglas Groothuis, *The Denver Journal* 2 (1999).
9. Roger Lancelyn Green and Walter Hooper, *C. S. Lewis: A Biography* (New York: Harcourt Brace, 1974, 1994), 116–18.
10. Ibid., 116.
11. William Lane Craig, *Reasonable Faith* (Wheaton, IL: Crossway, 1984, 1994), 301–2.

CHAPTER 2
DOES GOD EXIST?
THE COSMOLOGICAL ARGUMENT

Definitions

The cosmological argument for the existence of God tries to show that because anything exists there must be a God who brought it into existence. In other words, without a God to create it, nothing could or would exist. It is possible for God to exist without the universe, but it is not possible for the universe to exist without God. Thus the cosmological argument tries to show that the universe is not a necessary being and therefore cannot account for its own existence. The thrust of the argument is to show that the universe was caused by some agent that was neither part of the universe nor itself was caused.

The word "cosmos" is a Greek word that refers to everything that exists—the universe itself and all its constituents.

We will look at each of these philosophical arguments as well as at a scientific example of the cosmological argument in the real world.

There are three basic kinds of cosmological arguments: Kalam, Thomist, and Leibnizian.

It is possible for God to exist without the universe, but it is not possible for the universe to exist without God.

Distant Spiral Galaxy—Jeffrey Newman (Univ. of California at Berkeley) and NASA.

The Kalam Cosmological Argument

This argument was first formulated by Christian philosophers, but it was not until medieval Islamic thinkers devoted attention to the argument that it found its full force.[1] Kalam is an Arabic word meaning "talk" or "speech." Its connotation, however, is much

The Kalam argument tries to show that the universe is not eternal—that it had to have a beginning.

broader and encompasses something closer to philosophy or theology.[2]

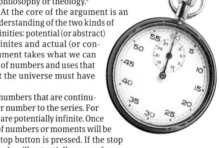

At the core of the argument is an understanding of the two kinds of infinities: potential (or abstract) infinites and actual (or concrete) infinites. The Kalam argument takes what we can know about these infinite series of numbers and uses that knowledge to demonstrate that the universe must have had a beginning.

Potential infinites are sets of numbers that are continually increasing by adding another number to the series. For example, seconds on a stopwatch are potentially infinite. Once the start button is pressed, a set of numbers or moments will be generated (1, 2, 3, etc.) until the stop button is pressed. If the stop button is never pressed, the seconds will potentially accrue forever.

However, potential infinites are never actually infinite. A potential infinite is always a finite set of numbers to which another increment can be added. It will never reach a point where it becomes infinite no matter how long it is added to.

Actual infinites are sets of numbers to which no increment can be added since, by nature of their infiniteness, the set includes all numbers—there is nothing to add. If this is hard to imagine, there is good reason: actual infinites do not exist and cannot exist in the physical world. If actual infinites did exist in the physical world, we would see absurdities and effects we could not live with, literally.

For instance, let's say you had a compact disc collection that was infinitely large, and each CD had an infinite number of songs on it. If you listened to one CD, you hear as much music as if you had listened to all of the CDs—an infinite amount— and yet those infinites are of different sizes—a nonsensical notion. Let's also say that there were only two artists in your CD collection, Bach and the Beatles, and that every second CD was by the Beatles. This would mean that you had as many Beatles CDs as you would Beatles and Bach CDs combined; they would both be an infinite number. But at the same time they would be different-sized infinites. And would the number of Beatles CDs be odd or even? It must be one or the other, but to speak of infinity in such a way is irrational.

Or imagine a racecar driver and his son. The racecar driver is making circuit after circuit on a track a mile long. Meanwhile in the infield, his three-year-old son is on his tricycle going in circles. The son is completing a dozen or so circuits to his dad's one. But if they had each been going for an infinite amount of time, they would have completed an equal number of circuits!

If this makes your brain hurt or is confusing at all, then you are beginning to understand why actual infinites do not exist in the physical world. These examples are not just interesting brain teasers or puzzles. The fact that if X = Y, then X cannot also be twelve times greater than Y is extremely important. You would never want to cross a bridge, ride in a car, or live in a house designed by an engineer who didn't recognize or didn't care about the absurdities of actual infinites.

This demonstration of the nonexistence of actual infinites can be applied in two real-world areas, time and causality. The best way to show that time is not infinite, that it had a beginning, is to observe that there is a "now." If now exists, then time cannot be infinite. To show this, picture the moment "now" as a destination, like a train station. Then picture time as train tracks that are actually infinitely long. If you were a passenger waiting on the train to arrive, how long would you have to wait? The answer is: forever. You can never reach the end of infinity; thus, infinitely long train tracks cannot ever be crossed. There is no end to arrive at, no station. If infinitely long train tracks could be crossed, they would be the equivalent of a one-ended stick, a nonsensical notion. In fact, this is the opposite limitation of potential infinites. Just as potential infinites are finite numbers that can never turn infinite, actual infinites could never reach the end of their infiniteness and turn finite. But there is an end, a "now"; the train did arrive at the station. This means the tracks of time cannot be infinitely long. There cannot be an infinite number of preceding moments prior to the present moment. The past is not an actual infinite. Thus, time had to have a beginning.

Time, however, did not cause itself to spring into existence. If it had a beginning, then something initiated it. This is where causality comes into the picture. There is no such thing as an effect that was not caused. You are an effect of the biological process caused by your parents. These words you now read were caused by my typing on a keyboard. The current state of the universe is an effect caused by various astronomical and physical conditions. Note, however, that each of the causes mentioned is also an effect. For example, your parents are not only your cause, but they are the effects of their parents who were the effects of their parents, and so on. But, as the nonexistence of actual infinites shows, the chain of causes cannot regress forever. The train station in this case is made of present causes; because we have causes now, there must be a beginning to the sequence. Thus there must be a cause that is not an effect, an uncaused cause, or first cause. Since the universe is an effect, it must have had a cause itself.

The Kalam argument tells us that the universe had a beginning and that the beginning was caused by an uncaused cause. At this point there are only two options: either the cause was personal or it was impersonal. Reflection on what this uncaused cause would look like leads us to a conclusion rather quickly. The first cause would require an ability to create. Without this ability, nothing could be created. It would also require an intention to create, a will to initiate the universe. Without this will to create, nothing would be created. It would require a noncontingent being, one whose existence depends on nothing but itself. If it were contingent, then it would simply be one more effect in the chain of causes and effects. And it must be transcendent. The cause of the universe must be outside of and apart from the universe. Now add all these things together. What kind of thing

- relies on nothing for its existence,
- has the power to create something from nothing,
- has a will to do it or not do it, and
- has the characteristic of existing outside of the creation?

Does this sound like a personal or impersonal being? Personal, of course. Thus the Kalam argument brings us to the conclusion that the universe had a beginning that was caused by a personal, powerful, transcendent being.

A question that frequently arises at this point has to do with God's infinite characteristics.

When we speak of God's infinite characteristics, we are speaking in more of a metaphorical manner. We do not mean that God has an infinitely large quantity of goodness and love with which he funds his grace and mercy. We mean he is the ultimate embodiment of goodness and love. These characteristics are without measure and speak to the quality of his character, not the quantity of his characteristics.

If there is no such thing as an actual infinite, then how can God be infinitely good or loving?

The Thomist Cosmological Argument

In the thirteenth century, Thomas Aquinas gave three forms of the cosmological argument in his *Summa Theologica* as a part of his "five ways" of proving the existence of God. He wrote:

> Since nature works for a determinate end under the direction of a higher agent, whatever is done by nature must be traced back to God, as to its first cause. So also, whatever is done voluntarily must also be traced back to some higher cause other than human reason or will, since these can change and fail. For all things that are changeable and capable of defect must be traced back to an immovable and self-necessary first principle.[3]

Aquinas first tried to demonstrate God's existence from motion. Motion is an effect and, as such, needs a cause. According to Aquinas, "whatever is moved must be moved by another."[4] This chain of one thing moving another that moves another cannot regress infinitely.

Whatever is moved must be moved by another.

As we have shown above, this is impossible. There must be a first cause that sets all others into motion—an unmoved mover. Although everything may be fully capable of functioning, without a first, uncaused cause to initiate the action, everything would remain idle and useless. Without the unmoved mover to open the lid, the universe would become like a wound music box that remained forever closed, motionless, and silent. Furthermore, to suggest the music box needs no unmoved mover to open the lid is to suggest that the wood and metal assembled themselves into the music box without the need of a craftsman. This first cause or unmoved mover is what we call God.

Aquinas employed a variation of this argument to arrive at his second proof. This argument, rather than being based on motion, is based on existence or what he calls "efficient cause."[5] Everything that comes into existence owes its existence to something else. There is nothing that brings itself into existence or causes itself. Thus existence is an effect of a cause that is itself an effect of a cause, and so on. But once again we cannot trace this lineage of causes back infinitely. There must be a first cause to explain why any cause exists. This first cause must be a self-existent being that

Thomas Aquinas (1225/27–1274) from *The Demidoff Altarpiece* by Carlo Crivelli.

does not rely on anything for existence. This self-existent, non-contingent being is called God.

Third, Aquinas based an argument on the possibility of existence. Nothing we see in the universe has to exist. Everything we see could just as well not have existed. This makes everything that exists simply possible, not necessary. But something does exist. "Therefore," says Aquinas, "not all beings are merely possible, but there must exist something the existence of which is necessary."[6] Thus we know that a necessary being must exist to account for the possible beings that do exist; it makes the possible beings possible. A being that is necessary for the existence of all things is called God.

> *Everything that comes into existence owes its existence to something else.*

The Leibnizian Cosmological Argument

This is the famous question of philosopher G. W. F. von Leibniz, whose cosmological argument took a slightly different approach than Aquinas's. Instead of arguing from cause itself, Leibniz argued there must be a sufficient reason for the existence of the universe.

> *"Not all beings are merely possible, but there must exist something the existence of which is necessary."*

Leibniz bought into Aquinas's arguments regarding cause but saw that they did not address the why of the cause. Things that are caused and states of affairs do not just happen without reason. And in the same way that everything that is caused has a prior cause, Leibniz observed that everything that exists has a reason outside of and prior to its existence. And just as there can be no infinite chain of causes, there can be no infinite chain of reasons. Thus the universe cannot provide a sufficient explanation for its own existence or state of affairs. The only sufficient reason must be found outside of the universe in a being whose existence is "self-explanatory . . . (and) logically necessary."[8] And this being is who we call God.

> *"Why is there something rather than nothing?"[7]*

Scientific Arguments

There are a number of examples of how these various forms of the cosmological argument play out in the real world. The second law of thermodynamics, for instance, is often used as an illustration.[9] However, the best and most easily understood example may be the big bang theory.

> *Just as there can be no infinite chain of causes, there can be no infinite chain of reasons.*

In the 1920s, astronomer Edwin Hubble discovered that our universe was bigger than previously thought. In fact, it was much bigger. Until he saw outside our galaxy, the prevailing thought was that our galaxy was the entire universe. Hubble was the first to recognize that ours was only one of billions of galaxies.

Late in the decade, he was studying the light from distant galaxies and found it was not what he expected it to look like. The light he saw did not correspond to any known element or combination of elements. Then he noticed the light was uniformly shifted to the red side of the spectrum. All the characteristics he expected were still there, just at a slightly different location on the color spectrum, the red end. This phenomenon became known as the red shift.

Star cluster photo:
NASA

Edwin Hubble, 1949

Hubble found an explanation for the red shift by applying the Doppler effect. The Doppler effect says that if sound is emitted from an object moving toward you, the sound waves are compressed or shortened. The shortening of the wavelength increases the pitch of the sound; it is shifted to a relatively higher place on the register. The farther away the object is as it moves toward you, the shorter the wavelength and the higher the pitch. Conversely, if the object is moving away from you, the sound waves are lengthened. The lengthening of the wavelength decreases the pitch, shifting the sound to a relatively lower spot on the register.

The Doppler effect is what describes the change in pitch you hear in sirens from ambulances. As the ambulance gets closer to you, the sound you hear drops toward its natural pitch. When it is next to you, you hear the siren at its natural pitch. As the ambulance gets farther away, the siren drops progressively lower than its natural pitch.

The Doppler effect says that if sound is emitted from an object moving toward you, the sound waves are compressed or shortened.

The Doppler effect can also apply to light waves, and this is just what Hubble did to solve the mystery. The blue end of the light spectrum is composed of the shorter wavelengths, while the red end is composed of the longer wavelengths. Everywhere he looked in the universe, he saw a red shift in the light. This meant the objects emitting the light—stars—are all moving away from each other. Thus the universe is expanding.

Other scientists took this discovery and built on it. If the universe is expanding, it must have a point of origin from which it was expanding. Other discoveries were made that showed the expansion is slower now than it was when it began—like an explosion. This explosion became known as the big bang, the beginning of the universe.

The Doppler effect can also apply to light waves, and this is just what Hubble did to solve the mystery.

The two primary challengers of the big bang theory are the steady state theory and the oscillating theory. The steady state theory argues the universe has always existed and always will exist. Not only do the observations that support the big bang militate against this view, but it would require the existence of actual infinites. The fact that there is a now makes the theory of an infinite number of preceding moments an impossibility.

The oscillating theory says that the universe will eventually stop expanding and contract back to a singularity that will then explode and continue a cycle that will forever repeat. Again, the theory would require the existence of actual infinites, a series without beginning or end. But since we exist in the current oscillation, there must be a start to the cycle. The other limiting factor is the second law of thermodynamics. The energy in the universe is

NASA, ESA, and The Hubble Heritage Team (STScI/AURA)

not infinite. Just as a rubber ball bounces lower and faster with each bounce until it stops, an oscillating universe would eventually run down. Again, an oscillating universe must have a beginning.

The big bang remains the best explanation for the current state of the universe. But if the big bang was an explosion, why did it explode? What exploded and where did it come from? Explosions are effects and effects need causes; they do not cause themselves. The cause of the big bang is not to be found in the physical universe, because that is precisely what exploded. Also, the matter that exploded did not create itself. The nonexistence of actual infinites shows that matter cannot be eternal.

If the universe is expanding, it must have a point of origin from which it was expanding . . . like an explosion.

Because the universe had a beginning, something must have initiated it. It did not start itself. The cause of the universe must be found outside of the universe; it must be transcendent. The cause must be powerful to create the entire universe *ex nihilo*, out of nothing. The cause must not be an effect but is an uncaused cause. Otherwise we would fall into a nonsensical chain of infinite regress. And this cause must not rely on anything else for its existence; it must be non-contingent—or necessary.

This explosion became known as the big bang, the beginning of the universe.

Note that this description describes only what is necessary for the big bang to work. But if there is such an entity as the one described, it is still not sufficient for the creation of the universe. Just because this entity does exist does not mean the universe must exist. Something is still missing—intentionality, a will to make it happen.

Because the universe had a beginning, something must have initiated it. It did not start itself. The cause of the universe must be found outside of the universe; it must be transcendent.

A car that has a working engine, a healthy battery, a properly connected electrical system to start the engine, and is full of gas has all the necessary conditions for running. Yet parking lots are full of cars that have the necessary conditions but are not running. Although they have the necessary conditions, they lack sufficient conditions. Cars that are moving down the street have necessary and sufficient conditions for running; that is why they are moving. What do the moving cars have that the parked cars do not? They have

drivers. And what is a driver? It is a being that is not part of the car, that has the power to start the car, that does not rely on the car for its existence, does not rely on anything outside itself to be able to operate the car, and has the will to start and direct the car. And if particularly clever, the drive may have even built the car.

Thus the universe needs a driver, an intelligent agent that is capable of choosing whether to create the universe or not. This necessary and sufficient cause of the universe is what we call God.

Conclusion

The cosmological argument has a long history and is employed effectively by numerous religions. It does not seek to show all of the attributes and characteristics of God, only that God does exist. But while the argument does not show which of those religions is true, it does expose several religions and worldviews being incompatible with the features of the universe that the cosmological argument brings to light. These will be examined in chapter 5. Islam, Judaism, and Christianity, however, hold a view of God that is compatible with the characteristics of our universe on which the cosmological argument is based.

> *The universe needs a driver, an intelligent agent that is capable of choosing whether to create the universe or not.*

Notable Quote

Do not be afraid of being free thinkers! If you think strongly enough you will be forced by science to the belief in God, which is the foundation of all religion. You will find science not antagonistic but helpful to religion.[10]

—*Sir William Thompson, a.k.a. Lord Kelvin*

Composite radio light image and rendition of our galaxy as seen in visible light. Image composite by Ingrid Kallick of Possible Designs, Madison, Wisconsin. The background Milky Way image is a drawing made at Lund Observatory. High-velocity clouds are from the survey done at Dwingeloo Observatory (Hulsbosch & Wakker, 1988).

Notes

1   William Lane Craig, *Reasonable Belief* (Wheaton, IL: Crossway, 1984, 1994), 80.

2   J. P. Moreland, *Scaling the Secular City* (Grand Rapids: Baker, 1987), 18.

3   Thomas Aquinas, *Great Books of the Western World*, vol. 19, *Summa Theologica* (Chicago: Encyclopedia Britannica, 1952), 14.

4   Ibid., 13.

5   Ibid.

6   Ibid.

7   G. F. W. von Leibniz, "Nature and Grace," in *Leibniz Selections*, ed. P. Weirner (New York: Scribner's, 1951), 527; quoted in Craig, *Reasonable Belief*, 83.

8   Moreland, *Scaling the Secular City*, 17.

9   Cp. Craig, *Reasonable Belief*, 113–16; Moreland, *Scaling the Secular City*, 34–38.

10 Lord Kelvin quotation, http://www.zapatopi.net/kelvin/quotes/#theo.

CHAPTER 3
DOES GOD EXIST?
THE DESIGN ARGUMENT

The Watchmaker

Imagine you are walking through the woods and find a watch lying on the ground. What would your first thought be? That random factors over time just happened to form a watch and then cough it up from the ground? That stray bits of metal chanced to assemble themselves in a way that just happened to be useful? That a spring was formed with no purpose and inadvertently came across a cog that was formed with no purpose and then were joined accidentally to a number of other gears, springs, and cogs, eventually forming a fully functioning and accurate instrument that could measure time? Of course not. You would assume someone had dropped it. This is because of its obvious design features.

The precision and intentionality of the mechanism betray a purpose, a plan. There must have been an intelligence who conceived of the watch and its workings and then created the watch.

The Argument

This analogy, often used to illustrate the argument from design, tries to show that when we observe nature, whether on a tiny level (like cells or proteins) or on a grand scale (like whole organisms or even the universe), we can see precision and intentionality, a purpose, a plan. And from that observation we can infer that there must be an intelligence behind it all. Just as fingerprints are the product of fingers touching something, intentionality and purpose are products of a mind acting, not chance. As one natural scientist has put it,

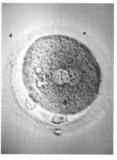

There are no facts yet wrested from the intriguing mysteries of this strange, onrushing cosmos which can in any degree disprove the existence and intelligent activities of an unconditioned, personal God. On the contrary, when as careful scientists we analyze and synthesize the data of the natural world, even by analogical inference, we are observing only the phenomena of the operations of that unseen Being who cannot be found by mere scientific seeking, but who can and did manifest Himself in human form. For science is indeed "watching God work."[1]

Aristotle

The History

The design argument is formally called the teleological argument. Telos is a Greek word meaning purpose or ultimate end.

Thus teleology is the study of a thing's purpose or design. The design argument predates Christianity. Ancient Greeks such as Plato and Aristotle argued for the existence of God based on their observations of the stars. In the thirteenth century, Thomas Aquinas used the design argument as one of his five ways of proving the existence of God.[2] In 1802, William Paley published what is probably the most famous articulation of the argument, *Natural*

William Paley

Theology. In fact, the watchmaker example comes from this book. In recent years, the design argument has been rechristened "intelligent design" or "ID." Champions such as Michael Behe, Philip Johnson, William Dembski, and Hugh Ross have used the latest scientific discoveries and advances to cast the design argument in the most contemporary terms.

Different Flavors of the Argument

The design argument has been used in a variety of ways to argue for the existence of God. Proponents have pointed to order, information, purpose, complexity, simplicity, sense, and even beauty as evidence of design in the universe. In this chapter, we will look at three

On Christmas Day 1968, the crew of Apollo 8 took this photo of the "Earthrise," showing for the first time how our planet looks from space. The night before astronauts Frank Borman, Jim Lovell, and William Anders, the first humans to leave Earth's orbit, took turns reading from Genesis in a live television broadcast.

examples of these arguments: the fine tuning of the universe (order as design), DNA (order as information), and irreducible complexity (order as complexity).

Fine-Tuning as Design: The Anthropic Principle

Scientists have come to understand the universe as having a great deal of precision. In fact, the degree of precision is so great that to alter any of the parameters even minutely would destroy life as we know it. This precision leads some scientists to make an argument based on order that the universe was actually designed to accommodate life. Also called "fine tuning," the anthropic principle has two classes of parameters: one set for the features of the universe, the other for the features of a sun-planet-moon system.

In his book *The Creator and the Cosmos*, astrophysicist Hugh Ross lists twenty-five parameters that must each fall within a very narrow range to make life possible. A partial list is noted here.[3]

- Strong nuclear force constant
- Weak nuclear force constant
- Gravitational force constant
- Electromagnetic force constant
- Ratio of electromagnetic force constant to gravitational force constant
- Ratio of electron to proton mass
- Ratio of protons to electrons
- Expansion rate of the universe
- Entropy level of the universe
- Mass density of the universe
- Velocity of light
- Age of the universe
- Initial uniformity of radiation
- Fine structure constant
- Average distance between stars

What would happen if any one parameter fell outside its narrow, life-friendly range? Take the expansion rate of the universe as an example. If the expansion rate were faster than one part in 10^{55}, galaxies could not have formed; if the expansion rate were slower than one part in 10^{55}, the universe would collapse before galaxies had a chance to form. Without galaxies, stars could not form; without stars, planets could not form; without planets, there could be

Artist's conception of an asteroid belt. NASA/JPL-Caltech/T. Pyle (SSC)

no life.[4] The extraordinary balance and precision exhibited by each of the above parameters demonstrate an order that points to an orderer, a being who designed the universe with a specific purpose.

The second set of thirty-two parameters has to do with our sun-planet-moon system.[5] Some of these parameters include:

- If the axial tilt of the earth were greater or lesser, the surface temperatures would be too harsh to support life as we know it.
- If the distance of the earth from the sun were greater, the earth would be too cool for a stable water cycle. But if the distance were less, the earth would be too warm for a stable water cycle.
- If the earth's crust were thicker, too much oxygen would be transferred from the atmosphere to the crust. But if the crust were thinner, there would be too much volcanic and tectonic activity.
- If the gravitational interaction with the moon were greater, the tidal effects on the oceans, atmosphere, and rotational period would be too severe. But if it were any less, Earth's orbital obliquity would change too much, causing climatic instabilities.
- If the gravity on the surface of the earth were stronger, the atmosphere would retain too much ammonia and methane, which is poisonous. But if the gravity were less, the atmosphere would lose too much water.
- If the length of a day were greater, the temperature differences would be too great to sustain life. But if the day were shorter, the atmospheric wind velocities would be too great to survive.

Again, according to Ross, "Each of these thirty-two parameters cannot exceed certain limits without disturbing a planet's capacity to support life."[6]

But is this just an egocentric view of the universe? Just because we humans happen to require the universe to have these parameters in order to live does not mean it was made with us in mind, does it? This is a possibility, of course. However, we should be mindful of a couple of things: first, that we have no evidence whatsoever of life of any kind anywhere else in the universe; and second, that even if we did find life elsewhere in the universe, it wouldn't necessarily change anything about the nature of human beings or the truthfulness of Christianity.

Let's say we find some form of primitive life on Mars and it resembles some form of life on Earth. What would that mean? That life on Earth somehow came from Mars? It's possible. But where did the life on Mars come from? Ultimately the discovery would answer nothing about man's origin; it would simply take our knowledge one step back in a chain of regression that must have a beginning, as we showed in the cosmological argument. Also, would it not be more likely that the life on Mars came from Earth (where we know life to have been for quite a while)? A meteor crashing into the earth could have shot debris into space that eventually contaminated Mars just as easily as the other way around.

Most important, discovery of life elsewhere would not take away our need for salvation. The human condition would still be fallen, whether we are alone in the universe or not; our having an ancestor or contemporary on some distant planet is irrelevant.

Parenthetically, this does not mean we should not continue space exploration or other scientific endeavors. The knowledge gained from these projects is extremely valuable. Even

A panoramic picture of Mars taken by Spirit, November 11, 2004.

more, the technology developed to accommodate these missions contributes greatly to the quality of our everyday lives and to the economy. For example, the spin-off technology from the space shuttle contributed to the development of the artificial heart, the in-ear thermometer, prosthetic material, and auto tracking systems, among others. The technology of the Apollo missions contributed to CT scans and MRIs, kidney dialysis, cordless power tools, and the insulation in cars and trucks; the blow molding used to make space suits was adapted to make athletic shoes.[7]

Information as Design: Information Theory and DNA

To understand this form of the argument, we must first understand the different kinds of order. Some order is the product of chance and random factors, while other kinds of order can have no other explanation than intelligent design.

Specified order is simply a string of repeating information, CAT CAT CAT, for example. This is a naturally occurring kind of order and can be found in things like crystals, nylon, or snowflakes.

Unspecified complexities are nonrepetitive and random. They are also naturally occurring. The sound of howling wind and the shape of a rock are good examples.

Specified complexities are nonrepetitive and nonrandom. They are not naturally occurring. In contrast to the howling wind and the shape of a rock, examples of specified complexities would be music or a statue. Even the sentence you are reading is an example of specifically complex order. The way we recognize a specified complexity is if it is contingent. "Contingency," says William Dembski, "is the chief characteristic of information."[8]

A rock's shape is determined by the laws of nature that are brought to bear on it by its circumstances. There are no other possibilities for its shape. However, a statue can be any shape its sculptor wants it to be. It is not determined, it is contingent.

If you were asked, "Is there any information on this page," what would your answer be? If you answered no, then you are correct; there is no information on this or any other page in the world. The only things on this page are squiggles of ink (albeit specifically ordered). In fact, you could have exhaustive knowledge about the printing process

Contingency is the chief characteristic of information.

and know all about paper and the chemistry of ink but still not know what was said on the page. If information was a property of the page, then we would never have to learn to read; the information would just fly off the page and impose itself onto our minds whenever we looked at it.

So what is information? It is communication between minds. But for minds to communicate, there must be a common language. The language must exist and be understood prior to any ability to communicate. For example, the language of written music (the staffs, notes, and values) must exist prior to attempting to play or even write the music. The music may exist in a composer's head, but it cannot be communicated without the convention of notation. Every language is a set of tokens and a set of conventions for the use of the tokens. A token stands in for something intangible. For example, the number "1" is not really an actual number "1" but a token or symbol representing the number "1" which is a nonphysical entity. There are no actual letters on this page, simply tokens representing the letters.

Information is communication between minds.

In English, the tokens are A, B, C . . . X, Y, Z. Because letters and numbers are nonphysical entities, they have no location or appearance. That is why we need tokens to represent them. Each token has a convention or way in which to use the token. The letter "A" has certain usages that when connected to other tokens make words. Then the words are connected to make sentences, and so on. The point is this: the rules of language were established before we could use them to communicate even on the most primitive level.

So if you were eating alphabet soup and the letters in your bowl spelled I LOVE YOU, you would immediately understand that this is not a communication from another mind. Your soup would not be declaring its passionate affection for you. The same is true if you were to go to the Grand Canyon and you saw STEVE WAS HERE etched in the canyon wall,

and you knew it was made naturally with wind and water through erosion; you would also know it contained no information. In fact, it would not even be English, just squiggles cut into rock that resemble the tokens and conventions used in English. But this resemblance would be entirely unintentional and therefore communicate nothing.

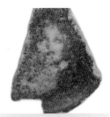

This grilled cheese sandwich, said to contain an image of the Virgin Mary, was sold on eBay for $28,000 in 2004 to internet casino GoldenPalace.com.

This is why when you are on eBay you should not bid on a grilled cheese sandwich that contains the face of the Virgin Mary. There is no mind behind the alleged image.

What about an unlimited number of monkeys with typewriters? Given an unlimited amount of time, could these monkeys ever write *Hamlet?* The answer is no. Even if at some point they happened upon the exact same sequence of letters as *Hamlet,* it still would not be *Hamlet.* It would be a string of letters that resembled *Hamlet,* but it would be void of any information. This is because there was no intention to communicate behind the monkey's actions; there was no true use of language, only its tokens. The tokens would be empty.

A great example of how scientists make use of this understanding of information theory is seen in the Search for Extraterrestrial Intelligence (SETI) project. SETI listens to radio waves and searches for a specifically complex string of information.

Recently our understanding of DNA has given new force for those making an information-based argument for design. That DNA contains information is not in dispute. In fact, it stores and retrieves information, corrects any errors when it copies itself, contains redundant information so that if a gene mutates it can be turned off and not cause any damage, overlaps so that it can provide information to more than one protein, is expressible in mathematical terms (it's digital), and houses as much information as an average volume of an encyclopedia. But, as we have seen, information is not intrinsic to naturally occurring physical objects.

The idea is that specifically complex signals (such as the first twenty-five prime numbers in a row, as in Carl Sagan's novel Cosmos) can only come from an intelligent agent wishing to communicate.

Just as a sound is an agent that carries the tokens and conventions used in speech for communication, DNA is simply an agent housing a set of tokens used to convey and store information that is necessary for the body to develop and function. But before DNA could be useful, there had to be a language established. The genetic code had to exist prior to the existence of DNA and come from outside the DNA.

Information did not emerge from DNA itself any more than a bowl of alphabet soup can say I LOVE YOU. The best explanation for the information found in DNA is that it was imposed on the DNA by a mind.

The best explanation for the information found in DNA is that it was imposed on the DNA by a mind.

The primary objection to this conclusion is a presupposition that all things are a product of random, nondirected forces. We call this worldview "naturalism." But as we have seen, this position is bankrupt in terms of explaining how the information came to be included in the DNA and how the language of the genetic code came to be at all. As Dembski points out, "Neither algorithms nor natural laws, however, are capable of producing information."[9] Information needs an informer, someone who orders things in a certain way to communicate specific content.

Complexity as Design: Irreducible Complexity

The irreducible complexity argument states that some things are as simple as they could possibly be and still function. As biochemist Michael Behe puts it, "An irreducibly complex system cannot be produced directly (i.e., by continuously improving the initial function, which continues to work by the same mechanism) by slight, successive modifications of a precursor system, because any precursor to an irreducibly complex system that is missing a part is by definition nonfunctional."[10] In other words, these things had to be created; they could not have evolved through undirected forces or chance. To illustrate the argument, Behe uses the example of a mousetrap.[11] Which part of a mousetrap can be removed and still leave you with a functioning mousetrap?

Some things are as simple as they could possibly be and still function.

The answer is that nothing can be removed without completely disabling the mechanism. It did not start out as a piece of wood that caught a couple of mice and then mutated to include a spring, which caught a few more mice, which then adapted to include a hammer, which caught even more mice. The mousetrap is made of individual components, which, apart from the whole of the mousetrap, are useless. And if any individual component is subtracted from the whole, then the mechanism is rendered useless. Successive stages of development did not arrive at a mousetrap. The mousetrap could not have possibly evolved. It was first conceived by a mind, then created by an intelligent agent with the power and will to act.

The implications of this are huge. If there are examples of irreducible complexity in biology, then macroevolution, the idea that evolution explains life's origins and that species evolve from one kind to another, must be false. Behe's book

Darwin's Black Box makes just such a case using the examples of cilium, bacterial flagellum, blood clotting, animal cells, and antibodies among others. Though these are some of the most basic biological mechanisms that we know of, Behe argues that each of these biological machines is irreducibly complex. And that each of the components of the mechanisms is also irreducibly complex and useless apart from the whole.[12]

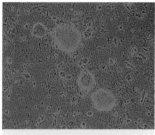

Culture of embryonic stems cells

Even the most basic biological mechanisms that we know are irreducibly complex.

For example, the bacterial flagellum is the whip-like part of a bacterium that allows it to move—much like an outboard motor—except this motor is water cooled, features a universal joint, has gears for forward and reverse, can reach speeds of 100,000 rpms, and can do self-assembly and repair. It demonstrates an economy of construction and a precision that cannot be accounted for by evolution. The far better explanation is that it was designed and created by an intelligent designer.[13]

Another biological machine often used to illustrate irreducible complexity is the human eye. The eye is made of more than forty different components, each of which contains a number of subcomponents. If any one component fails, then vision is impaired. Again, the economy of parts and the precision necessary for vision betrays a designer.[14]

A common objection to the use of the eye as an example of irreducible complexity is that there are a number of different kinds of eyes found in nature, and they exhibit a wide variety of complexity. This observation is used to make a case for evolution. But what we see in nature is not a series of steps in an evolutionary chain. Rather, we see a variety of irreducibly complex biological machines.

Just for the sake of argument, let us say the eye did evolve as a result of random processes. What does that give us? An interface with no receiver—like a keyboard that is not attached to a computer. After all, just as there is no actual input without the keyboard being attached to the computer, sight is not sight without a brain to receive it. The eye must connect to the brain somehow. But how does the eye know where the brain is or what a brain is or that it even exists or that it is required to make the eye useful? And how did the eye then wire itself properly to the brain? Why did it not connect itself to the nose or a knee? And even if it did connect to the brain properly (a feat in itself given all the different parts and functions of the brain), how did the eye know how to speak a language that the brain would understand, and vice versa? Again we need a language created prior to and apart from the existence of the things that will speak the language. And again, an intelligent designer is the best explanation. The eye could not have been self-directed or self-organized.

Tactical Note

Understand that the design argument does not prove that Christianity alone is true, but the God described by the Bible is consistent with the intelligent designer described by the argument. Christianity, Judaism, and Islam all describe an intelligent designer. Eastern religions have no place for such a being, as will be shown later.

Just as there is no actual input without the keyboard being attached to the computer, sight is not sight without a brain to receive it.

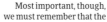

Most important, though, we must remember that the truth of Christianity ultimately does not stand or fall based on the truth of macroevolution. If macroevolution were irrefutably proven to be true tomorrow (in the sense that all species have a common ancestry and could evolve from one kind into new kinds), it would not and could not rule out the possibility of God using it as the agent through which he accomplishes his design. An intelligent agent would still be required to initiate and direct the process, create the languages and codes necessary for the exchange of information, and provide the purpose and design of the biological machines. In short, nothing about human nature will have ultimately changed. We would still be sinners in need of a savior regardless of how God chose to create us.

Conclusion

The different approaches to the design argument all try to show the same thing: that naturalism can account for only so much; at a certain point its explanatory power fails. But it is not this failure that points to an intelligent designer (the so-called "God of the gaps" theory). The precision of the universe, the nature of information, and the observation that random and undirected forces cannot account for the complexity of living things all lead to a transcendent, personal, intelligent designer.

Notable Quote

The world is too complicated in all its parts and interconnections to be due to chance alone. I am convinced that the existence of life with all its order in each of its organisms is simply too well put together. Each part of a living thing depends on all its other parts to function. How does each part know? How is each part specified at conception? The more one learns of biochemistry the more unbelievable it becomes unless there is some type of organizing principle—an architect for believers.[15]

—Allan Sandage

Notes

1   Merritt Stanley Congdon, "The Lesson of the Rosebush," in *The Evidence of God in an Expanding Universe*, ed. John Clover Monsma (New York: Putnam, 1958), 35–36.

2   Thomas Aquinas, *Great Books of the Western World*, vol. 19, *Summa Theologica* (Chicago: Encyclopedia Britannica, 1952), 14.

3   Hugh Ross, *The Creator and the Cosmos* (Colorado Springs: NavPress, 1994), 111–14.

4   Ibid., 109–10.

5   Ibid., 129–32.

6   Ibid., 114.

7   NASA—Scientific and Technical Information, http://www.sti.nasa.gov/tto/spinoff.html.

8   William Dembski, *Intelligent Design* (Downers Grove, IL: InterVarsity, 1999), 160.

9   Ibid., 153.

10 Michael Behe, *Darwin's Black Box* (New York: Simon & Schuster, 1996), 39.

11 Ibid., 42–43.

12 Ibid., 51–161.

13 Ibid., 70–72.

14 Ibid., 16–21.

15 Allan Sandage, "A Scientist Reflects on Religious Belief," Leadership U., at http://www.leaderu.com/truth/1truth15.html.

CHAPTER 4

DOES GOD EXIST?

THE MORAL ARGUMENT

Definitions

Are right and wrong objective realities with claims on all people at all times, or are they subjective realities only—matters of opinion? Was Adolph Hitler evil, or did he simply have a different opinion about things? The study of morality and values is called axiology (*axios* is Greek for worth or value). The moral, or axiological, argument tries to show that moral values must be objective and universal to make any sense.

And if moral values are objective, the source must be a transcendent, personal being for whom human actions and motives are not a matter of indifference.

The most widely held moral view in our culture is called "relativism." Relativism holds that societies and/or individuals decide what is right and wrong and that those values vary from culture to culture or person to person. There are no objective, universal moral truths—just conventions for behavior that are created by people for people and that are subject to

The study of morality and values is called axiology.

change. There are three different forms of relativism: cultural relativism, conventionalism, and ethical subjectivism.

Relativism holds that societies and/or individuals decide what is right and wrong and that those values vary from culture to culture or person to person.

Cultural Relativism

Cultural relativism is based on the observation that different cultures seem to have different values. And since they all have different value systems, there must be no right system, no objective morality. For example, some cultures, as evident in select states in Mexico, declare abortion to be abhorrent and have passed laws prohibiting it. Other cultures, like the United States, permit abortion as a legal option. Still other cultures, like China, actually require abortions under certain circumstances. Cultural relativism says that because each culture is holding to its own view of morality, and because these views differ, there must be no objective morality.

There are several problems with this line of thinking. One is that observing how cultures behave is just that—observation and nothing more. At best, these observations are simply statements of fact. Morals are not descriptions of the way things are. Morals are prescriptions of the way things ought to be. Just because things are a certain way does not mean they should be that way. When Popeye says, "I am what I am," he is making a statement of fact, not a moral claim. If he said, "I ought to be what I am," he would be making a moral claim.

Cultural relativism says that because each culture is holding to its own view of morality, and because these views differ, there must be no objective morality.

Another problem with cultural relativism is its premise that different answers to a given question mean that there is no right answer. Just because Mexico, the United States, and China disagree on the issue of abortion does not mean there is no right or wrong approach to abortion. If two golfers disagreed on how many strokes one of them took on a hole, it does not mean there is no incorrect answer. Either both are wrong or one of them is right. They cannot both be right. As Francis Beckwith and Gregory Koukl have put it, "The simple fact of disagreement on morality does not lead to the conclusion that there is no moral truth."[1]

Just as cultures develop languages, idioms, and slang that differ from one another, the cultural relativist sees morality as a convention of behavior that is molded by the hands

of each culture. And just as there is no wrong language, there can be no wrong morality. But to make this argument, cultural relativism must presuppose relativism, discounting the very possibility of objective morality.

Finally, let's say someone disagrees with cultural relativism. If the cultural relativists are to remain consistent, they must agree that the fact that there is a disagreement means that there is no wrong view of moral theory. But as cultural relativists, they are claiming there

is a correct view of moral theory, cultural relativism, and that other views are incorrect. As a result, they cannot live their own philosophy. On the other hand, if cultural relativists claim that the opposing view is a wrong way to think about the issue, then again they show they are not actually relativists. Thus cultural relativism fails to be an adequate explanation of morality. The difference in morality from culture to culture is an interesting anthropological phenomenon, but it cannot give a satisfactory account of the basis of morality.

Conventionalism

The view that each society decides what is right or wrong is called conventionalism. In contrast to cultural relativism, which says that there is no right or wrong answer, conventionalism claims there are a right and wrong, but they vary from society to society. The majority rules and morality becomes simply what is legal.

If conventionalism is true, the results are counterintuitive and very hard to live out. For example, let's say a law was passed that made having blue eyes illegal and that the penalty

> *The view that each society decides what is right or wrong is called conventionalism.*

for having blue eyes is death. There would not only be nothing immoral about the law, but it would in fact be immoral to have blue eyes!

But we do not need to employ absurd hypothetical situations to see what a conventionalist society would look like. This philosophy was adopted in Germany in the 1930s and '40s. When the Nazis declared Jews to be subhuman and deserving of death, there was no recourse for the Jews. The law was the law; by definition it was "moral." The large community of countries that protested was ignored. After all, what grounds did they have to critique German society? As a result, six million Jews were systematically killed. The defense given by Nazis tried at Nuremberg was conventionalism. "It couldn't have been wrong; it was the law," they said. "We were only following orders."

"It couldn't have been wrong; it was the law," they said. "We were only following orders."

Conventionalism is made even more difficult by its inability to be reformed. The German concentration camps were not populated only with Jews, but also with Germans who protested the law and policies of the Nazis. If society defines morality, then a person who protests against the laws of that society is, by definition, immoral and criminal. If a society were to change a law, it would not change from immoral to moral or from unjust to just. The law could only change from one rule to another. It would simply be different, not better or worse.

Furthermore, if conventionalism were true, then the Hebrew prophets, Gandhi, Jesus, Gautama Buddha, William Wilberforce, Mother Teresa, Abraham Lincoln, and Martin Luther King Jr. would be among the most egregious criminals who ever lived! Their crime? They pointed to what they saw wrong in society and declared that it should be changed, that it ought not be that way. The criminalization of such moral reformers is, of course, wildly counterintuitive and is a further indication of the bankruptcy of the conventionalist view.

In this view, too, relativism must be presupposed and objective morality dismissed out of hand. Objectivists say morality is like the North Pole—fixed, immovable, and a point that can be used for navigation. Conventionalists can plant the North Pole anywhere the majority says it goes. And it can move if the majority decides it belongs somewhere else. Not only that, anyone who does not orient himself to the pole is acting immorally.

Ultimately conventionalism is about power not morality. Whichever way the wind blows, the will of the majority is what is moral. Like a gang of bullies forcing into submission those who would dare oppose them, conventional-

Auschwitz-Birkenau concentration camp.

ism forces its preferences on everyone by defining itself into power. And like cultural relativism, this is an inadequate explanation of morality.

Ethical Subjectivism

By far the most widespread form of relativism is ethical subjectivism. In this view, individuals decide what is right or wrong for themselves and themselves only. Morality becomes fluid and privatized, changing to fit circumstances and conforming to convenience. Morality is nothing more than personal preference and opinion. "What's true for you is true for you, and what's true for me is true for me" is a familiar refrain of ethical subjectivism. "Who are you to judge?" is another. Alister E. McGrath observes this type of relativism as when "the signifier has replaced the signified as the focus of orientation and value."[2]

The first casualty of ethical subjectivism is language. Conversation about values and moral topics is rendered completely incoherent. No longer could anyone say something was right or wrong. The best one could say is "I choose not to do that because it is wrong for me" or "I do not prefer that." An ethical subjectivist could not call the terrorist attacks on September 11, 2001, evil or even wrong. And nothing could ever be called right or good. This is because not only is condemnation ruled out, but so is praise. An ethical subjectivist could say that those who risked their lives and perhaps suffered significant injury rescuing people from the World Trade Center did a good thing. But what they mean by "good" is very different from what most English speakers mean when they ascribe good to such actions. If someone contradicted them, saying, "I think it was evil to rescue people," they could only say, "Well, that's your view. And your view is as valid as mine." Truth is—very few people would be comfortable with this position.

> "What's true for you is true for you, and what's true for me is true for me" is a familiar refrain of ethical subjectivism.

Perhaps the fatal flaw in this view is that it is unabashedly self-refuting. Is all truth relative? If the answer is yes, then what are we to do with that statement itself, since it would be universally true? And if it is not true for everybody, then why are relativists pushing their morality on other people? Either way, it falls on its own sword. Paul Copan points out the claim of relativism commits the "self-excepting fallacy," claiming a statement holds true for everyone but oneself.[3]

"Something can be true for one person but false for another" fails to meet its own criterion for truth. Think about it: while a worldview can be internally consistent or logical yet still be false, no worldview can be true if it contradicts itself.[4]

A very effective way to expose the bankruptcy of ethical subjectivism is by using examples of obvious moral clarity that apply to all people at all times in all places. "Torturing babies for fun is wrong" is one well-used example. When confronted with this statement, an ethical subjectivist would then be in the unenviable position of having to argue against it. They may not personally think it is right, but they could not say it is wrong and be consistent. Just imagine what kind of people this system produces. In this system, an ethical subjectivist must walk past a rape in action since they cannot condemn it. After all, what is right for the rapist may not be what is right for an ethical subjectivist. Ethical subjectivists must allow trespassers into their home, thieves to burgle it, and arsonists to burn it as long as the trespassers, thieves, and arsonists do not believe their acts are wrong. But nobody lives this way. Or do they?

One way to gauge a moral system is to look at the kind of heroes the system produces. Take the objective moral stance of the Judeo-Christian view. The heroes are many and mighty: Jesus, Mother Teresa, and Martin Luther King Jr. immediately come to mind.

But what about ethical subjectivism? What kind of hero best exemplifies the ideals of believing that individual human beings define right and wrong? The heroes of ethical subjectivism go far beyond slackers, egocentrics, and individualists. Lived consistently, ethical subjectivism produces moral monsters, people who see no need to care about others, people who are unchecked and unaccountable to anything but personal fiat. As Beckwith and Koukl point out, "The quintessential relativist is a sociopath, one with no conscience."[5] Jack the Ripper. Charles Manson. Ted Bundy. Albert Fish (one of the models for Hannibal Lector). Ed Gein (the real-life model for *Psycho*'s Norman Bates, *Texas Chainsaw Massacre*, and *Silence of the Lambs*'s Buffalo Bill). These are the heroes of ethical relativism.

Objective Morality

Morals are not opinions. They are not personal, private decisions, and they are not descriptions of behavior. They are prescriptions for behavior and motive that have the force of a command. They contain a sense of obligation and oughtness that is universal, and authoritative and outweighs considerations of culture, time, and place.

> *Morals contain a sense of obligation and oughtness that is universal, and authoritative and outweighs considerations of culture, time, and place.*

To understand what our moral obligations are, we do not go about it scientifically. Science investigates the physical world, collects facts, and draws conclusions from those facts. Scientific laws do not tell us what ought to happen, only what will probably happen under certain circumstances. Scientific laws are simply descriptive.

If morality can't be based on descriptions of the world, neither can it be derived from reason. Reason helps us recognize contradictions, but not the morality of the propositions. For example, if someone told you, "I always lie," you would use reason to understand that this is a paradoxical statement. If it is true, then it is false, and if it's false, then it's true. But reason does not tell us anything about whether lying is right or wrong or whether truthful confession is virtue or not.

One way we come to moral knowledge is directly. We know it through intuition. This immediate knowledge is important because some things are known only in themselves. No investigation of facts or reasoning is required. This is precisely what is demonstrated by clear case examples, such as torturing babies for fun is wrong. Reason does not help us respond to this claim. And nobody has to investigate what torture is, what babies are, and what fun is before they can take a moral stance on it. This is self-evident; knowledge and our intuition equip us to recognize it as such. (Note that moral intuition does not mean some vague suspicion, premonition, or nagging feeling. Moral intuition is a genuine form of knowledge.)

There are several ways to demonstrate that all people, even self-professed relativists, actually believe in objective morality at their core. As we have shown, one way is through clear case examples. These examples need not be confined to outlandish claims like the torture example. Often conversations present opportunities to make this point in a much more personal way:

Christian thinker Francis Schaeffer once had a conversation with several students, one of whom disagreed with Schaeffer's moral objectivism. The student believed there was ultimately no difference between cruelty and noncruelty. Another student who was listening decided to put that belief to the test. He picked up a teakettle full of boiling water and held it over the first student's head as if he were about to pour it onto the student. He then said, "There is no difference between cruelty and non-cruelty."

The first student got up and left the room.[6]

Philosopher J. P. Moreland tells of a time he spoke with a student in a dorm room about relativism. The student basically said what was true for him was true for him and what was true for Moreland was no less legitimate even though it might be different. Moreland thanked the student for his time, picked up the student's stereo and began to leave. The student, predictably, protested. Moreland said he agreed with the student, that morality was a personal issue, and went on to say he didn't think stealing was wrong. It is fine for the student to think stealing is wrong, but he shouldn't push his morality on those who think it is okay.[7]

John Silber, president (1971–1996) and chancellor (1996–2003) of Boston University, was one of America's most innovative educators. Before going to Boston, Professor Silber was chairman of the philosophy department at the University of Texas and subsequently dean of the College of Arts and Sciences. While at Texas, he taught an honors course annually for some of the brightest freshmen at Texas. Silber gives the following account of a student's coming to see the inadequacy of relativism.

The class had been assigned Plato's dialogue *Protagoras*, in which Protagoras argues that man is the measure of all things. Writing on this paper an excellent student concluded that the individual is the measure of all things, and that whatever one's opinion is on any subject, it is as valid and true as the opinion of anyone else. I gave the paper an F.

When this fine student received the F, he was shocked and came in to talk to me about it. I said, "What are you complaining about? I found your argument convincing, and my grade strictly follows from your own argument. Since anyone's opinion is valid, my opinion is that your paper deserves an F." The student finally saw the devastating implication of his conclusion. He saw that the assertion that all judgments are relative is in fact self-refuting.[8]

What makes the examples of Schaeffer, Moreland, and Silber so powerful is that they saw opportunities to take their conversations out of the abstract and put them into the everyday world we all live in. In this light, the force of the objectivist position is undeniable no matter how hard someone tries to resist it.

> According to relativism, an individual is the measure of all things;
> whatever one's opinion is on any subject, it is as valid and true as the
> opinion of anyone else.

Another demonstration would be to show that a relativist expects to be treated with respect and dignity. An objectivist could ask whether there were any reason they should not verbally abuse, demean, and ridicule the relativist. A relativist would have to take the abuse or give no response to remain consistent. Yet the relativist most certainly will protest if they receive this kind of treatment because their moral intuition cries out that it is wrong to treat people this way.

A third way of exposing objectivism in a relativist is to discover that person's passion and relativize it. Let us say, for example, a relativist believed deeply in animal rights and was heavily involved in PETA, People for the Ethical Treatment of Animals. A moral objectivist could tell the relativist how she is trying to find a new shampoo and just tested out a couple of brands by rubbing the shampoo into the eyes of the relativist's dog to see whether there were any adverse reaction. Relativists will betray what they say they believe and object to these actions. And rightly so. But by objecting, they have demonstrated the reality of moral objectivism: moral laws are not personal opinions.

So ethical subjectivism joins cultural relativism and conventionalism as an inadequate moral theory. Furthermore, objectivism stands as the only coherent view of morality and the only way that can be consistently lived out.

Where Does Morality Come From?

At this point in the argument, all that has been shown is that there are good reasons for believing that objective morality exists. Two questions now arise: where did morals come from? and why should we obey them? To find the source, we should look at the characteristics of morality.

- *Morality consists of prescriptions for behavior and motives— not descriptions of the world.*
- *Morality consists of commands, not suggestions. Morality says, "Do this" and "Don't do that," not "It would be nice if you did this or refrained from doing that."*
- *Morality is universal in scope. Morality applies to all people in all places at all times.*
- *Morality is objective. Right and wrong exist outside of, and regardless of, our beliefs.*
- *Morality is authoritative. We are obliged to obey its commands.*

What kind of a being has these characteristics? Prescriptions and commands are forms of communication, and communication happens only between minds. As Beckwith and Koukl have written, "There can be no command if no one is speaking."[9]

Morals come from a transcendent person who has the power and authority to impose a moral law on us.

Also, because morals deal with purpose and will, the source of morality must also have purpose and will. Again, these things come only from minds. Because morals are universal and transcend individuals, societies, and time, the source must be universal and transcendent. Since morals are authoritative they must come from an authority, and authority can be held only by a person. Finally, this person must have the power to impose his moral will on us. This person must also be able to provide us with an ability to know this moral will through intuition. Thus morals come from a transcendent person who has the power and authority to impose a moral law on us. And we call this person God. (A variation of this argument is Aquinas's "Fourth Way" for proving the existence of God.)[10]

Another indication of where morals come from is found in what happens when we violate the moral law. Not only do we all have the ability to ignore our intuition and do what we know is wrong, but we all have done so many times. The result is guilt.

Toward whom do we feel guilty? Sometimes it is obvious to us. If we have lied to someone, we feel guilty to the person we deceived. At other times, the object of our guilt is not so obvious, for example, when our guilt stems

from our own thoughts or motives. To whom do we feel guilty then? The answer involves *whom* not *what*. We feel guilty toward persons, not objects. It is difficult to imagine feeling guilty to a broken window or a wrecked car, but easy to imagine feeling guilty to the owner of the window or the car. And we do not just feel guilt toward the person we deceived or harmed, but we understand the law came from someone, not something, and we feel guilty toward that person.

Without God, guilt is a passing state of mind that lacks substance and is ultimately illusory.

It is reasonable to suggest that moral laws come from a moral lawgiver, and it is to this lawgiver that the guilt owes its force. And if the moral law is transcendent, universal, and authoritative, so must be the lawgiver. If morals bring obligations, then it is to the lawgiver we are obliged. If morals are prescriptive, it is the lawgiver who prescribes them. And a transcendent, immutable, authoritative, prescribing, moral person to whom we are obliged is what we call God. Without God, guilt is a passing state of mind that lacks substance and is ultimately illusory.

Where Do God's Morals Come From?

Some philosophers, such as Plato, have raised the question about whether God is the ground of morality.[11] The first possibility is that morals are merely God's opinion or personal fiat. This means things are good or bad just because God said they are, and that what is good could just as easily have been declared to be bad. Thus morals are arbitrary and have no real force or obligation. The other possibility is that God understands what is good because goodness exists apart from him. This would make God answerable to a law outside of himself. On this view, God would not be sovereign and would be very different from God as revealed in Scripture. The source of morality would be impersonal, which would remove its authoritative nature. Either way, the objectivist position is in trouble. Or is it? Are those two scenarios really the only possibilities?[12]

There is a third possibility that answers both objections and shows moral objectivism to be completely coherent. This explanation says that goodness is a reflection of God's character. Goodness is not external to God, nor is it something that has authority over God. Rather, that which corresponds to his character is called good. His preferences

are extensions of his character, not an arbitrary decision on his part. Because his character does not change, morality is grounded in the very character of God.

What about Conflicting Morals?

The majority of moral conflicts actually have nothing to do with morality. In fact, there is great agreement on moral issues when the moral systems of other cultures and religions are surveyed.[13] They are, at their core, factual disputes. Again, let us take the issue of abortion. The prolife position argues that it is wrong to take the life of an innocent human being. The prochoice position actually agrees with the prolife position on this essential point. The difference is that the prochoice position doesn't agree that the fetus, blastocyst, or embryo is a human being. At its core, the debate is factual. Once that question is answered, morality's prescriptions can enter into the discussion, and abortion either is recognized as a morally neutral, completely acceptable procedure or as murder.

Genuinely conflicting duties should be dealt with on a case-by-case basis. In each case, we will probably find that morals appear to have a hierarchical property. There always seems to be a greater good or lesser evil to choose between. For example, imagine your baby is being held hostage by a man with a gun. The man says he will shoot the baby unless you rob the bank across the street and bring him the money. Stealing is always wrong, but killing a baby is a far more egregious wrong. Recognizing that hierarchy informs us what we should do.

Conclusion

In conclusion, moral relativism turns out not to be a moral system at all but merely a set of opinions. These opinions carry no sense of ought or authority and could change at any time. It seems clear that though many people give lip service to this philosophy, no one lives it. As Paul Copan has pointed out,

- Relativism . . . isn't merely emotionally offensive. It doesn't hang together logically. As a worldview, it cannot be sustained.[14]
- Relativism is a sunny-day morality, but as soon as a person is wronged, he instantly believes in moral absolutes.
- Objectivism is the only coherent view of morality. Only objectivism makes sense of our experience, of our perception of society and laws, our intuition and guilt. It is the only view of morality that can be lived consistently. And it points very strongly toward the existence of a transcendent, powerful, personal God.

Notable Quote

Whenever you find a man who says he does not believe in a real Right and Wrong, you will find the same man going back on this a moment later. He may break his promise to you, but if you try breaking one to him he will be complaining 'It's not fair' before you can say Jack Robinson. A nation may say treaties don't matter; but then next minute, they spoil their case by saying that the particular treaty they want to break was an unfair one. But if treaties do not matter, and if there is no such thing as Right and Wrong, . . . what is the difference between a fair treaty and an unfair one? Have they not let the cat out of the bag and shown that, whatever they say, they really know the Law of Nature just like anyone else?[15]*
—C. S. Lewis*

Notes

1   Francis J. Beckwith and Gregory Koukl, *Relativism: Feet Firmly Planted in Mid-Air* (Grand Rapids: Baker, 1998), 46.

2   Alister E. McGrath, *Intellectuals Don't Need God* (Grand Rapids: Zondervan, 1993), 175–76.

3   Paul Copan, *True for You, but Not for Me* (Minneapolis: Bethany House, 1998), 24.

4   Ibid., 24.

5   Beckwith and Koukl, *Relativism*, 31.

6   See Francis A. Schaeffer, *The God Who Is There* (Downers Grove, IL: InterVarsity, 1968), 101.

7   J. P. Moreland, "Arguments for the Existence of God," Biola University lecture.

8   Correspondence with John Silber, October 19, 2005.

9   Beckwith and Koukl, *Relativism*, 167.

10 Thomas Aquinas, *Great Books of the Western World*, vol. 19, *Summa Theologica* (Chicago: Encyclopedia Britannica, 1952), 13.

11 Plato, "Euthyphro," *The Dialogues of Plato*, vol. 2, trans. B. Jowett (Oxford University Press, 1892), 75–93.

12 In Islamic ethics, this is indeed the dilemma since the objective moral standard to obey is whatever God wills and is thus either arbitrary or subject to a moral law that exists apart from God. This differs from Christian ethics, in which the objective moral standard is grounded in God's character, not simply his will. Cp. Norman L Geisler and Abdul Saleeb, *Answering Islam* (Grand Rapids: Baker, 1993, 2002), 138.

13 One such survey was done by C. S. Lewis and included as the appendix to *The Abolition of Man* (New York: Macmillan, 1947, 1955), 95–121.

14 Copan, *True for You, but Not for Me*, 23.

15 C. S. Lewis, *Mere Christianity* (HarperCollins: New York City, 2001), 6–7

CHAPTER 5
WHICH GOD EXISTS?

The Elephant and the Blind Wise Men

Every religion paints a different picture of God. Though there are often similarities between these pictures, such as the claim that people are in need of salvation, these similarities amount to no more than a superficial common ground. There are important and fundamental differences, such as the way to attain that salvation. These fundamental differences are what make each religion distinct, for they cannot be reconciled. Logically, contradictory claims cannot all be true; either one picture of God is true or all of them are false.

Many have made the argument that each religion has a piece of the picture of God, and that all the pieces together form the full picture. This is illustrated by the story of the elephant and the blind wise men.[1]

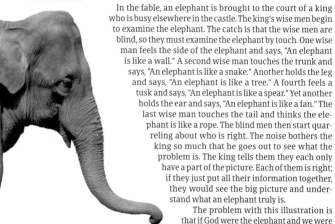

In the fable, an elephant is brought to the court of a king who is busy elsewhere in the castle. The king's wise men begin to examine the elephant. The catch is that the wise men are blind, so they must examine the elephant by touch. One wise man feels the side of the elephant and says, "An elephant is like a wall." A second wise man touches the trunk and says, "An elephant is like a snake." Another holds the leg and says, "An elephant is like a tree." A fourth feels a tusk and says, "An elephant is like a spear." Yet another holds the ear and says, "An elephant is like a fan." The last wise man touches the tail and thinks the elephant is like a rope. The blind men then start quarreling about who is right. The noise bothers the king so much that he goes out to see what the problem is. The king tells them they each only have a part of the picture. Each of them is right; if they just put all their information together, they would see the big picture and understand what an elephant truly is.

The problem with this illustration is that if God were the elephant and we were

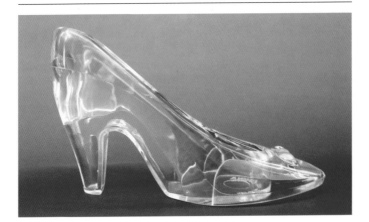

the blind wise men, there would be no one left to be the king who sees the full picture. No one is distanced enough from the situation to have a clear view. Ironically the illustration that tries to show that no one has a correct view of God actually illustrates just the opposite. To make this claim, a person would have to have a correct view of God, which is precisely what the claim denies. This brings us back to the question of which God exists.

> *If we can find the foot that fits, we will find a religion that holds to an accurate view of God.*

> *Atheism: God does not exist; if he does exist, we cannot know anything about him.*

The Glass Slipper

The arguments in the previous three chapters provide us not only with good reasons to believe in God's existence, but they also provide us with a partial list of God's attributes. The cosmological and design arguments show that God is necessary, powerful, transcendent, noncontingent, intelligent, and personal. The moral argument shows that God has a moral will, a purpose for how we are to live, that he is engaged in the world, and that the motives and actions of human beings matter to him. Finally, we must add that God is unique, that there is nothing and no one else like God. If God as described above does exist, there is nothing outside of himself that he did not create; no other god could exist.

As a result, these arguments provide us with a sort of Cinderella-type glass slipper, a set of criteria that must be met by any accurate description of God. If we can find the foot that fits, we will find a religion that holds to an accurate view of God. Any view that denies one or more of these attributes must be presenting a false view of God or must account for the discrepancy. Now, let us take the glass slipper in search of its owner.

Atheism

Atheism claims that God does not exist or that if he does exist we cannot know anything about him (which practically amounts to the same thing). The physical universe is all that exists, period. Obviously, this does not correspond to a single attribute of the glass slipper. Atheism rejects every finding of the cosmological, design, and moral arguments. But atheism does not provide adequate alternate explanations for how the universe came into existence, for the appearance of design in the universe, and for the existence of morality. The ideas of actual infinites in the real world, macroevolution, and relativism attempt to provide these explanations but are all deeply flawed.

The only religion proper to adhere to a form of atheism is Buddhism. Buddhism regards the existence of God as ultimately irrelevant. God is not necessary in the Buddhist system; if God did exist, nothing about Buddhism would change. It is a religion without a God.

Although the force of the arguments for the existence of God is powerful, many important, brilliant, even admirable people from all walks of life have rejected those arguments. Author Isaac Asimov seems unfazed by such arguments.

> The notion of an eternal universe introduces a great many difficulties, some of them apparently (at least in the present state of our scientific knowledge) insuperable, but scientists are not disturbed by difficulties; those all make up the game. If all the difficulties were gone and all the questions answered, the game of science would be over.[2]

A fascinating feature of claiming that there is no God is that its logical conclusion is self-refuting. To make the claim that God exists is simply to say that God is among the things that exist. But to say that God does not exist is to say that out of all the things that do exist, God is not among them. But who can honestly make such a claim? To make that claim honestly a person must have complete and exhaustive knowledge of everything that does exist. And the only person who can honestly make that kind of claim is God—the very person the atheist is trying to deny!

Atheist philosopher Bertrand Russell gave this rejection:

> Religion is based, I think, primarily and mainly upon fear. It is partly the terror of the unknown and partly, as I have said, the wish to feel that you have a kind of elder brother who will stand by you in all your troubles and disputes. Fear is the basis of the whole thing—fear of the mysterious, fear of defeat, fear of death. . . . Science can teach us, and I think our own hearts can teach us, no longer to look around for imaginary supports, no longer to invent allies in the sky, but rather to look to our own efforts here below to make this world a fit place to live in, instead of the sort of place that the churches in all these centuries have made it.[3]

To be fair, it must be said that many atheists merely claim that we cannot know anything about God. Sometimes known as "strong agnosticism," this form of atheism has its own troubles. Where does a "strong agnostic" get his information about God's unknowability?

EXISTS
IS NECESSARY
IS POWERFUL
IS TRANSCENDENT
IS NON-CONTINGENT
IS INTELLIGENT
IS PERSONAL
IS MORAL
IS ENGAGED
IS UNIQUE

ATHEISM

Karl Marx

Friedrich Nietzsche

Hellen Keller

As with atheism, a person would have to know everything to know with certainty that something is unknowable. Thus only God could know if God were unknowable.

Because atheism corresponds to none of the ten attributes we have learned about God, we can reject atheism as a valid way of understanding God. There is not a foot to even try to put the glass slipper on.

A quick sampling of other notable atheists include
- Sigmund Freud
- Charles Darwin
- Friedrich Nietzsche
- Karl Marx
- Francis Crick, co-discoverer of DNA
- Helen Keller
- Thomas Edison
- Woody Allen
- Ayn Rand
- Frank Zappa
- Kurt Vonnegut Jr.

Agnosticism

The word *agnostic* means to have no knowledge. The view that says God is unknown but not necessarily unknowable is agnosticism. This view is often characterized by its adherents as neutral ground—that they are neither for nor against the claim that God exists. For the agnostic the jury is still out; no verdict has been arrived at yet.

Weak agnosticism is not a view of God at all but rather is a description of an individual's current state of lack of knowledge and indecision. Agnosticism of either kind fails to address any attributes of the glass slipper.

Pantheism

Pantheism is the view that everything that exists is God. There are several different expressions of pantheism. One view holds that God is a force that is in all things (think *Star Wars*). Another view sees God as the totality of everything. All is one and one is all. Still others see God as manifest in many forms, each a part of the ultimate reality. (Hindus have as many as 330,000,000 gods!) Many pantheists believe nature is just part of the whole. Others believe material reality is only an illusion. Pantheists believe that God is impersonal. And since everything that exists is part of God, we ourselves are part of God, fragments of the divine whole. Because God is impersonal, our individual personhood is only illusion. When we die, we are absorbed into the impersonal whole.

In pantheism, dualities or opposites do not exist. Things either are or they are not; they are either real or illusion; they either exist or they do not. This means, for example, there

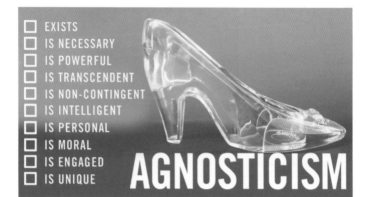

EXISTS
IS NECESSARY
IS POWERFUL
IS TRANSCENDENT
IS NON-CONTINGENT
IS INTELLIGENT
IS PERSONAL
IS MORAL
IS ENGAGED
IS UNIQUE

AGNOSTICISM

can be no right and wrong, good and evil, or true and false. Because God is impersonal, God cannot have a moral will. Whatever is reality; the rest is illusion. There are no moral distinctions. Some gods in the Hindu pantheon are both benevolent and malevolent. In pantheism, there is ultimately no difference between benevolence and malevolence. Logic and reason are also examples of illusions. Because logic and reason deal with opposites (things are either true or false), they do not exist. They are meaningless.

Pantheism: everything that exists is God.

Pantheism fails to account for features of reality that are expressed in the cosmological, design, and moral arguments. Because pantheism says God is impersonal, God cannot be intelligent, because only persons have intelligence. And God cannot be engaged in the world, because intentionality and engagement are also characteristics exclusive to persons. Too, if everything that exists is itself a part of God, then nothing can be transcendent. Finally, in pantheism the universe is eternal and unchanging; it has no beginning or end. This would necessitate the existence of actual infinites, something that is clearly false, as was shown in the Kalam cosmological argument in chapter 2.

A strain of pantheism is based on the observation that the same matter and energy that make the universe make us. We are made by the universe, sustained by the universe, destroyed by the universe, and returned to the universe after we die. The universe is all that exists. Awe, reverence, humility, and respect follow from a proper understanding of the universe.

This strain of thought is called scientific pantheism. One major differentiator of scientific pantheism is that it does not deny opposites. Rather, it relies heavily on logic and reason.

Looking at our list, we see that pantheism corresponds to only five of the ten attributes of reality that comprise our glass slipper.

Religions that have a pantheistic view of God include Hinduism, Taoism, some forms of Buddhism, the New Age movement, paganism, some forms of Unitarian Universalism, Christian Science, and Scientology.

Adherents to pantheism of one form or another include

- Carl Sagan
- Albert Einstein
- Henry David Thoreau
- Oscar Wilde
- Henri Matisse

EXISTS
IS NECESSARY
IS POWERFUL
IS TRANSCENDENT
IS NON-CONTINGENT
IS INTELLIGENT
IS PERSONAL
IS MORAL
IS ENGAGED
IS UNIQUE

PANTHEISM

Despite the fact that it has had some brilliant adherents, pantheism is fraught with difficult problems. One problem has to do with morality. If, when we die, we are all absorbed into the impersonal whole, then we all share the same fate. How we live makes absolutely no difference. There is no ground for morality. Mother Teresa and Adolph Hitler share the same fate. This is not only counterintuitive but an ineffective foundation for life.

Pantheists also claim that we are a part of God, and that God is unchanging. But if we can come to realize that we are a part of God, then we have changed. Thus God would change because we changed.

Pantheism has a convenient answer for this contradiction: there is no such thing as logic or reason. The problem with this solution is that it uses logic and reason to claim that logic and reason do not exist. Either there are such things as logic and reason or there are not. To make such a claim, or any claim, presupposes logic and reason. Christian apologist Ravi Zacharias, who grew up in Madras, India, points out that Hindus in India look both ways before crossing the street. They know that oncoming buses are real things that will cause real pain if they step out in front of them. Either they wait for the bus to pass, or they will get run over.[4] Logic is inescapable.

And, as mentioned above, pantheism would require the existence of actual infinites—an impossibility. So pantheism is a poor explanation for how to understand God. It fails to correspond with features of reality that can be known apart from religion. The glass slipper does not fit pantheism.

Albert Einstein

Oscar Wilde

Henry David Thoreau

Panentheism

Panentheism sees God as both distinct from and dependent on the world at the same time. God comes from the world, and the world comes from God. It is a symbiotic relationship. Ron Brooks and Norman Geisler describe panentheism by saying that "God is to the world what the soul is to the body."[5] God is ultimate reality (panentheism literally means "all in God"). Because our souls are our essence, which in turn is a part of the ultimate reality, we are all a part of God, though we are not God. And because the world is ever changing, God is also ever changing. As our souls learn and grow, God becomes more powerful. God then uses that power to create new things for us to learn. God is learning and growing just as we are.

One way to envision panentheism is to view God as both a seed and a tree. The tree represents everything God could possibly become. The seed represents the actual state that God (and, consequently, the world) is now in. But in panenthesim, the seed never actualizes a tree. Although God is always growing and changing, God will never attain all that is possible to become. This is why panentheism is also known as process theology; God is always in process.

In panentheism the universe, or God, has always existed and always will exist. Yet God is always changing. God is finite and temporal. A finite God always lacks something. That is why it can change at all. And change is a sequential phenomenon; things change from one thing to another over time. Thus in panentheism, God is simultaneously finite, bound by time, and yet eternal.

> *Panentheism: God comes from the world, and the world comes from God.*

Although it was not fully articulated until the twentieth century, the ideas behind panentheism can be traced back to Plato and Socrates. Panentheism has been adopted by some forms of Judaism and Christianity. More recently, in the 1960s, Latin American rebels mixed panenthesim, Marxism, and Roman Catholicism to create liberation theology. Panenthesim can account for seven of the glass slipper's attributes.

The attributes of the glass slipper reveal that the idea of a finite and dependent God is inaccurate. And the idea of an eternally existing universe again runs into the problem of the existence of actual infinites. Panentheism fails to fit the glass slipper by giving no grounding for morality. If morals are rooted in God and God is always changing, then moral values are also changing, or at least they can change. They become fluid and lose their force, their "oughtness." Why change immoral behavior if morality itself may soon change and make the immoral moral? Panentheistic morality therefore has no authority to enforce morality, and thus is no morality at all.

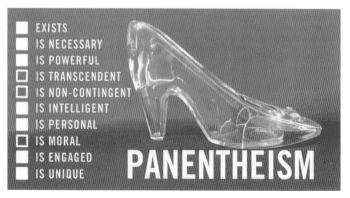

In the end, panentheism fails to account for the features of reality found in the cosmological, design, and moral arguments.

Finite Godism

Finite godism describes God as the first cause that is personal, loving, and good. But finite godism says that because evil exists, God must not be able to control or eradicate it. Therefore, God is not all-powerful and is limited in nature. God does not like evil, but he cannot prevent it from happening. Finite godism points to the imperfection of the universe and reasons that the source of the imperfection is an imperfect God. And since the universe is finite, the source of the universe is a finite God. Most adherents to finite godism do not believe that God performs miracles.

This statue of Freddie Mercury stands in Montreux, Switzerland, one of his homes.

Because God is finite, there is not any real certainty that morality falls within the scope of God's ability to ground it. The source of morality in finite godism is ultimately unknown. Some who embrace finite godism see God as the source of morality.

Though finite godism is found in some expressions of Reform Judaism, it is not a doctrine explicitly taught by any religion. Yet Zoroastrianism, which teaches that there is a duality of self-existing gods, one good and one evil, is ultimately a form of finite godism. In Zoroastrianism, the Wise Lord (God) is at war with the Destructive Spirit (the Devil). Since each of the gods is self-existing and each created different things—one good, the other evil—they are each finite. Each is something the other is not, and each has power the other does not.

Rabbi Harold Kushner's book *When Bad Things Happen to Good People* is a well-known articulation of finite godism.[6] Another famous adherent was Freddie Mercury, the now-deceased singer for the rock group Queen and a Zoroastrian.

Having missed on four and a half points, finite godism is thus faced with very serious questions. If God is finite, then where did God come from? And if God does not perform miracles, where did the universe come from? If God is not the source of morality, then what does it matter what we do? If God is the source of morality, then morality has limited force

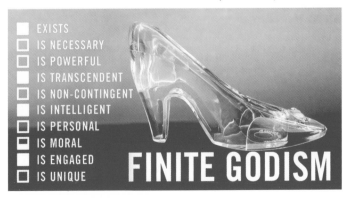

EXISTS
IS NECESSARY
IS POWERFUL
IS TRANSCENDENT
IS NON-CONTINGENT
IS INTELLIGENT
IS PERSONAL
IS MORAL
IS ENGAGED
IS UNIQUE

FINITE GODISM

since God is finite and may or may not be able to answer any wrongdoing with justice. And if, as in Zoroastrianism, God can be defeated by the Destructive Spirit, then God is not a necessary being since things could exist without him. But a God who is not necessary is no God at all. In short, finite godism has a number of internally incoherent features and falls far short of fitting the glass slipper.

Polytheism

Polytheism is the view that there are a multitude of gods. These gods either come from nature or were once human and became gods. As such, the gods are contingent and finite, but the universe is either eternal or made from eternal matter. Although there is no consensus, many polytheists are moral relativists and do not believe morality comes from the gods.

George Harrison

Religions that teach polytheism include Hinduism, Mahayana Buddhism, Confucianism, Taoism, Shintoism, paganism, and Mormonism. Mormons generally object to this characterization, claiming they worship only one God. But in Mormonism there are millions of gods, though they worship only one. This is a form of polytheism called henotheism.

Well-known polytheists include George Harrison, Joseph Smith Jr. (founder of Mormonism), and authors Aldous Huxley and J. D. Salinger.

Joseph Smith Jr.

The glass slipper is a poor fit for this view. The cosmological argument tells us that everything had a beginning and did not exist eternally. But polytheism teaches that the

Polytheism: there are a multitude of Gods.

universe (or matter) has always existed—an impossibility because of the nonexistence of actual infinites. Mormonism further requires actual infinites to accommodate the idea of gods coming from other gods who in turn came from other gods, and so forth. Again, this is an idea defeated by the nonexistence of actual infinites. Without a first god to begin the chain, we could not account for the gods of the present.

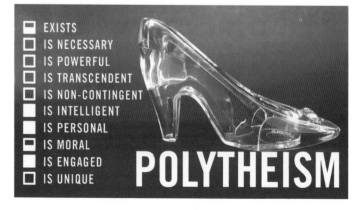

Voltaire

Thomas Jefferson

Benjamin Franklin

But even without the problem of actual infinites, polytheism cannot account for the existence of the universe because there are no transcendent beings in polytheism. All things, including gods, come from the universe. They do not exist apart from it. And the beings that do exist have limited power. Polytheism thus fails not only to correspond to the attributes of the glass slipper, but it is also internally incoherent.

Deism

Deism holds that God is not known through religion but only through reason and nature. God is a necessary, personal, powerful, transcendent being, and the world is his only revelation about himself. Thus there are no miracles. For us to understand him through his creation, he gave us reason. Basically, in deism God wound up the world and is passively watching it run down without interacting with it.

Deism: God is known only through reason and nature.

Deism is not taught by any religion. It is a system of belief held by individuals, including Voltaire, George Washington, Benjamin Franklin, and Thomas Jefferson. Jefferson even went so far as to physically edit his New Testament by cutting out all the miraculous content and leaving only the ethical teachings of Jesus.

In this view, for the first time the glass slipper gets close to fitting. It misses on only one of the ten attributes. The major problem with deism is that it requires the one thing that it denies—miracles. Or at least one miracle, anyway. The creation of the world was not a natural act. It required a miracle, an intervention by a transcendent, all-powerful, personal being. Without this miracle, the world could not exist. If the world could exist without God, God would not be all-powerful since he could not stop the world, would not be necessary, and would have no moral authority since he could not have a purpose for what he did not create.

The result is that deism, though close to fitting our glass slipper, still fails to account for the universe as we find it.

Monotheism

Monotheism sees God as the person who created all things and sustains all things but is different from those things. God interacts with creation in various ways and can reveal himself to us through morality, nature, reason, and even direct revelation. Monotheism is taught by three of the world's religions: Judaism, Islam, and Christianity.

Monotheism: God is the person who created all things and sustains all things.

Monotheism hits on every point of the glass slipper. The shoe fits perfectly.

Notable Quote

> Anyone who claims that all religions are the same betrays not only an ignorance of all religions but also a caricatured view of even the best-known ones.[7]
>
> *—Ravi Zacharias*

Conclusion

The way of thinking about God that best corresponds to the characteristics we can know through reason and the observation of the universe is monotheism. Now the question becomes, which monotheistic religion is the true one, or are they all false?

Interestingly enough, the monotheistic religions do not just have the same basic description of God; they all claim to be talking about the same God. The God who has revealed himself in the Old Testament is claimed by Jews, Christians, and Muslims alike. Islam, however, claims the Old Testament has become corrupted. And Christians believe the messianic promises in the Old Testament were fulfilled in Jesus. Judaism denies both claims.

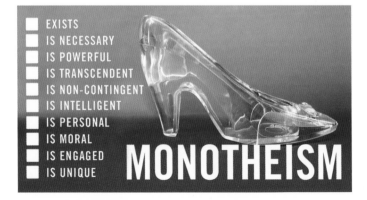

EXISTS
IS NECESSARY
IS POWERFUL
IS TRANSCENDENT
IS NON-CONTINGENT
IS INTELLIGENT
IS PERSONAL
IS MORAL
IS ENGAGED
IS UNIQUE

MONOTHEISM

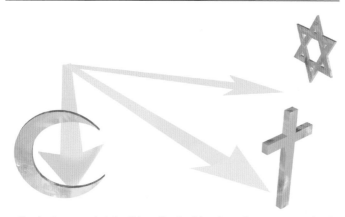

Also, the three monotheistic religions all make claims about who Jesus was. To Islam, he was a great prophet, but the Gospel accounts of him are corrupted and do not show who he really was. To Judaism, he was a pretender claiming to be the Messiah promised by the prophets. To the Christians, he was the long-awaited Messiah.

To see our way forward, then, we will next look at the authenticity and trustworthiness of the New Testament. If it is not a reliable account of the person and work of Jesus, we can narrow down our options to Judaism and Islam. But if the New Testament is reliable and trustworthy, then Islam can be rejected as inaccurate, because it contradicts the New Testament. We can then look at the Tanak, what Christians call the Old Testament, to see whether it has changed or is trustworthy. If it is trustworthy, what does it say about the Messiah, and does the Messiah look like Jesus? If the answers do not correspond to what we know about Jesus, then we can reject Christianity and embrace Judaism. On the other hand, if what we know about Jesus does correspond to the teachings of the Tanak, then we can discount Judaism's view of Jesus. So our next step is to investigate the New Testament.

Notes

1   This ancient Indian fable was retold by Lillian Fox Quigley in her children's book *The Blind Men and the Elephant* (New York: Charles Scribner's Sons, 1959). Her version is used as an illustration by Francis J. Beckwith and Gregory Koukl, *Relativism: Feet Firmly Planted in Mid-Air* (Grand Rapids: Baker, 1998), 47.

2   Isaac Asimov, *In the Beginning* (New York: Crown, 1981), 12.

3   Bertrand Russell, *Why I Am Not a Christian* (New York: Simon & Schuster, 1957), 22.

4   This illustration is a staple of Ravi Zacharias's talks.

5   Don Brooks and Norman Geisler, *When Skeptics Ask* (Grand Rapids: Baker, 1996), 47.

6   Harold Kushner, *When Bad Things Happen to Good People* (New York: Schocken, 1981).

7   Ravi Zacharias, *Jesus among Other Gods* (Nashville: Word, 2000), 7. This method of comparing the different ways of how people think about God to what we can know of God through nature is deeply indebted to the Brooks and Geisler approach in *When Skeptics Ask*.

CHAPTER 6
WHERE DID THE NEW TESTAMENT COME FROM?

The Challenge

The twenty-seven books that make up the New Testament record the teachings and events that are the foundation of Christianity. Of any ancient source, they contain by far the greatest amount of information about Jesus and the people he charged with spreading his message. These writings, called the New Testament, make both assumptions and overt claims about the world and why it is the way it is. They provide a unique perspective on what human beings are, why they are that way, and two potential destinies—eternal life or eternal death. The New Testament writings describe a fallen world whose inhabitants have rebelled against the purpose for which they were made. They also prescribe a solution to remedy that problem— the person and work of Jesus, the Messiah. The

claims of the New Testament are powerful and demand to touch every area of our lives. If we were to take it seriously, the New Testament would require a radical shift in how we view the world and ourselves.

The New Testament's claims are far reaching both in depth and scope, but are they true? How do we begin to assess their truth? Who wrote these books? Are the authors trustworthy? Are these accounts historically accurate? When were they written? How were they chosen to be included in the New Testament and who chose them? And what about the books that were rejected for inclusion into the New Testament? If these questions can be answered satisfactorily in favor of the New Testament, then its content has profound implications for our lives and must be taken seriously. Otherwise, we can cross Christianity off our short list of religions that claim to view God correctly.

Who Chose the Books and How Were They Chosen?

The councils of Carthage, in 393, and Hippo, in 397, fixed the list of New Testament books into its final form. But these books were not arbitrarily selected; they each had to meet certain criteria. They had to have apostolic origin, meaning each book had to have been written by an apostle or by an associate who preserved an apostle's teachings. The only exceptions were granted to James and Jude, brothers of Jesus who became his followers after his death. This requirement also means the books had to have been written during the apostolic age, the time when the apostles were still alive (ending with John's death probably in the late 90s). They had to have been generally accepted by the church and in continuous use in worship services. The teaching of the books had to cohere and agree with accepted and undisputed Scripture. Last, the books must be inspired by God. As such, they must display a self-evidencing quality and the power to transform lives. This criterion is a little tougher to nail down. Some thought the books were inspired because of their apostolicity. Others focused on inspiration rather than apostolicity. Whatever the reason for belief in inspiration, the books comprising the New Testament were set apart from all other books because they were believed to be inspired. The books meeting the criteria formed what is called the canon of the New Testament ("canon" comes from the Greek word *kanōn*, meaning measure or rule) because all teaching had to bow to its authority.

Prior to the councils at Carthage and Hippo, there had been much discussion on the issue. In a letter dating from 367, Athanasius, bishop of Alexandria, was the first to compile a list of the twenty-seven books as we now have them. He was also the first person in the church to use *kanōn* in this sense around AD 353. In *De decretis* 81.3, Athanasius says that the Shepherd of Hermas "does not belong to the canon." About ten years later, the Synod of Laodicea made a distinction between canonical and noncanonical books. The first appearance of the phrase "canon of the NT" appears about

This Greek copy of the Bible, Codex Sinaiticus, is dated about AD 350 and can be viewed at the British Library in London.

Athanasius

Eusebius

Tertullian

The writings of the church fathers are important because they quoted so heavily from the writings they considered authoritative because of their apostolic origin.

AD 400 in Macarius Magnes's *Apocriticus* 4.10. Athanasius was no doubt informed by the work of Eusebius, the father of church history.

In 325, Eusebius, spurred by Constantine's desire for unity and uniformity in Christianity, began investigating the history of the books that were being used as Scripture or had advocates who said they should be used as Scripture. Eusebius had access to large libraries of Christian writings both in Caesarea Maritima, his home, and in Jerusalem. These librar-

SPURIOUS

WIDELY ACCEPTED

CANONICAL
The 4 Gospels
Acts
14 letters of Paul
(including Hebrews)
1 John
1 Peter
Revelation

James
Jude
2 Peter
2 & 3 John

Acts of Paul
Barnabas
Shepherd of Hermas
The Didache
The Apocalypse of Peter

Eusebius's division of the books.

ies contained the works of church fathers dating back to the first century. The writings of the church fathers are important because they quoted so heavily from the writings they considered authoritative because of their apostolic origin. For example, Tertullian (ca. 150–ca. 229) quotes from twenty-three of the twenty-seven New Testament books. In fact, the vast majority of the New Testament can be reconstructed on quotations from the church fathers alone. Taking his cue from the importance given to these certain writings and the criteria of the canon, Eusebius divided the books into four categories:

- *canonical*
- *widely accepted*
- *rejected (also called "spurious")*
- *heretical*[1]

The canonical books were books whose authorship and authority had rarely been in question. Eusebius counted twenty-two books in that category:

- *the four Gospels*
- *Acts*
- *the fourteen letters of Paul* (Hebrews was counted among the works of Paul)
- *1 John*
- *1 Peter*
- *Revelation* (though he notes there were those who doubted John's authorship)

Among the books that were widely accepted but were attended by some debate were

- *James*
- *Jude*
- *2 Peter*
- *2 John*
- *3 John*

These five books in addition to Eusebius's twenty-two canonical books make up the New Testament.

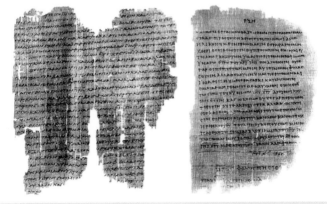

The Gospel of John (left) and parts of Galatians and Philippians (right) date to ca. AD 180 to 200—about the same time as the Muratorian Canon. It is part of a near-complete New Testament called the Chester Beatty Papyrii and can be seen at the Chester Beatty Library, Dublin, Ireland.

There were several books that had the appearance of Scripture, and that some churches used for instruction and worship, yet failed to be included in the New Testament. These books ultimately fell short of the canon requirements in one way or another. Eusebius mentions five of them:

Marcion

- *The Acts of Paul*
- *The Letter of Barnabas*
- *The Shepherd of Hermas*
- *The Didache* (or the Teaching of the Twelve Apostles)
- *The Apocalypse of Peter*

Although Eusebius does not attempt an exhaustive list of books cited as Scripture by heretics, he does mention the Gospels of Thomas, Peter, Matthias, and any other Gospels besides the accepted four; the Acts of Andrew, John, and any of the other works claiming to document the life of an apostle.

Somewhere around AD 180 to 200 the oldest-known list of New Testament canon books was compiled. It was discovered in the 1700s by Antonio Muratori and counted twenty-two books as Scripture. The Muratorian Canon, as it has come to be known, includes

- *the Gospels*
- *Acts*
- *the thirteen letters of Paul* (not counting Hebrews)
- *Jude*
- *1, 2, and 3 John*
- *Revelation*[2]

Marcion argued that the God of the Old Testament and the God of the New Testament were two different Gods.	The question of what was and was not Scripture really did not begin in earnest until about AD 140. The question was sharpened and made more urgent by a development in the church at Rome.

In AD 135, Marcion, a wealthy shipbuilder and son of a Christian bishop from Sinope in the province of Pontus, came to Rome and gave the church a large gift—200,000 sesterces. Almost immediately, Marcion became highly influential in the Roman church. But it soon became obvious that Marcion's theological views differed significantly from those widely held by the Christians not only in Rome but throughout the Mediterranean world.

Marcion argued that the God of the Old Testament and the God of the New Testament were two different Gods. Where most Christians saw a continuity between the Hebrew Scriptures and the teachings of Jesus and the apostles, Marcion saw irreconcilable discontinuity. For almost a century, Christians had accepted the Hebrew Scriptures as Scripture.

To challenge this deeply held view that Jesus is the fulfillment of the Hebrew Scriptures, Marcion created his own canon of Scripture that completely excluded the Old Testament and any reference to God as presented in the Old Testament. Marcion's canon included ten of Paul's letters and the Gospel of Luke. But even these were edited to remove elements of Judaism and God who is wrathful and retributive.[3]

One of the values of Marcion's and other heresies in the second- and third-century churches was that they forced Christians to think through the tradition that had been handed down to them and to reassess the grounds for its truthfulness.

As early as AD 115, twenty years before Marcion appeared in Rome, Ignatius, bishop of Antioch, referred to "The Gospel" as an authoritative writing. The Gospel circulated as a unit bound together as a codex like books as we now know them and not on separate scrolls.

Ignatius of Antioch was fed to the lions in the Roman Colosseum.

"The Gospel" was the title of this book and each component had a subtitle, "According to Matthew," "According to Mark," and so on. Paul's letters were also collected into a single codex early in the second century.

For Marcion, the supreme God was the Father of Jesus, not God as presented in Judaism. But the preaching of the early church and its presentation of Jesus showed that Jesus took Hebrew Scripture to be God's Word and to be strongly continuous with God's revelation in Jesus. To maintain his position, Marcion had to claim that apostolic preaching of Jesus was a distortion. Marcion's task then was to purge from the Gospel of Luke and the Pauline Epistles those elements that supported the view that God the creator of Abraham, Isaac, and Jacob was identical with the God and Father of Jesus.

Again, Marcion served a valuable function in setting forth a canon of New Testament Scripture. Had he not done this and challenged the thinking of his contemporaries, the canonization process might have proceeded much more slowly with the issues less sharply defined.

Marcion's canon appeared against the backdrop of a firmly developed, though not quite final, tradition of what books were authoritative. According to Bruce Metzger,

> During the course of the second century most churches came to possess and acknowledge a canon which included the present four Gospels, the Acts, thirteen letters of Paul, 1 Peter, and 1 John. Seven books still lacked general recognition: Hebrews, James, 2 Peter, 2 and 3 John, Jude, and Revelation. It is hard to say if this was the cause or the effect of the divergent opinions concerning their canonicity.[4]

In the 1950s, a cache of papyrus scrolls and codices, as well as vellum codices, was found in Egypt. The copies dated from about AD 200 and are known as the Bodmer Papyrii. The papyrii pictured contain the oldest complete copies of 1 Peter and Jonah. (The Schøyen Collection MS 193, Oslo and London)

John

Polycarp

Irenaeus

When questions arose or the teachings of Christianity needed defending, these were the books that the church looked to as the sole authority and judge. The reason these books were given such weight was that they preserved the teaching of the apostles, those personally commissioned by Jesus to spread his teaching.

Who Wrote the Books?

At this point, the origin of the books must be investigated. If we are to submit to their authority and use them as our rule to judge theological matters, as they require and as the early church would have it, what credentials can these books demonstrate? Is there any reason to think the apostles actually had a hand in their writing?

One of the more striking attestations of the authority and origin of the Gospels is in a writing of Irenaeus, bishop of Lyons, preserved by Eusebius. Irenaeus was the student of Polycarp, the bishop of Smyrna, who had personally been a disciple of the apostle John. In about AD 180, Irenaeus passed on the history of the Gospels that he had learned from Polycarp, who had in turn received his information from John. According to Irenaeus:

John told the history of the Gospels to Polycarp, who told Irenaeus.

The four Evangelists as portrayed by the Book of Kells ca. AD 800.

> Matthew published his Gospel among Hebrews in their own language, while Peter and Paul were preaching and founding the church in Rome. After their departure Mark, the disciple and interpreter of Peter, also transmitted to us in writing those things which Peter had preached; and Luke, the attendant of Paul, recorded in a book the Gospel which Paul had declared. Afterwards John, the disciple of the Lord, who also reclined on his bosom, published his Gospel, while staying at Ephesus in Asia.[5]

This history is corroborated by Papias, an associate of Polycarp. Papias may have been a "hearer" of John, or even a disciple of his, and claimed to know many of John's intimate friends. Papias wrote that John taught the following:

> Mark, having become the interpreter of Peter, wrote down accurately, though not indeed in order, whatsoever he remembered of the things said or done by Christ. For he neither heard the Lord nor followed him, but afterward, as I said, he followed Peter, who adapted his teaching to the needs of his hearers, but with no intention of giving a connected account of the Lord's discourse, so that Mark committed no error while he thus wrote some things as he remembered them. For he was careful of one thing, not to omit any of the things which he had heard, and not to state any of them falsely. . . . So then Matthew wrote the oracles in the Hebrew language, and every one interpreted them as he was able.[6]

Clement, who assumed a leadership role in Rome in the latter part of the first century, wrote a letter to the Corinthians sometime around AD 95 that quoted from ten different New Testament books. Clement, according to Eusebius, also recorded how the Gospel of Mark was written and that it had Peter's blessing.

> And so greatly did the splendor of piety illumine the minds of Peter's hearers that they were not satisfied with hearing once only and were not content with the unwritten teaching of the divine Gospel, but with all sorts of entreaties they besought Mark, a follower of Peter, and the one whose Gospel is extant, that he would leave them a written monument of the doctrine which had been orally communicated to them. Nor did they cease until they had prevailed with the man, and had thus become the occasion of the written Gospel which bears the name of Mark. And they say that Peter, when he had learned, through a revelation of the Spirit, of that which had been done, was pleased with the zeal of the men, and that the work obtained the sanction of his authority for the purpose of being used in the churches.[7]

It should be noted that most modern scholars do not agree with the ancient history of Matthew as stated above. The majority, though not the unanimous, opinion currently is that Mark was written first and that Matthew relied on Mark's account when he wrote his Gospel. This is because the two Gospels share many exact or near exact wordings of the same accounts. Where they differ in their treatments of the same event, Matthew is generally the more extensive and detailed account. Most scholars believe that Matthew embellished Mark rather than Mark editing Matthew's accounts. Interestingly, this reliance of Matthew on Mark speaks to the authority with which Mark wrote since Mark was not an apostle like Matthew. Why would Matthew rely on Mark unless he had accurately preserved the teaching of another apostle? Also, the oldest fragments of Matthew that we have are not in Hebrew or Aramaic, as Papias and Polycarp say, but in Greek. However, the scholars who believe that Matthew was the first Gospel written suggest that there was an earlier, abbreviated or more primitive version of Matthew that was written in Hebrew or Aramaic. Mark may have used this for some material when composing his Gospel. Matthew then revised and expanded his account using material from Mark's Gospel.[8] According to New Testament scholar Craig Blomberg, the tradition found in Papias and Polycarp is so "persistent in the early church that there is probably something to it."[9] How that plays out, however, remains a matter of conjecture.

One of the more interesting arguments for the authorship of the Gospels is simply who they are credited to. John, an intimate friend of Jesus, is the type of prominent person whose name we would expect to find attached to an account of the life of Christ. But who was

Matthew

Mark

Matthew? Though he had the privilege of being an apostle, he is, frankly, not of much note in the narratives. Would the book not carry more weight if it were attributed to Peter or James? The fact that it bears a "lesser" apostle's name is itself a good reason to accept the tradition. This is even more so with Mark and Luke since they were not apostles at all and commanded no authority themselves. And yet their writings were immediately considered authoritative. According to tradition, as we saw above, Peter knew about Mark's writings and gave them his blessing. Likewise, Paul is said to refer to Luke's Gospel as "my Gospel."[10]

There is a good argument that all four Gospels were written prior to AD 70.

Another interesting feature of the Gospels is that the names of the authors are nowhere found in the texts. Yet all the books were accepted very early as the teachings of the apostles. In contrast to that are the apocryphal writings, such as the Gospel of Peter and the Gospel of Thomas. These writings and dozens of others explicitly claim apostolic authorship in their texts and yet were rejected as being unauthoritative and, in many cases, declared heretical because of their teachings. The claim of apostolic authorship was not enough to attain an authoritative status. The best explanation for the names affixed to the four Gospels is that these were in fact the authors. The best explanation for their early and quick acceptance is that they preserved the teachings of the apostles accurately.

According to Eusebius, the Gospel of Peter was a forgery condemned by Serapion (d. AD 211). This copy dates from the seventh to ninth centuries.

Dating the Gospels

There is an extremely strong and very early tradition that not only did John write the Fourth Gospel, but that he wrote it after the other three Gospels had been written. According to Clement, bishop of Rome late in the first century, John wrote his Gospel because he was urged by others to aug-

Luke

John

ment the first three Gospels.[11] In his Gospel, John mentions landmarks in Jerusalem as if they still existed at the time of writing, such as the Sheep Gate (John 5:2). Since Jerusalem was razed in AD 70 and the Sheep Gate was among the great destruction, there is a good argument that all four Gospels were written prior to AD 70. This position is further supported by the complete absence of any mention of Jerusalem's destruction in the Gospel or in any other New Testament book, for that matter. As a fulfillment of a prophecy made by Jesus himself, it seems unlikely that it would be omitted by John. However, it has been pointed out that elsewhere in his Gospel, John uses the present tense when referring to things of the past. This leaves the question of the date of writing open to any time just prior to the destruction of Jerusalem to around AD 98, when John died. Many scholars who reject a pre-AD 70 date place the writing sometime between AD 80 and 85. They argue that by then enough time had passed for the destruction of Jerusalem to be a given and therefore not necessary to mention. They also point out that John wrote his epistles because the gnostics had taken John's Gospel and misinterpreted it. Thus a good amount of time must have passed between the writing of the Gospels and the Epistles. This makes the window of AD 80 to 85 a good candidate for those who hold a post-AD 70 view.[12]

Luke's Gospel was likely conceived as a two-volume set consisting of the Gospel of Luke and the Acts of the Apostles. Generally speaking, the books of the New Testament were probably written to fit on whatever size parchment was at hand. The biggest piece of parchment used fairly easily as a scroll was about thirty to thirty-five feet.[13] Both Luke's Gospel and Acts require some thirty to thirty-five feet of parchment each. That and the narrative flow between the end of the Gospel

An inkwell and stylus found at Qumran from the first century BC to AD 68. (The Schøyen Collection MSS 1655/2 and 5095/3, Oslo and London)

Mamertime Prison in Rome where both Peter and Paul were held prior to execution. The hole in the ceiling was the only entrance in their day.

and the beginning of Acts suggest to many scholars that Luke intended his writings to be seen as a whole.

The book of Acts ends with Paul in a Roman prison. Prior to that, Luke documents many of Paul's other imprisonments, trials, persecutions, and various other abuses that he suffered. But Luke does not document the beheading of Paul under Caesar Nero at the end of the imprisonment mentioned at the end of Acts. Nor does he mention any other event that fell after about AD 62.[14] This suggests that Acts was written before Paul's execution. It seems highly unlikely that Luke would mention other such persecutions and not Paul's martyrdom. Thus Acts can be reasonably dated before the death of Paul sometime between AD 62 and 65. And the Gospel of Luke shortly preceded Acts, probably in the very early 60s.

It seems apparent that Luke had access to, and borrowed material from, the Gospel of Mark. If the indications that Luke's Gospel was written in the early 60s are correct and if Luke indeed used Mark, then Mark was written no later than AD 60. This goes against some early tradition that says Mark wrote his Gospel after Peter's death around AD 64 to 65. But other tradition, as noted above, says Peter blessed the work of Mark. Some scholars place the work in the 40s. They argue that some of the fragments found among the Dead Sea Scrolls are from Mark.[15] This may eventually be shown to be true, but it has two hurdles to clear before being accepted. One is that the fragments are disputed. In fact, they may be from Mark or they may be from an even earlier tradition that Mark used. The fragments are just too small to be conclusive. Also, many of Paul's writings predate the Gospels. It seems likely that if the Gospel of Mark did exist in the 40s that Paul would have appealed to it as an authority in his writings. Although these arguments are by no means conclusive, given what we know, the date for the writing of Mark that seems to make the most sense is the late 50s.

7Q5, this tiny fragment of papyrus, a part of the Dead Sea Scroll finds, dates between 50 BC and AD 50 and is claimed by some to be a fragment of Mark.

Many modern scholars place Matthew between AD 70 and 100. However, there are a number of good reasons to hold to an earlier date. Tradition dating back to the first century attributes the writing of the Gospel to Matthew, a point rejected by those holding to a later date. Also, like John, Matthew makes mention of customs and landmarks that were no longer reference points after the destruction of Jerusalem. This makes a date prior to AD 70 reasonable. The oldest tradition, as mentioned earlier, sees Matthew as written prior to Mark rather than relying on Mark. But this would make the overlapping material between Matthew, Mark, and Luke more difficult to explain. Because Matthew and Luke have far more in common with Mark than with each other, it appears they both used Mark rather than Luke and Mark using Matthew. A popular solution to this problem suggests that there is a difference between the canonical Matthew of the Bible and the Matthew mentioned by the church fathers. Matthew then, if he used Mark for some of his material, can be dated no earlier than AD 60. Though it is by no means conclusive, the weight of evidence places the authorship of the canonical version of Matthew sometime in the 60s.

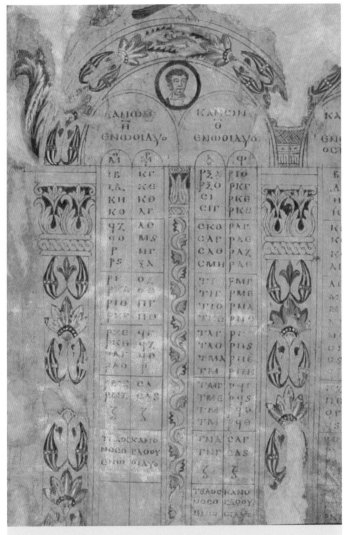

A list of biblical books, called a Canon Table, from the sixth century and housed in the British Library.

Dating Paul's Writings

The earliest parts of the New Testament were written by Paul. Though not all his writings pre-date the Gospels, some do. To date Paul's writings, we can take the evidence from his letters and from Acts and try to reconcile them with what we know from archaeology and other historical indications. We know that Paul died during the persecution of Nero around AD 64–67 so the writings must be dated no later than that. Many scholars believe Galatians, 1 Thessalonians, and 2 Thessalonians are probably Paul's earliest writings and date in the early 50s. Galatians may be dated even in the late 40s.

The main anchor used in dating Paul's chronology is found in Acts 18:12: "While Gallio was proconsul of Achaia, the Jews made a united attack against Paul and brought him to the tribunal." In 1905, a letter from Emperor Claudius to Gallio was discovered in Paris by a doctoral student sorting through a collection of inscriptions. This letter, known as the Gallio or Delphi inscription, was later dated around AD 51 to 52 and fixed the date of Gallio's proconsulship at AD 51 to 52.[16] Thus the events of Acts 18:12-17 took place somewhere in that span. With that time frame, scholars can then work backward. Because Paul's encounter with Gallio happened a year or so into his second missionary journey, the Jerusalem Council mentioned in Acts 15:6-30, which preceded the second missionary journey, probably took place around AD 48. The Jerusalem Council was preceded by Paul's visit to Jerusalem for the purpose of famine relief (Acts 11:27-30). First-century historian Josephus dates this famine around 45 or 46, which puts Paul's visit between AD 45 and 47.[17] In Gal. 2:1, Paul says that after fourteen years he went up to Jerusalem again. But fourteen years from what? Fourteen years since his conversion or fourteen years since his first visit, three years after his conversion? Although it is debated, many scholars prefer the view that the fourteen years should be counted from the time of Paul's conversion, because the conversion is the main temporal reference point in the passage, and it makes the most sense of all the events that must be accounted for in a chronology of Paul. Starting with the famine relief visit in 45 to 47, we then arrive at Paul's conversion in AD 32 to 35. In the ancient world, it was common to count spans of time inclusively. For example, if Jesus died on a Friday and was raised on Sunday, it could be reckoned as three

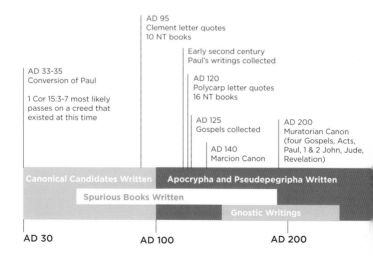

AD 33-35
Conversion of Paul

1 Cor 15:3-7 most likely
passes on a creed that
existed at this time

AD 95
Clement letter quotes
10 NT books

Early second century
Paul's writings collected

AD 120
Polycarp letter quotes
16 NT books

AD 125
Gospels collected

AD 140
Marcion Canon

AD 200
Muratorian Canon
(four Gospels, Acts,
Paul, 1 & 2 John, Jude,
Revelation)

Canonical Candidates Written   **Apocrypha and Pseudepegripha Written**

Spurious Books Written

Gnostic Writings

AD 30   AD 100   AD 200

The Gallio inscription, a.k.a. the Delphi inscription, is a main key to dating Paul.

days just as well as a day and a half. The two most likely dates for the crucifixion of Jesus are AD 30 and 33 (for reasons we will discuss in chapter 10, which deals with prophecy). Thus this span of AD 32 to 35 fits in with either date and shows how early Paul's conversion was.

This exercise in formulating a chronology of Paul is important because of passages like 1 Cor 15:3-8:

For I passed on to you as most important what I also received: that Christ died for our sins according to the Scriptures, that he was buried, that he was raised on the third day according to the Scriptures, and that he appeared to Cephas, then to the Twelve. Then he appeared to over five hundred brothers and sisters at one time; most of them are still alive, but some have fallen asleep. Then he appeared to James, then to all the apostles. Last of all, as to one born at the wrong time, he also appeared to me.

AD 325
Eusebius records the history of the NT books:
22 canonical,
5 widely accepted,
various heretical

AD 393
Council of Hippo fixes the 27 books

AD 397
Council of Carthage also fixes 27 NT books

AD 367
Athanasius lists all 27 NT books

300   AD 400

Note that Paul says he is passing down what he had received. Also note the grammatically unnecessary repetition of the word "that." Because this tradition was handed down to Paul, and because of the way "that" is used, the passage has the look and feel of a creed, a summation of the beliefs of the earliest Christians in a form that was easy to

This third-century fragment of the book of Romans is from Egypt. (The Schøyen Collection MS 113, Oslo and London)

This copy of the Didache is from the late fourth century and can be seen at the Sackler Library in Oxford, UK.

memorize. And because Paul's conversion was one to four years after the crucifixion, this creed is very likely one of the oldest parts of the New Testament, dating within three years of Jesus's death.

The importance of this is enormous because of the content of the creed. According to the creed, Jesus was a real person who died, was buried, was raised from the dead, and then appeared in a resurrected, glorified state to his followers both corporately and individually. Also important is the appeal to the Scriptures as the proper way to understand Jesus. What Scriptures were they talking about? After all, the New Testament did not exist at that point. The creed claims that Jesus is to be seen through the lens of the Old Testament. Critics of the New Testament who say that a legend developed many years after the fact that attributed divinity to Jesus are hard pressed to deal with this extremely early tradition.

What about the Books That Were Left Out?

Eusebius mentions five books he characterizes as spurious: the Acts of Paul, the Epistle of Barnabas, the Shepherd of Hermas, the Didache, and the Apocalypse of Peter. These were books that were considered authoritative by some but ultimately were left out of the New Testament canon.[18]

The Didache, also known as the Teaching of the Twelve, dates back possibly as far as AD 70.[19] The book claims to be the "Lord's Teaching through the Twelve Apostles to the Nations"[20] and was used basically as a handbook for new believers. As the church became more organized, this book eventually fell into disuse, which may have contributed, along with its unlikely attribution of authorship, to its noninclusion in the canon.

The Acts of Paul is a work often referenced by early Christian writers and is considered to contain much accurate information about Paul's history. However, Tertullian, a priest at Carthage at the end of the second century, writes that an elder at Carthage authored the book out of a great admiration for Paul and wanted to increase his fame, though in a misguided way. Because the book is pseudepigraphal, a forgery, the elder who wrote it was removed from office and the book was disqualified for inclusion in the canon.[21]

The Epistle of Barnabas dates from late in the first century or early in the second century. Nothing in its content is out of line with orthodoxy. It was even quoted by Clement of Alexandria and Origen. But the authorship of this book (it is not actually a letter) was thought to have been an early church father and not Paul's missionary partner Barnabas.[22] So it did not meet the criteria set forth for the canon.

The Shepherd of Hermas is an early second-century writing. It contains a series of visions received by a shepherd named Hermas. Like the Epistle of Barnabas, this letter contained nothing suspect. But its author was most likely a church father and not an apostle.[23]

The Apocalypse of Peter is a book well known for its graphic depictions of heaven and hell. But it was found to be written sometime in the first half of the second century, far too late to connect it to Peter himself.[24]

Outside these spurious books and those of the New Testament canon, no other books were ever seriously considered for inclusion. Though there are dozens of books bearing eyewitness names, such as the Gospel of Thomas, the Gospel of Peter, and the Acts of Pilate, none of them met the criteria to be included in the New Testament. These books were written well past the apostolic age (some as late as the Middle Ages) and most of them are clearly legendary and/or heretical. In fact, there are no ancient writings arguing for the acceptance of these second- and third-century books as Scripture except by heretics such as Marcion or the gnostics. The books that are falsely attributed to someone are called pseudepigraphal books. Apocryphal books, meaning books that were hidden away, comprise the rest. To advocates, these books are hidden from the uninitiated and simple-minded people. To the people who rejected these books, they were hidden because of their heresies. Either way, they were not candidates for the canon.

The Codex Bezae is from the sixth century and was once owned by Calvin's successor, Theodor Beza. It contains the Gospels, Acts, and a few verses from 3 John. It resides at the University of Cambridge.

Conclusion

It is interesting to note that the process of the creation of the New Testament made it far more likely to exclude authentic Scripture than to include false writings. The long process ensured a healthy debate from many different perspectives. And yet the majority of the books of the New Testament enjoyed a sustained and overwhelming support for inclusion. Bruce Metzger describes this process by saying, "In the most basic sense neither individuals nor councils created the canon; instead they came to perceive and acknowledge the self-authenticating quality of these writings, which imposed themselves as canonical upon the church."[25] Merrill C. Tenney agrees, saying, "The church did not determine the canon; it recognized the canon."[26]

We see the New Testament has a very strong chain of tra- dition surrounding its authorship by eyewitnesses or those who wrote down what the eyewitnesses reported. The books that are not included in the New Testament, useful though some may be, have no place in the canon given the criteria for inclusion. Thus the Bible was written by people who could reliably document the events they recorded.

The New Testament has a very strong chain of tradition surrounding its authorship by eyewitnesses or those who wrote down what the eyewitnesses reported.

- *But how were the books copied?*
- *Did the information in the books become corrupt?*
- *What about all the contradictions in the New Testament?*
- *And how old are the oldest copies of the New Testament that still exist?*

It is to these questions we must now turn our attention.

Notable Quotes

Even a casual acquaintance, however, of the apocryphal gospels and their credentials will prove that no one excluded them from the Bible; they excluded themselves.[27]   *—Bruce Metzger*

Notes

1 Alexander Roberts and James Donaldson, eds., *Nicene and Post-Nicene Fathers*, vol. 1, 2nd ser., *The Church History of Eusebius* (Peabody, MA: Hendrickson, 2004), 155–57.

2 Mark Knoll, *Turning Points* (Grand Rapids: Baker, 1997, 2000), 36.

3 Ibid., 35.

4 Bruce Metzger, *The New Testament: Its Background, Growth, and Content* (Nashville: Abingdon, 1965), 274–75.

5 Roberts and Donaldson, eds., *Church History of Eusebius*, 222.

6 Ibid., 173.

7 Ibid., 116.

8 An excellent overview of the "Synoptic Problem" is found in D. A. Carson, Douglas J. Moo, and Leon Morris, *An Introduction to the New Testament* (Grand Rapids: Zondervan, 1992), 19–60.

9 Craig Blomberg, "The Historical Reliability of the New Testament," in William Lane Craig, *Reasonable Faith* (Wheaton, IL: Crossway, 1984), 204–5.

10 Roberts and Donaldson, eds., *Church History of Eusebius*, 136–37.

11 Ibid., 153.

12 Carson, Moo, and Morris, *Introduction to the New Testament*, 166–68.

13 Metzger, *The New Testament*, 278–79.

14 Carson, Moo, and Morris, *Introduction to the New Testament*, 116.

15 Randall Price, *Secrets of the Dead Sea Scrolls* (Eugene, OR: Harvest House, 1996), 185–89.

16 Charles Ludwig, *Ludwig's Handbook of New Testament Rulers and Cities* (Denver: Accent, 1976, 1983), 133.

17 Josephus, *Antiquities* 20.2.5.17

18 Roberts and Donaldson, eds., *Church History of Eusebius*, 156–57.

19 Craig A. Evans, *Noncanonical Writings and New Testament Interpretation* (Peabody, MA: Hendrickson, 1992), 157.

20 Alexander Roberts and James Donaldson, eds., *Ante-Nicene Fathers*, vol. 7, *The Teaching of the Twelve Apostles* (Peabody, MA: Hendrickson, 2004), 377.

21 Alexander Roberts and James Donaldson, eds., *Ante-Nicene Fathers*, vol. 3, Tertullian, *On Baptism* (Peabody, MA: Hendrickson, 2004), 677.

22 Craig A. Evans, *Noncanonical Writings and New Testament Interpretation* (Peabody, MA: Hendrickson, 1992), 158; cp. Alexander Roberts and James Donaldson, eds., *Nicene and Post-Nicene Fathers,* vol. 1, 2nd ser., *The Church History of Eusebius* (Peabody, MA: Hendrickson, 2004), 156, n. 20.

23 Evans, *Noncanonical Writings*, 158.

24 Alexander Roberts and James Donaldson, eds., *Ante-Nicene Fathers*, vol. 9, *The Apocalypse of Peter* (Peabody, MA: Hendrickson, 2004), 142.

25 Metzger, *The New Testament*, 276.

26 Merrill C. Tenney, *New Testament Survey* (Grand Rapids: Eerdmans, 1953, 1985), 405.

27 Metzger, *The New Testament*, 101.

CHAPTER 7
IS THE NEW TESTAMENT RELIABLE?

The Problem with the New Testament

When Johannes Gutenberg introduced movable type to Europe in the 1450s, he not only created a method that could mass produce writings relatively easily, but he also rendered obsolete the copying of books by hand—a method that was almost guaranteed to introduce errors into texts. That means for 1400 years or so the New Testament was highly vulnerable to corruption—both intentional and unintentional. If the New Testament is a document written by eyewitnesses of the life and teachings of Jesus, the accurate transmission of these documents over time is a real problem. How can we possibly know that what we now call the New Testament is in fact what was originally written? After all, we do not have the original writings.

Textual Criticism

To deal with the issue of recovering the original text of ancient writings, a discipline called textual criticism was developed. In textual criticism, all the extant copies of a manuscript are compared to one another, and certain techniques are then employed to parse the text in a way that will suggest which of the copies are the more primitive ones. For example, when a variation is found in the texts, the earliest copies are preferred to the later ones, since the change was probably introduced sometime after the early copies. Also, the shorter versions of manuscripts are given more weight than longer ones. This is because the scribes who made the copies were far more likely to add to the text for clarification or comment on the passages than to subtract from the text. When faced with variations themselves, the scribes frequently put what they believed to be authentic in the main

A page from the Gutenberg Bible.

body of the text and then documented the variation in the margins of the page. A third technique is to prefer the reading of the majority of texts. Each of these techniques is a general rule, not a strict standard.

The scribes copied the books in two ways. One way was for each scribe to have an edition of the book they wished to copy, called an exemplar, sitting in front of them. They then tediously copied word for word the text of the book. The other method required a lector to read aloud from the exemplar while several scribes took dictation. This was a much faster way to produce copies but also carried a liability not present in the first method. The liability was that certain words sound exactly the same, or very similar, but can be written two different ways. This is true of English as well. "To" and "too" or "here" and "hear," for instance, are indistinguishable by sound.[1]

Because the books of the New Testament were not officially considered Scripture until late in the fourth century, the scribes probably treated what they were copying with less reverence than was given to the Scripture of the Old Testament. The precautions, developed by scribes of the Old Testament to ensure a copy accurately reflected the exemplar (which we will talk about in the next chapter), were not used initially in the copying of the New Testament. The New Testament books were treated like other valuable letters and histories until the canon was finally formed. Thus the variations we find in the manuscripts were largely introduced into the texts before the fifth century.

Transmission

A common misconception about the New Testament is that it was transmitted like links in a chain, each book being copied, which was then copied by someone else, which was then copied by someone else, and so on. This is often likened to the "telephone game" where one person whispers a message to another, then that person whispers it to another, and it goes around the room. By the time it reaches the last person, the message is often corrupt.

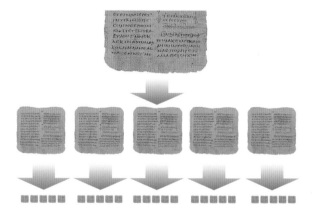

But this is not how the New Testament writings were handed down. As we saw in the last chapter, the books of apostolic origin were considered authoritative very early on. As a result, the books were highly valued. But each church did not have each book. So when a church received a document from an apostle, it shared the book by making a number of copies to send to other churches. The recipients also made multiple copies and sent them to other churches, and so on. We even see Paul directing that copies be made and shared (Col 4:16). As a result, the number of copies grew in an exponential way, with each copy spawning a number of copies.

> When a church received a document from an apostle, it shared the book by making a number of copies to send to other churches. The recipients also made multiple copies and sent them to other churches, and so on.

This fragment of John dates between AD 125 and 130.

Manuscript Authority

Because textual criticism relies entirely on extant manuscripts, the more manuscripts we have, the more accurately the original text can be recovered. In the case of the New Testament, if we limit ourselves to only the original-language manuscripts, we have more than 5,300 copies, including fragments.[2]

Most of these manuscripts were found in monastery libraries around the Mediterranean, and more continue to be discovered. The oldest complete New Testament, which also contains about half the Old Testament, was found in a monastery on Mount Sinai. Codex Sinaiticus, as it is known, dates from AD 350. Note that this is before the canon was officially formed. Codex Vaticanus is dated AD 325 to 350 and contains almost the entire New Testament. The Chester Beatty Papyrus dates to AD 180. It comprises the complete writings of Paul. The Bodmer Papyrus is a copy of most of John's Gospel, from AD 150 to 200.[3]

The oldest universally accepted fragment of the New Testament was found in Egypt in 1920. It is from John's Gospel and is dated AD 125 to 130. If John wrote his Gospel shortly before AD 70, then the span between writing and the copy is 60 years or so. If John wrote the book around AD 80 to 85, then the span is fifty years or less.[4]

There are two notable copies whose dates are debated. The Magdalen Papyri, also called the Jesus Papyri, is a set of five fragments that contain parts of Matthew, originally dated as third or fourth century AD; they have recently been dated prior to AD 70. The other, mentioned in the last chapter, is called 7Q5, indicating that the fragment was the fifth fragment documented at the seventh cave of Qumran near the Dead Sea. It has been dated between 50 BC and AD 50. The text is highly disputed, because the content preserved on this very small fragment contains mostly common words, but a good case has been made for identifying it as a fragment from Mark.[5]

Even if we exclude the last two disputed copies from consideration, compared with other writings of the ancient world, the New Testament has an enormous amount of manuscripts and an extremely short period of time between the writing and the oldest copy.

Homer's *Iliad* probably has the next greatest manuscript authority compared to the New Testament. Homer wrote the *Iliad* around

The Magdalen Papyrii

MANUSCRIPT AUTHORITY OF THE NEW TESTAMENT COMPARED TO OTHER CLASSICAL WORKS

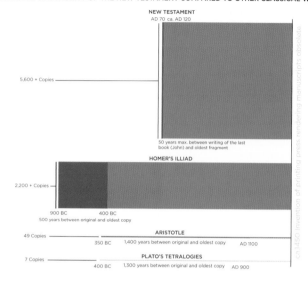

900 BC. The oldest copy we have is from 400 BC—a 500-year span. The total number of manuscripts is 643, and the readings agree about 95 percent of the time.[6]

Aristotle wrote between 384 and 322 BC. The oldest copy is dated AD 1100—1,400 years later. The total number of original language manuscripts is forty-nine of any one book.[7]

Plato wrote his *Tetralogies* between 427 and 347 BC. The earliest extant copy is from AD 900—1,300 years later. We know of only seven manuscripts.[8]

In addition to original language manuscripts of the New Testament, we have about 8,000 Latin Vulgates (a common Latin version translated by Jerome in the fourth century) and 9,300 other early versions. These other early versions are translations into languages such as Coptic, Syriac, Armenian, and Nubian.[9]

The more manuscripts we have, the more accurately the original text can be recovered.

The third piece of the puzzle used in recovering the text is the citations of Scripture in the writings of the early church fathers. As mentioned in chapter 6, the whole of the New Testament can very nearly be reconstructed just from the quotations found in their letters.

Thousands of Errors?

When the original language manuscripts are compared with one another, we find there are about 200,000 variants or errors in 10,000 different places.[10] Variants are, simply, disagreements between texts. These variants can be divided into two categories: unintentional and intentional.

The vast majority of variants are unintentional and are misspellings, interpolations of words or lines, or orthographical in nature.[10] Each time a certain word is misspelled in a certain point in the text, it is counted as an error. For example, if a certain word in a certain verse had the same misspelled word in 537 copies, that would count as 537 errors or variants. Orthographical variants refer to the way words are spelled differently in different places.

A fourth-century fragment of a writing by Melito, a second-century bishop of Sardis. (The Schøyen Collection MS 2337, Oslo and London)

The difference between "theater" and "theatre" is orthographical. Both spellings are correct, but each is preferred in a different geographical location.

Because they preserve the errors of their exemplars, early translations of the New Testament help locate where certain textual variants were mainly known and probably occurred. Also, the writings of the early church fathers are a great help at this point, because when they quote the New Testament, they essentially have tagged the errors they preserved with a time and place. If the oldest occurrence of a variant is found in Augustine, for example, we would know the error was from no later than the late fourth or early fifth centuries and was known in North African copies. If a different error from the same time period is preserved by Chrysostom, we would know that the error was found in copies in the Byzantine region. And if a variant is found in Justin Martyr's writings, we know the variant was no later than the mid-second century and known to the Romans.

These observations led scholars to divide the copies into three major text types, each with its own peculiarities. The Western text type is named for the versions found around Rome. The Byzantine text type encompasses modern Turkey, Greece, and the Middle East. The Alexandrian text type is named for the copies found in North Africa.[11]

The Alexandrian text type has the oldest manuscripts. It is the text type found in the almost ninety surviving papyri and date back to the second (and possibly first) century. The vast majority of English translations are based on the Alexandrian text type, since it is considered by most experts today to be the oldest form of the New Testament.

The text type with the most copies by far is the Byzantine. These manuscripts were written on vellum, a much more durable medium than papyri. The Byzantine texts date from the ninth century onward. This text type was used by Erasmus to compile the first published

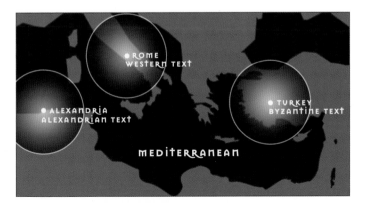

A fifth-century copy of Romans written in Syriac. (The Schøyen Collection MS 2530, Oslo and London)

Greek New Testament. The King James Version was based on Erasmus's work. This accounts for the variation seen between the King James Version and almost any other major English translation.

Whether the Byzantine is the latest and the Alexandrian is the oldest text type is still debated. The majority opinion is that the Byzantine is a combination of the Alexandrian and Western types. But the argument that at least some parts of the Byzantine text date just as far back as the other text types is a strong one.

The other kind of error found in Scripture is an intentional error. These are deliberate changes to the text by the scribes. It was probably not the scribes' intention, however, to corrupt the text. They would sometimes try to correct what they saw as an error or to improve the text in some other way.

A good example of an intentional error is found in Mark 1:1–3 (emphasis added):

> The beginning of the gospel of Jesus Christ, the Son of God. *As it is written in Isaiah the prophet:* See, I am sending my messenger ahead of you; he will prepare your way. A voice of one crying out in the wilderness: Prepare the way for the Lord; make his paths straight!

The above CSB translation uses the Alexandrian (also known as Egyptian) text type as its source.[12] Compare its translation with the New King James Version, based on the Byzantine text type (emphasis added):

> The beginning of the gospel of Jesus Christ, the Son of God. *As it is written in the Prophets:* "Behold, I send My messenger before Your face, Who will prepare Your way before You. The voice of one crying in the wilderness: 'Prepare the way of the Lord, Make His paths straight.'"

Note that the CSB attributes the quote to Isaiah, but the NKJV attributes the quote to "the prophets." Apparently at some point a scribe recognized the quote was not only from Isa. 40:3, but also from Mal. 3:1, and sought to correct the attribution. Whether Mark intentionally, for whatever reason, made the attribution solely to Isaiah is unknown.

This dilemma does, however, illustrate another principle used in recovering the original writing: prefer the more difficult reading. Between the two renderings of Mark 1:1–3, it is easier to explain the difference as a correction from "Isaiah" to "the Prophets" than to explain it as a corruption from "the Prophets" to "Isaiah." The more difficult reading is "Isaiah"; therefore it is considered to have a higher probability of being the original.

Regardless of the value of the techniques described above, there are some parts of the New Testament where we are just not sure what the original writing said. About 400 words fall into this category and comprise about forty verses. The content of these verses contains no basis for any essential doctrine of the Christian faith. As a result, scholars can recover 97 to 99 percent of the original content of the New Testament with certainty.[13]

As it turns out, rather than being disadvantaged by not having the original writings, we find ourselves in a position of good fortune. If we had the originals, a critic of the writings would need only to call into question one document. Instead, a critic needs to deal with more

The ossuary of Caiaphas was found just outside Jerusalem in 1990.

The Sergius Paulus inscription corroborates Acts 13:7-12.

Flavius Josephus

than 5,300 documents that agree substantially 99.5 percent of the time. This ultimately carries as much or more weight than having the originals.

Archaeology and Non-Christian Writings

Because the New Testament purports to document history—events that it claims happened to real people in real places at certain points in time—one of the ways we can test for its reliability is to compare the writings with archaeological finds. Do the findings corroborate or contradict the New Testament?

This test became especially necessary with the rise of liberal theology and "higher criticism" in the early nineteenth century. Biblical scholars and theologians of this stripe ignored the tradition and testimony preserved by the early church fathers and dated the books of the New Testament largely to the second century or even later. With the emergence of archaeology as a scientific discipline (also in the nineteenth century), the historical veracity of the New Testament could be tested.

Do archaeological findings corroborate or contradict the New Testament?

Since that time, archaeology has repeatedly and consistently confirmed the New Testament. Much information about the Mediterranean world at that time that was found only in the New Testament has now been corroborated by archaeological finds. Titles, names of local rulers, time periods, and landmarks that were once thought to be in error or even fictional are now considered to be fact.

There are many books written on this subject detailing the ever-growing number of finds, and even a brief survey would be woefully insufficient. Two of the more important finds have already been mentioned—the Pilate Stone (chap. 1) and the Gallio or Delphi inscription (chap. 6). Other notable finds include the Caiaphas Ossuary (a box used to bury the bones of Caiaphas), found outside Jerusalem in 1990; the Sergius Paulus inscription documents the existence of Paul's first convert on Cyprus

(Acts 13:7); the Pool of Siloam (John 9:1–11);[14] the Pool of Bethesda (John 5:1–15); and inscriptions documenting Lysanias as the tetrarch of Abilene at the time John the Baptist began his ministry according to Luke 3:1.

In addition to archaeological finds, there are a number of writings from non-Christian sources that have survived and corroborate the New Testament. Again, there are too many of these to detail all of them in this context.

The most famous of these non-Christian sources is Josephus (AD 37–100), a Jewish historian in the employ of the Romans. In his work *Antiquities*, book 18, chapter 3, Josephus writes the following:

Cornelius Tacitus

> Now there was about this time Jesus, a wise man, if it be lawful to call him a man; for he was a doer of wonderful ***works, a teacher of such men as receive the truth with pleasure.*** He drew over to him both many of the Jews and many of the Gentiles. He was the Christ. And when Pilate, at the suggestion of the principal men amongst us, had condemned him to the cross, those that loved him at the first did not forsake him; for he appeared to them alive again the third day; as the divine prophets had foretold these and ten thousand other wonderful things concerning him. And the tribe of Christians, so named from him, are not extinct at this day.

Because Josephus was Jewish, it seems extremely unlikely that this passage has been preserved as he wrote it. It is widely regarded to have been added in later, probably by Christian scribes. The remainder of the text, however, is considered by most scholars to be authentic. In the work of Josephus, we also find mentions of James (Jesus's brother), John the Baptist, Herod the Great, and many other people and events documented in the New Testament.[15]

Pliny the Younger

Roman historian Tacitus (AD 55–117) mentions Jesus and Christianity in a passage recording Nero's burning of Rome.

> Consequently, to get rid of the report, Nero fastened the guilt and inflicted the most exquisite tortures on a class hated for their abominations, called Christians by the populace. Christus, from whom the name had its origin, suffered the extreme penalty during the reign of Tiberius at the hands of one of our procurators, Pontius Pilate, and a most mischievous superstition, thus checked for the moment, again broke out not only in Judea, the first source of the evil, but even in Rome, where all things hideous and shameful from every part of the world find their centre and become popular.[16]

Pliny the Younger, governor of Bithynia in Asia Minor from 109 to 111, wrote to Emperor Trajan explaining, among other things, how he handled the Christians.

> I have asked them if they are Christians and if they admit it, I repeat the question a second and a third time, with a warning of the punishment

awaiting them. If they persist, I order them to be led away for execution; for, whatever the nature of their admission, I am convinced that their stubbornness and their unshakable obstinacy ought not to go unpunished.... They also declared that the sum total of their guilt or error amounted to no more than this: that they had met regularly before dawn on a fixed day to chant verses alternately among themselves in honor of Christ as if to a god, and also to bind themselves by oath, not for any criminal purpose, but to abstain from theft, robbery, and adultery.... This made me decide it was all the more necessary to extract the truth by torture of two slave-women, whom they call deaconesses. I found nothing but a degenerate sort of cult carried to extravagant lengths.[17]

Lucian of Samosata

Second-century Greek satirist Lucian wrote:

[Christians] still worship, the man who was crucified in Palestine because he introduced this new cult into the world. ... The poor wretches have convinced themselves, first and foremost, that they are going to be immortal and live for all time, in consequence of which they despise death and even willingly give themselves into custody; most of them. Furthermore, their first lawgiver persuaded them that they are all brothers of one another after they have transgressed once, for all by denying the Greek gods and by worshiping that crucified sophist himself and living under his laws. Therefore they despise all things indiscriminately and consider them common property, receiving such doctrines traditionally without any definite evidence.[18]

Just from the four non-Christian citations quoted above, we see that Jesus was a real person who lived in Palestine during the time of Tiberius and Pontius Pilate. He had a reputation for working wonders and teaching radical doctrine. He was worshiped as God. His followers met on a certain day of the week and exhibited an extreme devotion, even to the point of enduring torture and welcoming death. There was a communal culture that cared for the welfare of all believers. His followers were bound by oath to adhere to a high ethical standard.

All of these things, written by neutral parties at best, corroborate the New Testament. And many other ancient non-Christian writings join these in supporting the history documented in the New Testament.[19]

Is the New Testament the Inspired Word of God?

The word "inspiration" literally means "God-breathed." It does not mean divine dictation where each author became an automaton mechanically recording the words of God. Rather, God used the personalities, experiences, and talents of each writer to reveal himself. It is because man is sinful and prone to error that God superintended the writing of Scripture. That is, in fact, what separates authentic Scripture from any other body of literature.

God used the personalities, experiences, and talents of each writer to reveal himself.

But a claim to be the inspired Word of God is not unique to the New Testament (see 2 Tim. 3:16; 1 Thess. 2:13). The Quran, for example, is among other sacred writings that

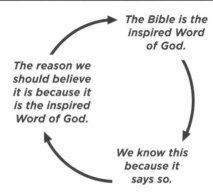

The Bible is the inspired Word of God.

We know this because it says so.

The reason we should believe it is because it is the inspired Word of God.

make this claim. However, the content of the books that claim inspiration cannot be reconciled with one another; they are incompatible. Either one of them is the inspired Word of God, or all of them are uninspired.

The claim that a body of writing is inspired can easily fall into circular reasoning or question-begging where the conclusion of the argument is assumed in the premises. It goes like this: "The Bible is the inspired Word of God. We know this because it says so. The reason we should believe it is because it is the inspired Word of God." This circular reasoning is of no use whatsoever. You can take any set of documents and argue for their divine authority using such fallacious reasoning.

To test for inspiration we must first determine whether the New Testament is a reliable historical document since it purports to be. Some religious documents don't make these kinds of claims. Archaeology and non-Christian writings attest to the historical elements of the New Testament, verifying the times, names, and titles of people who were once thought by critics to be fictional or inaccurate. The Pilate Stone, the Gallio inscription, the writings of Josephus, Lucian, and the like are but a few of the ancient evidences that corroborate the testimony of the New Testament.

Jesus claimed that he was God incarnate, the Word made flesh, so we must focus our investigation on Jesus's claims about himself.

In addition, the vast manuscript authority, as described above, gives us good reason to believe we know the original text with remarkable certainty. Also, the chain of evidence and tradition that traces the New Testament back to eyewitness accounts is very strong. In fact, it is unparalleled in ancient literature.

Jesus claimed that he was God incarnate, the Word made flesh. This claim will be examined in chapter 12. If it can be shown that Jesus made such an outlandish claim, he surely must have also provided a way to authenticate the claim. This authentication came in the form of the resurrection, which he himself predicted and which will be examined in chapter 11. If the arguments for the resurrection are compelling, then we must take seriously what Jesus said about the Old and New Testaments.

According to the New Testament records, Jesus took the Old Testament as the authoritative Word of God spoken through the prophets. He spoke of Abraham, Moses, David, Noah, Jonah, the prophets, and others as real people in history, people whose very existence has been questioned by critics. He spoke of miracles as acts of God that really happened. He spoke of prophecy as a genuine phenomenon.

If the arguments for the resurrection are compelling, then we must take seriously what Jesus said about the Old and New Testaments.

A twelfth-century depiction of the apostle Paul.

Jesus took the Old Testament as the authoritative Word of God spoken through the prophets.

Thus if it can be shown that the New Testament is real history accurately preserved by eyewitnesses, handed down to us in a way in which we can have a good degree of certainty of the original writings, and that there is good reason to believe the resurrection took place, then we must take the words and beliefs of Jesus seriously. Because he considered the Old Testament to be the authoritative Word of God, we have good reason to accept it as well. This is why the apostles often appealed to the Old Testament—because Jesus did. For the first Christians, the Bible was the Old Testament.

Jesus also said that after his death, God the Father would send the Holy Spirit to the apostles. The Holy Spirit would teach them and bring to remembrance all that Jesus taught. After the Holy Spirit came on the day of Pentecost and empowered

For the first Christians, the Bible was the Old Testament.

them, the apostles began teaching what they had been taught. Eventually these things were written down by them and that body of work is what we call the New Testament.

Thus if it can be shown that Jesus claimed to be God, and if it can be shown to be reasonable to believe the resurrection is a historical event, then we have good reason to believe the Bible is the inspired Word of God. If the case can be made for the Bible's inspiration, then it is also reasonable to believe that the Bible is infallible in its original writings. The whole idea of inspiration is that God ensured the writings of the authors to contain certain accounts that convey the truth accurately. Infallibility is a by-product of inspiration.

After the Holy Spirit came on the day of Pentecost and empowered them, the apostles began teaching what they had been taught.

The New Testament is no ordinary work of men, but the infallible, ever-reliable Word of God spoken through instruments of his choosing.

Conclusion

The New Testament commands a manuscript authority that far outstrips any other ancient writing and allows us to have a very high degree of certainty of the original text. In addition, the claim of inspiration that the New Testament makes is not an idle boast. It is a claim that can be investigated. Thus the New Testament is no ordinary work of men, but the infallible, ever-reliable Word of God spoken through instruments of his choosing.

Notable Quote

> If I were the devil (please, no comment), one of my first aims would be to stop folk from digging into the Bible. Knowing that it is the Word of God, teaching men to know and love and serve the God of the Word, I should do all I could to surround it with the spiritual equivalent of pits, thorn hedges and man traps, to frighten people off.[20]
> —*J. I. Packer*

Pentecost as portrayed in the Ingeborg Psalter from before AD 1210.

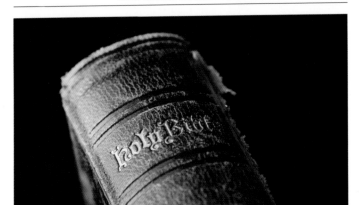

Notes

1   Bruce Metzger, *The New Testament: Its Background, Growth and Content* (Nashville: Abingdon, 1965), 280.

2   Ibid., 283.

3   Norman Geisler, *Christian Apologetics* (Grand Rapids: Baker, 1976), 306.

4   Craig Blomberg, "The Historical Reliability of the New Testament," in William Lane Craig, *Reasonable Faith* (Wheaton, IL: Crossway, 1984), 194.

5   Randall Price, *Secrets of the Dead Sea Scrolls* (Eugene, OR: Harvest House, 1996), 185–89.

6   Josh McDowell, *Evidence That Demands a Verdict* (San Bernardino: Here's Life, 1972, 1979), 43.

7   Ibid., 42.

8   Ibid.

9   Metzger, *New Testament*, 283.

10 Ibid., 281.

11 David Allen Black, "Key Issues in New Testament Textual Criticism," Biola University lecture, cd; Larry W. Hurtado, "How the New Testament Has Come Down to Us," in *Introduction to the History of Christianity*, ed. Tim Dowley (Minneapolis: Fortress, 2002), 132.

12 The CSB uses the *Novum Testamentum Graece*, 27th ed., as the textual base for its translation of the New Testament. The *Novum Testamentum Graece* is primarily reliant on the Alexandrian text type.

13 Black, "Key Issues in New Testament."

14 John 9:1–11; cp. Hershel Shanks, "Where Jesus Cured the Blind Man," *Biblical Archaeology Review* 31, no. 5 (September/October 2005): 16–23.

15 Blomberg, "Historical Reliability," 215.

16 Tacitus, *Annals* 15.44.

17 Pliny the Younger, *Epistles* 10.96.

18 Lucian, *The Passing of Peregrinus*, 11–13.

19 An excellent compilation and study of such writings is found in Gary R. Habermas, *The Historical Jesus* (Joplin, MO: College Press, 1996), 143–255.

20 J. I. Packer, foreword, in R. C. Sproul, *Knowing Scripture* (Downers Grove, IL: InterVarsity, 1977), 9.

CHAPTER 8
IS THE OLD TESTAMENT RELIABLE?

Why Pay Attention to the Old Testament?

With the death of Jesus, the earliest Christians were not left in a crisis of authority. Jesus had prepared for his absence by commissioning apostles, men whose mission it was to preserve and spread his teachings and oversee his church. Their teachings were soon codified into writings that would eventually become known as the New Testament. But the apostles and other Jews of the first century already had a body of writings they viewed as canonical. Jesus confirmed and upheld this view that the Hebrew Bible was Scripture,[1] the written Word of God, an authority for their lives.

According to Jesus, the Old Testament was God's specific revelation of himself; as such, it was only through the Old Testament that they could correctly perceive God, the world around them, and, most important, Jesus himself. The framework of the Old Testament was absolutely essential for understanding Jesus and his teachings. And, in turn, Jesus's teachings, life, and death shed great light on the Old Testament.

As a result of the Old Testament's importance to Christianity, the same questions must be asked of it that were asked of the New Testament. What is it? Where did it come from? Is it reliable?

What Is the Old Testament?

Not surprisingly, Jews do not refer to their Scriptures as "the Old Testament." Although the writings are between 2,400 and 3,400 years old, for Jews the writings are not old in the sense of having been augmented by a newer body of work such as the writings of the apostles about Jesus.

An eleventh-century Targum, an Aramaic translation of the Old Testament.

Therefore the term "Old Testament" is considered by Jews to be, at best, a misnomer. The Hebrew Bible is known as the Tanak. The word *Tanak* is an acronym created from the first letter of each of the three sections of Scripture. The first section is the Torah, meaning "the Law." The first five books of the Bible, all attributed to Moses, comprise the Law. The second section is the Neviim, meaning "the Prophets." This section documents the lives of the prophets and their messages. The third section is called the Ketuvim, meaning "the Writings." Wisdom literature, songs, and miscellaneous stories are found in this section.

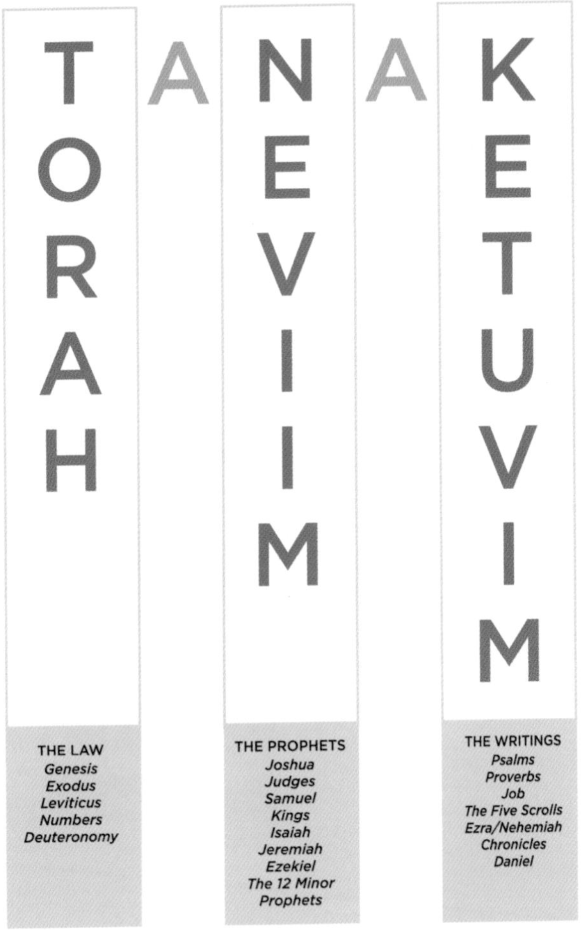

T A N A K

TORAH

NEVIIM

KETUVIM

THE LAW
Genesis
Exodus
Leviticus
Numbers
Deuteronomy

THE PROPHETS
Joshua
Judges
Samuel
Kings
Isaiah
Jeremiah
Ezekiel
The 12 Minor
Prophets

THE WRITINGS
Psalms
Proverbs
Job
The Five Scrolls
Ezra/Nehemiah
Chronicles
Daniel

How Was the Old Testament Written?

In the nineteenth century, the prevailing view was that there were no large masterpieces of literature at the time Moses lived. Since the nineteenth century, archaeologists have uncovered masterpieces that pre-date Moses by many centuries, such as *The Epic of Gilgamesh*. There are no Hebrew texts outside the Bible from the time of Moses except a very few short inscriptions in the Sinai that may be Hebrew. Moses himself was most likely literate because of his privileged upbringing and could have been literate in as many as three languages.[2]

Just as Luke worked with multiple sources in writing the Gospel that bears his name, so Moses likely had numerous documents that had been passed down from generation to generation. The Hebrews' consciousness of their unique role as God's people would have been a motivating factor in conveying what God had earlier revealed. We now know that people from this time often kept extensive written records of business deals and communications, and that the early Israelites probably had written stories and other sources regarding the events of the patriarchs' lives.

This tablet is one of six known records that contain a list of kings and cities from before the great flood. It dates between 2000 and 1800 BC and is from Babylonia. (The Schøyen Collection MS 2855, Oslo and London)

> *The Hebrews' consciousness of their unique role as God's people would have been a motivating factor in conveying what God had earlier revealed.*

There are a couple of reasons Moses's writings were accepted by the nation of Israel as the inspired Word of God. One reason is the many miracles they observed that Moses either did or was a player in. These miracles were not for the benefit of Moses, but for those who were witnesses. They were not gratuitous in nature, but done to authenticate Moses as one who spoke for God. Another reason is that he conducted his ministry openly with no attempt to hide things from anyone. No one had any grounds to question his motives or his methods. The nation of Israel took what they saw at face value: Moses was a man through whom God had chosen to reveal himself.

The writings of the prophets therefore had a criterion to meet. There would have to be some sign, primarily predictive prophecy, that would authenticate those who claimed to speak for God. The messages and histories of

Moses receiving the Law as depicted in the Ashburnham Pentateuch, a Spanish Torah from the sixth century.

these people were preserved and accepted ultimately for the same reasons as Moses's works. According to tradition, from Moses to Nehemiah there appears to be a chain of prophets whose messages were recorded. After Nehemiah, the canon of the Neviim (the prophets) was, for all intents and purposes, closed. The chain of prophets came to an end.

The remaining books in the Tanak were, for one reason or another, treated as scriptural. A primary indication of the high esteem held for these books, such as Psalms, Job, and Proverbs, is that there were commentaries written about them. Many examples of such commentaries were found among the Dead Sea Scrolls. Noncanonical books did not inspire such ancillary literature.

A great witness to the canonicity of the books is provided by the New Testament. As mentioned in the last chapter, Jesus referred to many people and events in the Tanak as actual history. Following his lead, the New Testament writers also reference and appeal to the figures and events documented in the Tanak as actual and reliable. Norman Geisler makes the following observation:

A passage from Exod. 20 taken from a Pentateuch at the British Library.

Jesus and the New Testament writers did not have specific occasion to quote every book in the Old Testament, but when they did cite a specific book it was often with introductory phrases that indicated their belief in the divine authority of that specific book. Of the twenty-two books numbered in the Jewish Old Testament some eighteen are cited by the New Testament. There is no explicit citation of Judges, Chronicles, Esther, or the Song of Solomon, although Hebrews 11:32 refers to events in Judges, 2 Chronicles 24:20 may be alluded to in Matthew 23:35, Song of Solomon 4:15 may be reflected in John 4:15, and the feast of Purim established in Esther was accepted by the New Testament Jews.[3]

Historian Josephus preserves in his writings what Jews of the first century AD thought about the Tanak. He mentions the Scriptures of the Jews in a way that implies the books were not in dispute, that they were a de facto canon. This view was corroborated by Jewish leaders who met at Jamnia in AD 90 and 92. Their goal was not to fix a canon necessarily, but to envision what Judaism should look like without the temple and its sacrificial system. Certainly the books were discussed, but no formal authority for fixing the canon was given or claimed by them. The point of their authority to officially determine is probably moot since they ultimately suggested no change to the canon.

With the destruction of the temple in Jerusalem in AD 70, the Jews became decentralized. As they began to disperse to other regions, the need for a standardized text became paramount if they were to remain a distinct people at all. As the people through whom God revealed himself, they needed to

As the people through whom God revealed himself, they needed to ensure that all the people had access to and a reminder of the revelation that had been given to them.

ensure that all the people had access to and a reminder of the revelation that had been given to them. They were people of the Book and as such instituted measures to ensure its accurate transmission.

The Difference between the Tanak and the Old Testament

When you compare the Tanak and the Old Testament, you will immediately notice a difference. The Old Testament has thirty-nine books, but the Tanak has only twenty-four or twenty-two (depending on whether Ruth was considered the end of Judges and whether Lamentations was considered the end of Jeremiah). And the books that share the same names are often in a different order. A closer look, however, reveals that they contain identical text and differ only in formatting.

The longer books of the Tanak, such as Chronicles, Kings, and Samuel, have been segmented in the Old Testament. Also, the minor prophets ("minor" meaning prophets that did not write very much, not that they were of lesser importance) are collected in one book in the Tanak but are individual books of the Old Testament. This reformatting was not an

This fragment from the Septuagint dates between 50 BC and AD 50.

innovation of the early Christians but, in fact, was done by the Jews themselves when the Tanak was translated into Greek, some 250 years or so before the birth of Jesus.

The Septuagint

After the Hellenization of Palestine and Egypt in the fourth century BC under Alexander the Great, many but not all Jews found themselves speaking Greek as their common language. Sometime about halfway through the third century, according to legend, Ptolemy Philadelphus, the king of Egypt, commissioned a translation of the Torah into Greek. To do the work, he contacted Eleazar, the chief priest in Jerusalem at the time.

Eleazar arranged for six translators from each of the twelve tribes of Israel.[4] These seventy-two men became the namesake of the translation—"Septuagint" means seventy (apparently they rounded down) and is often referred to now as the "LXX," the Latin form of 70. By 200 to 150 BC, the Neviim and Ketuvim were also translated into Greek, completing the work. Later versions also include apocryphal books, books rejected by the Jews as canonical but still considered important. Whatever the actual history behind the translation of the Septuagint, it is clear that it was translated from Hebrew into Greek in Alexandria beginning in the third century BC.

By the first century BC, the Septuagint was the standard version of Scripture used by the Jews in the Diaspora. It is likely that Palestinian Jews, especially around Jerusalem, used the Hebrew Old Testament and Aramaic Targums. Hellenistic Jews would more likely use the LXX.

Septuagint Books

Genesis	2 Chronicles	Daniel
Exodus	Ezra	Hosea
Leviticus	Nehemiah	Joel
Numbers	Esther	Amos
Deuteronomy	Job	Obadiah
Joshua	Psalms	Jonah
Judges	Proverbs	Micah
Ruth	Ecclesiastes	Nahum
1 Samuel	Song of Solomon	Habakkuk
2 Samuel	Isaiah	Zephaniah
1 Kings	Jeremiah	Haggai
2 Kings	Lamentations	Zechariah
1 Chronicles	Ezekiel	Malachi

Tanak Books

Genesis	Samuel	Proverbs
Exodus	Kings	Job
Leviticus	Isaiah	The Five Scrolls
Numbers	Jeremiah	Daniel
Deuteronomy	Ezekiel	Ezra/Nehemiah
Joshua	The 12 Minor Prophets	Chronicles
Judges	Psalms	

The Talmudists

When a document is purposed to be the Word of God, one of the questions that arises is how we know that the manuscripts we now have accurately accord with the original manuscripts. What do we know about the transmission of the Tanak?

A group of men called the Talmudists took on the responsibility of copying the Tanak in Hebrew in the years following AD 70. The Talmudists developed a very strict set of rules governing the ways in which the copies were made. Each page of the codex must have the same number of text columns. The columns had to be at least 48 lines long, but no longer than sixty lines. Each line had to be thirty letters long. The spacing between letters, lines, sections, and books had to follow very specific rules as well. The Torah had to end exactly at the end of a line. Nothing, not even a part of a letter, could be written from memory. The ink had to be black and had to be made in a very specific way. The name of God could not be the first thing written after dipping the pen in ink. The copyist had to wear specific clothes and follow certain rules about bathing.[5]

To the Jews, the newest, most unblemished copy was preferred, not the oldest. Thus, if a Tanak was found to be in error, damaged or blemished in any way, the copy was burned, buried, or given to schools for lessons. This partially accounts for the great lack of ancient manuscripts, a stark contrast to the New Testament's impressive manuscript authority.

The Masoretes

From AD 500 to 900, the task of preserving and transmitting the Tanak was assumed by the Masoretes. By the time they began their role, there was a concern that the proper pronunciation of the Hebrew could be lost. The problem was that the Hebrew alphabet did not contain any vowels. To ensure the accurate passing down of tradition ("masora" means tradition), the Masoretes developed a system of markings that surrounded the consonants and acted as vowels.[6]

Like the Talmudists, the Masoretes also developed a system for ensuring the accuracy of their copies. They would count the number of words and letters in each book and also calculate the middle word and middle letter. They even knew the number of times each letter of the alphabet appeared in each book.[7] If a copy did not agree exactly with the original, it was destroyed.

An example of a Torah case.

The result, called the Masoretic Text, is what is used today by both Jews and Christians. Because of the great pains that were taken by the scribes to ensure exact copies, it was long assumed that the text was very accurate, but there was no way to know for sure—until the discovery of the Dead Sea Scrolls, that is.

The Dead Sea Scrolls

Because of the frailty of writing materials and the climate of Palestine (which promotes the rotting of the materials), the Old Testament has a manuscript authority much like other ancient texts. Writings that have survived for any length of time have only done so because they were stored in vessels that were kept in dry and arid climates. This is precisely what happened in the case of the Dead Sea Scrolls. There are a number of versions of the story of how the scrolls were discovered. Although we will probably never know exactly how it happened with certainty, the basic features seem to be as follows.[8]

A second-century fragment from Numbers and Deuteronomy. This papyrus is a part of the Chester Beatty collection.

In 1947, seven ancient manuscripts were offered for sale by a Bethlehem dealer in antiquities. He had bought them from a Bedouin shepherd who had found them in a cave near Qumran on the Dead Sea. The shepherd had been looking for a lost goat.

Rather than crawl into every single cave in the area, he decided to throw rocks into the caves and try to scare the goat out. Instead, in one cave he heard the breaking of a clay jar. He let himself into the cave and found a number of large clay jars that contained ancient manuscripts written on parchment. The shepherd's first thought was that the old parchment could be used for sandal straps. So the scrolls were taken back to his tent and hung there for a time before being sold in Bethlehem. The scrolls were then resold, with some eventually finding their way to the international market.

The price of $250,000 for several of the scrolls in 1954 ignited a gold rush of sorts among the Bedouin. And the discovery itself ignited a number of archaeological expeditions. About

Parts of Amos, Zechariah, and Malachi can be seen in this eleventh-century copy of the Tanak that is an example of the Masoretic text tradition. (The Schøyen Collection MS 1630, Oslo and London)

Many of the caves contained scroll jars that were still intact and contributed to the preservation of the manuscripts. (photo courtesy www.HolyLandPhotos.org)

Cave 4, site of the biggest Dead Sea Scroll find.

270 caves in the area were explored; ten of them contained more manuscripts. In all, more than 40,000 fragments were discovered from 500 different books and writings. Of these books, every single book of the Old Testament except Esther was found. Most important, the writings dated from the third century BC (a portion of Samuel) to the first century AD—far older than the oldest previously known manuscripts.

Chief among the finds was one of the first scrolls discovered in Cave 1: a copy of Isaiah from about 150–100 BC. This discovery provided the opportunity to see just how accurately the Hebrew Scriptures had been transmitted. Comparison with a second, though incomplete, copy of Isaiah also found at Qumran showed more than a 95-percent agreement in the texts. The 5 percent of disagreement had to do with misspellings and copying errors.[9] More impressive, the Masoretic text, copied 1,000 years later, also agrees with the Isaiah scroll to an astonishing degree. For example, in Isa. 53, the difference between the two texts is an issue of seventeen letters, ten of which are spelling variances and four are stylistic changes. The three letters of real variance do not change the text in any substantial way.[10]

The Apocrypha

After the completion of the translation of the Tanak into Greek, other writings containing the history of the Jews from the time of Malachi (ca. 450 BC) to the birth of Jesus were translated as well. Although these books were held to be very important by the Jews, they were not considered scriptural. Their content not only contained some historical and factual errors, but also taught things that did not cohere with Scripture. They were, however, added to many versions of the Septuagint, creating what is sometimes referred to as the "Septuagint plus." When Jerome translated the Old Testament into Latin in the fourth century, he included these books, designating them as apocryphal. Like the Jews, he considered them as having some value but that they were not fit for the formulation of doctrine. With the caveat of their noncanonical status, the books continued to be included in Bibles until shortly after the

Reformation. After 1825 or so, the apocryphal books were largely dropped from inclusion in the Bible except in versions authorized by the Roman Catholic Church or the Eastern Orthodox churches.

During the Reformation, one of the complaints against Rome was that some of its teachings had no basis in Scripture. Rome responded in 1546 at the Council of Trent by declaring the apocryphal books to be scriptural, thus expanding its definition of the canon. The reason these books were incorporated is that Roman Catholic doctrines such as prayers for the dead, purgatory, and justification by faith plus works are derived from them.

Archaeological Corroboration

The accurate transmission of the text is, of course, irrelevant if the history it purports to preserve can be shown to be invented or contradicted by archaeological finds. Fortunately, there is no small number of sites that have yielded and/or continue to yield finds relating to the ancient Hebrews. As with the New Testament, many volumes have been dedicated to the cataloging of such finds. A very few selected highlights are mentioned below.

The Taylor Prism

The excavations at the biblical city of Nineveh have given archaeologists a great wealth of findings. From 705 to 681 BC, Sennacherib ruled Assyria from Nineveh and housed his great library there. This library included up to 100,000 texts[11] including what became known as the Taylor Prism. This prism is a six-sided clay cylinder with an inscription detailing Sennacherib's siege of Jerusalem. It also mentions Hezekiah as being "like a caged bird within his royal capital."[12] Second Kings 18–19, 2 Chron. 32, and Isa. 36–37 are all corroborated by the Taylor Prism. The Taylor Prism currently resides in the British Museum.

The Cyrus Cylinder

A sixth-century-BC clay cylinder found in the nineteenth century bears an inscription concerning Cyrus the Persian. After taking control of Babylon in 539 BC, he issued a decree allowing Babylonian captives to return to their homes and to worship their own gods.[13] This decree corresponds to an account regarding Cyrus in Ezra 1:1-3; 6:3 (cp. 2 Chron. 36:23; Isa. 44:28). It can be seen in the British Museum.

The Black Obelisk of Shalmaneser

In 1846, a 6.5-foot-tall pillar of black limestone was found in the biblical city of Calah. This four-sided monument commemorated, among other things, the receiving of a tribute by the Assyrian King Shalmaneser III from Jehu (2 Kings 9-10), son of Omri, in 841 BC. Part of the bas-relief depictions shows an Israelite prostrate before Shalmaneser and is the oldest known picture of an ancient Israelite.[14] The obelisk can be seen in the British Museum.

The Gilgamesh Epic

Also found in the library at Nineveh was a set of twelve tablets containing an epic poem about a king named Gilgamesh. Tablet XI was the first find that contained a non-biblical account of what is known in the Tanak as the flood for which Noah built the ark (Gen. 7–8). Gilgamesh is noted as the fifth king after the great flood. Though the stories do not totally agree, there is much similarity between them. Many ancient finds since then also tell this story or something very close to it. This likely indicates the actuality of a great flood, though the details of the flood vary from culture to culture.[15]

The Moabite Stone

In 1868, a stone was discovered in Palestine that contained an inscription in ancient Moabite. Not only does the inscription mention Mesha, the Moabite king who rebelled against Israelite rule in 2 Kings 3, but it also mentions the name "Yahweh."[16] The Moabite Stone is housed in the Louvre.

The Tel Dan Stele

Found in 1993/94 in Israel, this is an Aramaic inscription apparently commissioned by Hazael to commemorate his victory at Ramoth Gilead (2 Kings 8:28-29). It is noteworthy for referring to the kingdom of Judah as the "House of David." This is the first extra-biblical evidence for the fact that the dynasty of David ruled in Jerusalem.

Conclusion

In the end, we see that although the Old Testament was written as long as 3,500 years ago, its content has been extremely well preserved. The methods employed by the scribes who made the copies give us good reason to think that we have the same text that was written by the authors. Archaeological finds corroborate many of the historical events documented in the Old Testament, giving us good reason to think that the authors were accurately documenting historical events. We also find evidence that this history of the ancient Hebrews was documented and transmitted in written

Although the Old Testament was written as long as 3,500 years ago, its content has been extremely well preserved.

A Torah scroll being held in its wooden case at a celebration in Jerusalem.

form by Moses and others. In short, there is every reason to take the content of the Old Testament seriously.

This leads us to our next problem: how are we to take such things as miracles and prophecy? What exactly is meant by them, and do they really happen? These things factor heavily into both the Old and New Testaments and must be dealt with if we are to accept them as trustworthy, let alone authoritative. The next chapters will deal with miracles and prophecy respectively.

Notable Quote

> For the Hebrew Scriptures . . . are of a self-authenticating character, and do not derive their authority either from individual human beings or from corporate ecclesiastical pronouncements. . . . Ecclesiastical councils did not give the books their divine authority, but merely recognized that they both had it and exercised it.[17]
> — *R. K. Harrison*

Notes

1   The Sadducees accepted only the Torah as Scripture, however.

2   R. Laird Harris, *Inspiration and Canonicity of the Scriptures* (Greenville, SC: A Press, 1995), 128.

3   Norman Geisler, *Christian Apologetics* (Grand Rapids: Baker, 1976), 355–56.

4   Merrill C. Tenney, ed., *Pictorial Encyclopedia of the Bible* (Grand Rapids: Zondervan, 1975–1976), 5:343–44.

5   Josh McDowell, *Evidence That Demands a Verdict* (San Bernardino: Here's Life, 1972, 1979), 53.

6   Don Brooks and Norman Geisler, *When Skeptics Ask* (Grand Rapids: Baker, 1996), 158.

7   McDowell, *Evidence That Demands a Verdict*, 55.

8   This brief account closely follows the account found in Randall Price, *Secrets of the Dead Sea Scrolls* (Eugene, OR: Harvest House, 1996), 29–50.

9   Brooks and Geisler, *When Skeptics Ask*, 158–59. Brooks and Geisler are here citing Gleason Archer Jr., *A Survey of the Old Testament Introduction* (Chicago: Moody Press, 1964), 19.

10 McDowell, *Evidence That Demands a Verdict*, 58. McDowell is citing Norman L. Geisler and William E. Nix, *A General Introduction to the Bible* (Chicago: Moody Press, 1968), 263.

11 Howard F. Vos, *Archaeology in Bible Lands* (Chicago: Moody Press, 1977, 1982), 120.

12 E. M. Blaiklock and R. K. Harrison, *The New International Dictionary of Biblical Archaeology* (Grand Rapids: Zondervan, 1983), 436–37.

13 Ibid., 146.

14 Blaiklock and Harrison, *New International Dictionary of Biblical Archaeology*, 409.

15 Ibid., 214.

16 Ibid., 319.

17 R. K. Harrison, *Introduction to the Old Testament* (Grand Rapids: Eerdmans, 1969), 262–63.

CHAPTER 9
DO MIRACLES HAPPEN?

What Is a Miracle?

During the course of our lives, we see many things that amaze us, inspire us, and fill us with wonder. Cures are found for diseases that once seemed untamable. A child self-assembles in a mother's womb and is born to astonished parents. Extraordinary and highly unlikely plays and comebacks are made in different sports. All these things and others like them are commonly referred to as being miraculous. But the word "miracle" means something completely different than a highly improbable event. It may be that, but there is more. A miracle is an extraordinary event that is the product of a being that is intentional, purposeful, and benevolent. Such an event couldn't have happened apart from the agency of such a being.

Wayne Grudem says that miracles are "a less common kind of God's activity in which he arouses people's awe and wonder and bears witness to himself."[1] To be clear, this does not mean that God is only occasionally present and that every once in a while he chooses to interrupt or intervene. The God of the Bible is in control of all things and is powerful enough to create and sustain what we call normalcy and regularity. As defined above, miracles do mean that sometimes God works in a way that is outside the patterns that appear normal. He does this to instill awe at his nature and to achieve the end he desires.

The Context and Possibility of Miracles

God has created and sustains the universe in patterns that can be described as law-like and that we describe as natural laws. One of the most obvious regularities that make life possible is what we call the law of gravity. A miracle is often mischaracterized as a suspension or violation of these laws. However, miracles may be more accurately characterized as revealing an element that does not normally present itself in how the world works and is therefore not accounted for by the natural laws.

To illustrate this idea, picture a vase falling off a table in the middle of a room that contains no other furniture. The law of gravity says the vase will continue falling until it hits the floor. The fall of the vase is a naturally occurring event, and, in fact, it is predictable as long as no other factors are present or at work. But if you are standing next to the table and catch the vase, has the law of gravity been violated? Of course not. The law of gravity does not and cannot account for the behavior of a freely acting agent who chooses to interrupt the fall of the vase. Whether or not you choose to catch the vase, the law of gravity is still in force.

Miracles are "a less common kind of God's activity in which he arouses people's awe and wonder and bears witness to himself." —Wayne Grudem

If God does not exist, then there is no transcendent agent to act in nature, nothing to effect a miracle—and so there would be no miracles. But if God, a transcendent, personal, powerful, engaged being, does exist, then it is possible for miracles to exist. Even more important, God is actually required for what we call "natural laws" to exist in the first place. God creates the patterns that we call normal and against which we judge events to be ordinary or extraordinary. This does not mean, however, that miracles will happen, just that they are possible.

The existence of God as described by theism is necessary for miracles to occur but not sufficient. God's will is the sufficient cause of a miracle occurring. To continue the illustration of the vase, God is always in the room, always in control of the vase (he is all-powerful), and has the ability to act extraordinarily at any time. God's being all-powerful means that he is not only always in the room and can catch the vase, but also that he can change the patterns of the physical universe from what they are now, resulting in a wholly different physics. The arguments in chapters 2 through 5 provide good reason for believing that such a God exists.

Does Natural Science Show That Miracles Cannot Happen?

Natural sciences, such as physics, astronomy, and chemistry, study the physical universe. They are concerned with observing, exploring, and measuring the characteristics of matter and energy and how the two relate to each other. The methods used by scientists in their work are based on the principles of uniformity and regularity or predictability. Scientists

observe and document natural phenomena. Theories are then proposed to account for why the phenomena are the way they are. Tests are then developed to either corroborate or falsify the theories. As a result, theories are then refined and retested, adopted as sufficiently explanatory, or abandoned. The great value of this approach is that theories that describe the world accurately provide us with the ability to predict events with a high degree of reliability and provide explanations for why certain things happen physically.

It has been argued that if God occasionally intervened in the world, it would upset the natural order and thus render the scientific method useless. But there are almost always unknown factors and agents at work in the physical world, and many events cannot be predicted regardless of scientific knowledge. For example, for all we know about seismology,

we are still surprised when earthquakes happen. And regardless of our knowledge of civil and mechanical engineering and psychology, we still cannot predict car crashes. If I develop a brain tumor, it does not mean that medical science is worthless because it could not predict the irregular and nonuniform development of my brain. In the case of events that don't fall within patterns known to science at that point, one stratagem of science is to seek patterns at a deeper level. Anomalies at one level can become law-like phenomena if we probe to a deeper level.

Theories that describe the world accurately provide us with the ability to predict events with a high degree of reliability and provide explanations for why certain things happen physically.

Earthquakes, car crashes, and brain tumors differ, however, from miracles. Miracles are vehicles through which God communicates purposefully and specifically. They are not arbitrary events; they are not monkey wrenches thrown into the mix with no good reason. They are events that betray an intelligent action. Again, it is normalcy and regularity that equip us to recognize such extraordinary events. So when a claim of a miraculous event is made, such as the parting of the Red Sea, it is really a claim of intelligent action by a powerful, transcendent being in an extraordinary way.

Miracles are vehicles through which God communicates purposefully and specifically.

Natural science, though extremely important and useful for providing information about the normal, regular course of the physical world, is not in a position to comment on miracles. Miracles fall outside science's purview, its ability to speak with authority. Miracles need to be investigated as nonuniform, irregular, purposeful events. As such, natural science has no place at the table other than establishing what is normal and regular. Miracles are not part of the job description of scientists; it is not their department. Ron Brooks and Norman Geisler comment that "trying to explain miracles by means of natural causes is definitely unscientific!"[2] This means that miracles and natural science are necessarily incompatible. Science is not the sole method of explanation for this world, nor does it trump or carry more weight than other ways of knowing. Other methods of explanation, such as philosophy, are not subject to the dominion of natural science. Both science and philosophy exercise authority for offering explanations, but not in the same arenas. Explanatory disciplines conflict when one is used to try to explain what is outside its sphere and belongs to another. Thus natural science does not show that miracles cannot happen. It does, however, help to equip us to recognize miracles if they do occur.

Does Experience Show That Miracles Cannot Happen?

It is probably safe to say that the majority of people we know do not claim to have witnessed a miracle. Skeptics of God's existence have often seized on this as evidence against miracles. But just because something happens rarely or even only once in the course of history does not mean there can be no good reason to believe it occurred.

To demonstrate this, picture Ford's Theatre in Washington, D.C. We know with great certainty that plays were performed there regularly from 1863 to 1865. But we also know with great certainty that on April 14, 1865, Abraham Lincoln was shot while watching a play in Ford's Theatre. Just because Abraham Lincoln was assassinated only once does not make it historically suspect. And just because his assassination was improbable does not mean there is a lack of evidence regarding the facts. The frequency of an event and the evidence for the occurrence of a one-time event with an accurate description of it are two entirely different matters.

Consider another example: Based on a 2005 estimate, the odds of winning the Grand Prize in the Powerball lottery are 120,256,770 to 1.[3] Using the skeptic's reasoning, there is no good reason to believe that anyone has ever won the lottery. But a number of people have actually won the Powerball grand prize despite its being 120 million times more likely that they won nothing at all. The rarity of their feat says nothing about the ability to know it occurred.

The same can be said for miracles. Indeed it is the infrequency of miracles that gives them their force. After all, the parting of the Red Sea would cease to be news if it happened fairly often.

What Is the Purpose of Miracles?

If miracles are extraordinary, intentional occurrences performed by God, what is their purpose? If miracles exist, why do they exist? For this answer we can look to the source that in the last three chapters we have found is historically reliable and also contains accounts of miracles: the Bible. To begin, let us see what the New Testament has to say about miracles.

In John 11:38–44, we read of the raising of Lazarus:

> Then Jesus, deeply moved again, came to the tomb. It was a cave, and a stone was lying against it. "Remove the stone," Jesus said.
>
> Martha, the dead man's sister, told him, "Lord, there is already a stench because he has been dead four days."
>
> Jesus said to her, "Didn't I tell you that if you believed you would see the glory of God?"
>
> So they removed the stone. Then Jesus raised his eyes and said, "Father, I thank you that you heard me. I know that you always hear me, but because of the crowd standing here I said this, so that they may believe you sent me." After he said this, he shouted with a loud voice, "Lazarus, come out!" The dead man came out bound hand and foot with linen strips and with his face wrapped in a cloth. Jesus said to them, "Unwrap him and let him go."

Jesus indicates the purpose for the resurrection was to display God's glory. He also says the purpose of the miracle is to authenticate his ministry as being from God. The character of the miracle itself is good; Lazarus was raised from the dead and returned to the family that mourned him.

Mark 2:1–12 records the miracle of the healing of a paralytic:

> When he entered Capernaum again after some days, it was reported that he was at home. So many people gathered together that there was no more room, not even in the doorway, and he was speaking the word to them. They came to him bringing a paralytic, carried by four of them. Since they were not able to bring him to Jesus because of the crowd, they removed the roof above him, and after digging through it, they lowered the mat on which the paralytic was lying. Seeing their faith, Jesus told the paralytic, "Son, your sins are forgiven."

The traditional site of the tomb of Lazarus.

These ruins are the traditional site of Peter's house in Capernaum, possible site of this miracle. The octagonal walls remain from a church built by early Christians to mark the site. (www.HolyLandPhotos.org)

But some of the scribes were sitting there, questioning in their hearts: "Why does he speak like this? He's blaspheming! Who can forgive sins but God alone?"

Right away Jesus perceived in his spirit that they were thinking like this within themselves and said to them, "Why are you thinking these things in your hearts? Which is easier: to say to the paralytic, 'Your sins are forgiven,' or to say, 'Get up, take your mat, and walk'? But so that you may know that the Son of Man has authority on earth to forgive sins"—he told the paralytic— "I tell you: get up, take your mat, and go home." Immediately he got up, took the mat, and went out in front of everyone. As a result, they were all astounded and gave glory to God, saying, "We have never seen anything like this!"

The source of the miracle is God alone. The source of the miracle was understood by the audience since they praised God as a result. Also, for Jesus to claim the power to forgive sins is an indirect but powerful claim of deity.[4]

The purpose of the miracle is to authenticate Jesus's claim as "the Son of Man," a messianic title, and his claim of deity.

The character of the miracle, again, is good; a paralyzed man is healed.

Thus miracles in the New Testament have three attributes:
· They give God credit for being the source of the miracle.
· They authenticate the claims of the miracle worker.
· The miracles display a benevolent character.

The Red Sea

Much of this pattern is even expressed in Heb. 2:4:

> "At the same time, God also testified by signs and wonders, various miracles, and distributions of gifts from the Holy Spirit according to his will."

If the New Testament is truly the continued and final revelation of the God described in the Old Testament, then we should see the same pattern regarding miracles in the Hebrew Scriptures.

The parting of the Red Sea in Exod. 14:13–18 indeed shows the same pattern:

> But Moses said to the people, "Don't be afraid. Stand firm and see the LORD's salvation that he will accomplish for you today; for the Egyptians you see today, you will never see again. The LORD will fight for you, and you must be quiet."

> The LORD said to Moses, ". . . As for you, lift up your staff, stretch out your hand over the sea, and divide it so that the Israelites can go through the sea on dry ground. As for me, I am going to harden the hearts of the Egyptians so that they will go in after them, and I will receive glory by means of Pharaoh, all his army, and his chariots and horsemen. The Egyptians will know that I am the LORD when I receive glory through Pharaoh, his chariots, and his horsemen."

The power of the miracle is attributed to God. We see Moses obeying God's directions to accomplish the work. The purpose of the miracle is to demonstrate God's sovereignty and provision to the people of Israel as well as to their enemies. The character of the miracle is ultimately good because it frees an entire nation of people from bondage and slavery.

As an aside, some miracles in the Bible are described by the biblical writers as being part of expected natural patterns. For example, verses 21 and 22 reveal that one of the factors in the Red Sea's being made passable for the Hebrews is a strong east wind.

This Ishtar gate was built in sixth-century BC Babylon by Nebuchadnezzar.

Then Moses stretched out his hand over the sea. The LORD drove the sea back with a powerful east wind all that night and turned the sea into dry land. So the waters were divided, and the Israelites went through the sea on dry ground, with the waters like a wall to them on their right and their left.

In miracles of this kind, timing may constitute miracle rather than some unknown cause. The miracle of Shadrach, Meshach, and Abednego's survival in the furnace, recorded in Dan. 3:16–30, displays the same pattern. In the face of King Nebuchadnezzar's threat to have them thrown into a furnace if they did not worship his idol, the three men gladly refused and famous consequences followed.

Shadrach, Meshach, and Abednego replied to the king, ". . . If the God we serve exists, then he can rescue us from the furnace of blazing fire, and he can rescue us from the power of you, the king. But even if he does not rescue us, we want you as king to know that we will not serve your gods or worship the gold statue you set up."

Then Nebuchadnezzar was filled with rage, and the expression on his face changed toward Shadrach, Meshach, and Abednego. He gave orders to heat the furnace seven times more than was customary, and he commanded some of the best soldiers in his army to tie up Shadrach, Meshach, and Abednego and throw them into the furnace of blazing fire. So these men, in their trousers, robes, head coverings, and other clothes, were tied up and thrown into the furnace of blazing fire. Since the king's command was so urgent and the furnace extremely hot, the raging flames killed those men who carried Shadrach, Meshach, and Abednego up. And these three men, Shadrach, Meshach, and Abednego fell, bound, into the furnace of blazing fire.

Then King Nebuchadnezzar jumped up in alarm. He said to his advisers, "Didn't we throw three men, bound, into the fire?"

"Yes, of course, Your Majesty," they replied to the king.

He exclaimed, "Look! I see four men, not tied, walking around in the fire unharmed; and the fourth looks like a son of the gods."

Nebuchadnezzar then approached the door of the furnace of blazing fire and called: "Shadrach, Meshach, and Abednego, you servants of the Most High God—come out!" So Shadrach, Meshach, and Abednego came out of the fire. When the satraps, prefects, governors, and the king's advisers gathered around, they saw that the fire had no effect on the bodies of these men: not a hair of their heads was singed, their robes were unaffected, and there was no smell of fire on them. Nebuchadnezzar exclaimed, "Praise to the God of Shadrach, Meshach, and Abednego! He sent his angel and rescued his servants who trusted in him. They violated the king's command and risked their lives rather than serve or worship any god except their own God. Therefore I issue a decree that anyone of any people, nation, or language who says anything offensive against the God of Shadrach, Meshach, and Abednego will be torn limb from limb and his house made a garbage dump. For there is no other god who is able to deliver like this." Then the king rewarded Shadrach, Meshach, and Abednego in the province of Babylon.

The purpose of the miracle was for Shadrach, Meshach, and Abednego to be vindicated in their claim that the God of the Bible was the one true God and that no other god is worthy of worship.

Shadrach, Meshach, and Abednego gave the entire credit to God for the miraculous act that took place. The purpose of the miracle was for Shadrach, Meshach, and Abednego to be vindicated in their claim that the God of the Bible was the one true God and that no other god is worthy of worship. The character of the miracle was good, for it effected the protection of the innocent three men who otherwise would have burned to death. Also, God revealed himself to the spiritually blind king Nebuchadnezzar[5] and placed Shadrach, Meshach, and Abednego in positions of power and influence.

As in the New Testament, the Old Testament's miracles consistently attribute their source to God and are purposeful and benevolent in character. This becomes an extremely important point, because the existence of miracles and their accurate documentation in the Bible work to authenticate the Bible as an authoritative book whose teachings are worthy to be followed as the Word of God.

What about Miracles That Appear to Be Cruel?

Some miracles recorded in the Bible and attributed to God may, at first reading, seem cruel or contradictory to the idea of the benevolent God found throughout Scripture. The flood of Noah, for example, doesn't seem to correspond with the idea of a God of love. But we must remember that love is not God's only attribute. He is also righteous and just. Because God is righteous, he cannot tolerate evil. It is a good thing for evil to be punished, and its appropriate punishment is death—the wages of sin. Anything less than that is an act of benevolence on God's part. But to punish evil appropriately is also a good thing and is called justice. Thus the flood is not an act of a cruel God, but of a righteous, just God who loves us so much that he revealed to us a plan of salvation that can satisfy his righteousness while also justly punishing the evil we have done. Noah embraced the promises of God when no one else did, which resulted in their righteous judgment and destruction.

But some cases are even tougher. Take, for example, 2 Kings 2:23–24.

> From there Elisha went up to Bethel. As he was walking up the path, some small boys came out of the city and jeered at him, chanting, "Go up, baldy! Go up, baldy!" He turned around, looked at them, and cursed them in the name of the LORD. Then two female bears came out of the woods and mauled forty-two of the children.

At this point in Israel's history, God's prophets were not just ignored but hated and ridiculed. Second Chronicles 36:16 reports that God had let this situation go on long enough. The children in 2 Kings, by mocking God's messenger, were mocking God himself. And this they learned from their parents. Their destruction was righteous and it was just. The purpose of the miracle was to call Israel back to God, a good and loving thing. It was not cruel, capricious, or impulsive. It was a miracle of judgment designed to correct his people.

Ramesses II may have been the pharaoh Moses and Aaron dealt with.

What about Miracles Not Done by God?

The Bible also records miracles and signs that were not done by God or his prophets, but by those who rejected him or militated against him. For example, we find this in Exod. 7:11–12, when Pharaoh's magicians match the miracles of Moses and Aaron step for step (see also Lev. 19:26,31; Deut. 18:10–12). In the New Testament, we see this in a number of places as well. Acts 16:16–24 records a non-Christian girl's ability to foretell the future. And Revelation tells of the second beast who will perform many signs (Rev. 13:11–14).

A number of things must be taken into account when considering these miracles.

First, in every case *the God of the Bible is denied and a false gospel is proclaimed*.

Second, *their purposes are not benevolent but self-serving*. In the case of Pharaoh's magicians, it was the retention of valuable slaves and the refusal of Pharaoh to acknowledge a higher power than himself. The girl who divined the future did so to make money for her keepers. And the beast of Revelation is attempting to usurp the place rightfully held by God himself.

Third, in each case *God responds to these miracles with a demonstration of his power that proves his position of ultimate authority over these lesser powers*. Not only did Aaron's staff/snake eat the others who copied him, but God followed the incident by sending the ten plagues of judgment, an undeniable display of power that resulted in Israel's freedom. The fortune-teller of Acts had the spirit that gave her the power exorcised by Paul. And the beast of Revelation proves to be no match for the God of the universe. The miracles of God proclaim him to be Lord over all things, unbelieving thought included.

Fourth, *the power to do these signs and wonders is not denied by Scripture but at the same time the power is not supernatural*. The Bible speaks of a class of beings that are spirits not subject to what we call natural laws. These are angels and fallen angels or demons. They are capable of things that appear miraculous to human beings but are natural to them. When an angel does something, however, it is a supernatural act since it is done at the direction of God (e.g., appearing to Mary or Joseph to deliver a message). But a demon does these things for deceitful reasons meant to take away attention from God.

> *When a miracle is done outside of God's will, the God of the Bible is denied and a false gospel is proclaimed.*

The fortune-teller of Acts is an interesting case, because she is proclaiming the truth about Paul and his companions. However, she told the truth in a way that was distracting and harassed Paul, and that violated the commands of God against divination. As created beings, the demons' power is not supernatural but supernormal. They may act outside of what is normal to us but not outside what is normal to them. They are not transcendent from the world they manipulate and do not act on the direction of such a being.

Thus when we see signs and wonders in the Bible performed by those who deny the God proclaimed by the Bible, we may characterize them as false miracles. They are false not in the sense that they are not miraculous but in the sense that they reveal blasphemy and promote unbelief through deceit as to the nature of their power.

The Annunciation by El Greco, 1570–1575.

Miracles of Other Religions

The difficulty of making the claim that miracles authenticate the Bible, and therefore Christianity, is that almost all religions point to miracles to authenticate their scriptures and their view of God. But if each religion claims miracles as a method of authentication, then do the miracles not cancel one another out and ultimately prove nothing? To answer this question, we must look at the miracles of other religions. If they present the same characteristics as the biblical miracles, then we must admit that none of the miracles authenticates anything and all are useless for anything more than entertaining stories. However, if the miracles of other religions are substantially different in nature from the biblical miracles, then the Bible may not be so easily dismissed.

Buddhism

There are several schools of Buddhist thought, each with its own tradition of scripture. The

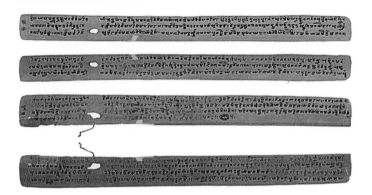

This Sanskrit manuscript of the Mahayana Sutra is from fifth-century India.
(The Schøyen Collection MS 2378/1, Oslo and London)

Dhammapada (loosely translated as "scripture verses") is among the earliest of these traditions and contains the sayings of Siddhartha Gautama, the Buddha, founder of Buddhism.[6] The Dhammapada is divided into twenty-six chapters and contains 423 verses. The verses are accompanied by stories intended to illuminate and explain them. Whether these stories are myth or history is apparently somewhat debated among Buddhist scholars.

Chapter 4, section 12 of the Dhammapada stories (illustrating vv. 58–59) contains an account of a miracle by the Buddha himself. A man wishing to make the Buddha look foolish and expose him as a false teacher sets a trap for the Buddha. The man makes several empty pots look as though they contain food. (He is pretending to invite the Buddha to a feast.) He also disguises a pit filled with burning coals and plans to have the Buddha fall into it. But the Buddha knows of the man's deceit and causes lotus flowers to grow up from the pit, rendering it harmless, and causes the man's pots to be filled with food.

The source of the power of the miracle in this story is the individual performing it. The purpose of the miracle is to bring glory to himself in order to create another follower. The character of the miracle is ultimately dubious, since the result was self-aggrandizing.

In chapter 25, section 12 of the Dhammapada stories (illustrating v. 382), we read of a young Buddhist monk who, because of his good karma, gained supernormal powers. Once when his master was sick, the monk flew to a faraway lake to fetch some water. Later, the monk was brought before the Buddha. The Buddha wished for his disciples to observe the young monk's rare qualities and so asked the monk to bring some water from the same faraway lake. Again, the young monk flew through the air to retrieve the water. The other

The first five disciples of Buddha paying respects to the wheel of Dhamma.

monks witnessed this miracle and reported it to the Buddha. The Buddha replied, "Monks, one who practices the Dhamma (concentrated meditation) zealously is capable of attaining supernormal powers even though he is young."

In this story, the miracle's power is not attributed to a transcendent, powerful God, but to the individual performing the miracle. The purpose of the miracle is to demonstrate that anyone who has the discipline to practice Dhamma can attain supernormal powers, a rather selfish endeavor, and the Dhamma leads to self-enlightenment, also a selfish endeavor. Although the character of the miracle in the first instance is good, in the second instance it is not inherently good but rather frivolous.

In Buddhism, a miracle's power is not attributed to a transcendent, powerful God, but to the individual performing the miracle.

The Vinaya Pitakas, another early Buddhist scripture, sets forth rules for monks and nuns. According to chapter 4, section 4, monks may be able to manifest themselves in more than one place at the same time, to appear in a different bodily form, create astral bodies, pass through solid matter, display clairaudience (the ability to "hear sounds both heavenly and human, far and near"), read minds, see beings pass from death in one level and be reborn in another, and remember previous lives. Later, however, in chapter 8, section 8, the Buddha condemns the display of such powers to lay people, saying they would believe the teachings for the wrong reasons and as a result hinder their enlightenment instead of fostering it.

Buddhist miracles focus on the aggrandizement of the individual while biblical miracles glorify a benevolent, transcendent, powerful God.

Thus the miracles found in Buddhism are not like the biblical miracles. They differ in their source, their purpose, and their character. Buddhist miracles focus on the aggrandizement of the individual, while biblical miracles glorify a benevolent, transcendent, powerful God.

Hinduism

Hinduism teaches that everything that exists is a part of God. Because nothing exists that is outside of God, God is not transcendent. And because God is not transcendent from the world, there can be nothing that is supernatural (outside of nature), only supernormal. That does not mean, however, that there are no miracles in Hinduism.

The Puranas, one of the Hindu scriptures, records the following in 2.5.5:

> The sages enquired from Sutji about the holiest city situated on the banks of river Yamuna. Sutji narrated the tale which Sage Saubhari had once told Yudhishthir: Once, Narad and Parvat were traveling through an aerial route; while they were flying over Khandav forest, they were lured by the beautiful sight of river Yamuna. They decided to take rest for a while. Both of them descended down and entered river Yamuna to take their bath.

Other such powers are mentioned in the Puranas 17.1.7 and include knowledge of past, present, and future events, the ability to hear abnormal sounds, the ability to make whatever one says come true, and seeing the invisible. To be fair, this list of "divine powers" is in the context of a warning—these powers may distract a man in the path of Yoga. But according to the scripture, these powers do exist.

The source of this miraculous power comes from the individuals involved. The purpose of the power is self-serving or self-aggrandizing. The character of these miraculous powers is not inherently good.

The source of this miraculous power comes from the individuals involved. The purpose of the power is self-serving or self-aggrandizing. The character of these miraculous powers is not inherently good.

A Sanskrit copy of the Rig Veda from nineteenth-century India. (The Schøyen Collection MS 2097, Oslo and London)

Interestingly, a famous Hindu miracle happened in our own time. On September 21, 1995, a miracle began in New Delhi and quickly spread around the globe. Apparently a man dreamed that the Lord Ganesha, a Hindu god who is portrayed in the form of an elephant, desired milk. The man went at once to the temple, not even waiting for daybreak, and convinced the priest to allow a spoonful of milk to be offered to the stone statue. As both men watched, the milk was consumed by the statue. It continued to accept offerings of milk for the rest of that day. By that time, word of the miracle had not only brought New Delhi to a standstill as people dropped whatever they were doing to make milk offerings, but all of India flocked to the temples. Offerings of milk were accepted by statues of other gods as well, not just Ganesha. Also, the statues varied in material; some were stone, and some were copper. Then, twenty-four hours after it began, the miracles in India stopped. During the next several days, the miracle was repeated around the globe in places such as New York, Los Angeles, and Canada.[7]

In this miracle, we see the source of the miracle attributed to one or more gods in Hindu's pantheon. The purpose of the miracle is unknown, and no good resulted from the miracle (except for those who sold milk).

Because Hinduism teaches that God is ultimately impersonal, miracles can have no purpose and no message can be conveyed through a prophet or any other way. Remember the argument from chapter 3 that information is communication from one person's mind to another. Also, the miracles found in Hinduism do not display a benevolent character. Rather, Hindu miracles are self-aggrandizing, magnifying the doer of the miracle instead of a God who wishes to make himself known and bring about good. Ultimately Hindu miracles are meaningless and lack goodness.

Islam

The sacred scripture of Islam is the Quran. It is attributed to Allah's prophet, Muhammad, and is said to be the final revelation of God. Surprisingly, the Quran attributes no

miracles to Muhammad, with one possible exception—the Quran itself. Sura 29:49-52 says the following:

> You did not read the previous scriptures, nor did you write them with your hand. In that case, the rejectors would have had reason to harbor doubts.
>
> In fact, these revelations are clear in the chests of those who possess knowledge. Only the wicked will disregard our revelations.
>
> They said, "If only miracles could come down to him from his Lord!" Say, "All miracles come only from GOD; I am no more than a manifest warner."
>
> Is it not enough of a miracle* that we sent down to you this book, being recited to them? This is indeed a mercy and a reminder for people who believe.
>
> Say, "GOD suffices as a witness between me and you. He knows everything in the heavens and the earth. Surely, those who believe in falsehood and disbelieve in GOD are the real losers."[8]

Allah written in Arabic.

Much has been made of Muhammad's being no more than a "plain warner." This has been pointed to by Muslims and non-Muslims alike as a clear statement in the Quran that Muhammad did no miracles. But many Muslims believe that this passage claims the Quran itself is his miracle. If the first interpretation is correct and Muhammad did no miracles, then he cannot be a prophet since there is no divine authentication. Sura 17:90-93 is used to support this view. In this passage Muhammad is challenged to do a miracle to authenticate his claim of being Allah's prophet to which he responds, "Glory be to my Lord, Am I any more than a human messenger?"

If the Quran is Muhammad's miracle, then the God it describes is not the God of the Bible (as Islam claims).

However, if the second interpretation is correct, then we see a circular argument. The reason given for believing that Muhammad is a prophet is that it is stated in the Quran, the final revelation of God. But the reason given to believe in the Quran as the word of God is that Allah's prophet Muhammad says it is the word of God. And around it goes. Further added to the predicament is that Muhammad did not receive this revelation in full view of a

Late sixteenth- to early seventeenth-century Quran from China. (The Schøyen Collection MS 4475, Oslo and London)

This copy of the Hadith is from Saudi Arabia and dates from 1329. (The Schøyen Collection MS 4470, Oslo and London)

nation of people like Moses. Rather, he received it in secret, making it suspect. If the Quran is Muhammad's miracle, then the God it describes is not the God of the Bible (as Islam claims). Unlike the God of the Quran, the God of the Bible, without exception, made a distinction between his message, his messenger, and the miracle that would authenticate the messenger.

But this challenge is taken up by writings that record the sayings and works of Muhammad. There are many such writings in Islamic literature, collectively called the Hadith. Some books in the Hadith are considered more accurate and valuable than others. The two most highly revered and early books are the Sahih Bukhari Hadith and the Sahih Muslim Hadith and date in the ninth century, 200 years or so after Muhammad's death.

According to the Sahih Bukhari Hadith 4.783, Muhammad did indeed perform miracles. "The prophet used to deliver his sermons while standing beside a trunk of a date-palm. When he had the pulpit made, he used it instead. The trunk started crying and the prophet went to it, rubbing his hand over it to stop its crying."

In Sahih Bukhari 5.208, Muhammad again performed a miracle. "That the Meccan people asked Allah's Apostle to show them a miracle. So he showed them the moon split into two halves between which they say is the Hiram Mountain."

If we overlook the problem of the Hadith and the Quran contradicting each other, we see miracles in the Hadith whose source may or may not be a transcendent God (no such attribution is made), whose purpose is not at all apparent (except to console a sad tree), and whose character is not benevolent. Whether the Hadith is considered in this discussion or not, the miracles of Islam are clearly not the same kinds of things as are found in the Bible.

Conclusion

We find that miracles in and of themselves are neither unscientific nor exempted from historical investigation. We also see that the miracles of the Bible are quite different from miracles of other religions. Biblical miracles uniquely point to a transcendent, personal God as their source, they are purposeful and intentional, and they are benevolent in character. Therefore, although other religions claim miracles in their traditions, they are speaking of different kinds of events that cannot cancel out the authenticating power of the miracles found in the Bible.

Pilgrims in Mecca during the Hajj.

Notable Quote

Those who assume that miracles cannot happen are merely wasting their time by looking into the texts: we know in advance what results they will find for they have begun by begging the question.[9]　　*—C. S. Lewis*

Notes

1　Wayne Grudem, *Systematic Theology* (Grand Rapids: Zondervan, 1994), 355. Grudem acknowledges in the footnotes that he has adapted this definition from the lectures of John Frame.

2　Ron Brooks and Norman Geisler, *When Skeptics Ask* (Grand Rapids: Baker, 1996), 82.

3　Powerball.com, http://www.powerball.com/powerball/pb_prizes.asp, accessed June 9, 2005.

4　This kind of claim will be dealt with in chap. 12.

5　Daniel 4:1-3 records Nebuchadnezzar's praise of the biblical God.

6　Clarence H. Hamilton, ed., *Selections from Buddhist Literature* (Indianapolis: Bobbs Merrill, 1952), 64.

7　"'It's a Miracle!' Rejoice Millions as Lord Ganesha Receives Milk," *Hinduism Today*, November 1995, at http://www.hinduismtoday.com/archives/1995/11/1995-11-01.shtml, accessed June 13, 2005.

8　*Quran, Authorized English Version*, trans. Rashad Khalifa (Tucson, AZ: Islamic Productions, 1989).

9　C. S. Lewis, *Miracles* (New York: Macmillan, 1947, 1978), 4.

CHAPTER 10
WHAT ABOUT PROPHECY?

What Were Prophets and What Is Prophecy?

Prophets were not fortune-tellers or mediums who were simply able to see the future. Prophets did not coax crystal balls into revealing a glimpse of events not yet come to pass. A prophet was someone who spoke a message from God. Prophets did not just report on what God thought; they actually spoke the very words of God. Sometimes this was a blessing, and sometimes this was a warning. Whatever message a prophet was given was called a prophecy. Prophecies did not always entail predicting some future event.

Moses is the first writing prophet mentioned in Scripture and the one who established the criteria for being accepted as a prophet. During Moses's experience at the burning bush, God commissioned Moses to act and speak on his behalf (Exod. 3:1–4:17). Moses was told the future of Israel, how the nation was to be brought out of slavery from Egypt and into the land of Canaan, and how the king of Egypt would resist but finally

Moses is the first writing prophet mentioned in Scripture and the one who established the criteria for being accepted as a prophet.

St. Catherine's Monastery is built on the traditional site of the burning bush, at the base of Mount Sinai.

be compelled by the miracles that God would do there. Moses was to tell these things to the nation of Israel, but he was not convinced they would believe him. They would ask for some evidence of his authority to speak for God. God then gave him two signs or miracles for him to perform to demonstrate his authority to speak for God. In addition to these and many other miracles, the liberation of Israel by Egypt was accomplished during Moses's lifetime, fulfilling his prophecy and authenticating Moses's position as one who spoke the very words of God.

With Moses as a prototype, the prophets who succeeded him also spoke the words of God and were sometimes authenticated by miracles—often predictive prophecy that came true during the prophet's lifetime. Deuteronomy 18:17–22 sets forth criteria for distinguishing between authentic and false prophets and how God's people are to respond both to true and false prophets (see also Num. 22:38; Jer. 1:9).

> Then the LORD said to me, "They have spoken well. I will raise up for them a prophet like you from among their brothers. I will put my words in his mouth, and he will tell them everything I command him. I will hold accountable whoever does not listen to my words that he speaks in my name. But the prophet who presumes to speak a message in my name that I have not commanded him to speak, or who speaks in the name of other gods—that prophet must die." You may say to yourself, "How can we recognize a message the LORD has not spoken?" When a prophet speaks in the LORD's name, and the message does not come true or is not fulfilled, that is a message the LORD has not spoken. The prophet has spoken it presumptuously. Do not be afraid of him.

Thus prophets were never wrong. The penalty for a prophet's false testimony was death. Also, the words of the prophet were to be obeyed as God's own words.

There are many occasions in the Bible, however, where prophecy takes the form of future events that are foretold. These prophecies are given so far ahead of their fulfillment that they cannot have possibly been intended to authenticate a prophet during his lifetime, though they all must come true if they are indeed from a true prophet. God uses these prophecies to reveal himself as a faithful God who keeps his promises and in whom we can place our trust. He also reveals himself as sovereign over all history and able to direct it and achieve his ends without violating the free choices of men and women.

In the end, studying prophecies becomes very much like the Design Argument we discussed in chapter 3. There we saw God as a designer and orderer of nature and its process-

There are many occasions in the Bible where prophecy takes the form of future events that are foretold.

es. In prophecy, we see God designing and ordering history using seemingly unconnected acts of people disconnected by time and purpose. Picture a person who accidentally spills tea on a white carpet. Many years later someone else enters the room, spills their tea and adds to the stain on the carpet. One hundred years later still another cup of tea is spilled. Now imagine finding that carpet and discovering the stains form a map that can be navigated.

Or picture a pond with a sandy bottom and flat rocks on the shore but no rocks in the water. Now picture a boy who accidentally discovers the lake and skips a few rocks. A century later, another boy also skips some rocks across the pond. Another century goes by

The remains of the triumphal arch at Tyre. (photo by David Bjorgen)

and another boy skips more rocks on the pond. Imagine then climbing a tall tree by the pond and discovering that there was an excellent portrait done in mosaic on the bottom of the pond made from the skipping stones. This is what prophecy is like.

Examples of Prophecy Fulfilled in the Old Testament

Given the advantage of hindsight and the advances of archaeology, we should be able to take a look at some of the predictive prophecies and test the accuracy of their fulfillment—if they were fulfilled at all. Many have taken up this task in the past hundred years or so, and there is no shortage of books on the subject. The lists of specific examples of fulfilled prophecy are fairly consistent from book to book. A couple of the more amazing and verifiable fulfillments are sketched out below.

The City of Tyre
Ezekiel 26:3–14, 21

³"Therefore this is what the Lord God says: See, I am against you, Tyre! I will raise up many nations against you, just as the sea raises its waves. ⁴They will destroy the walls of Tyre and demolish her towers. I will scrape the soil from her and turn her into a bare rock. ⁵She will become a place in the sea to spread nets, for I have spoken." This is the declaration of the Lord God. "She will become plunder for the nations, ⁶and her villages on the mainland will be slaughtered by the sword. Then they will know that I am the Lord."

⁷"For this is what the Lord God says: "See, I am about to bring King Nebuchadnezzar of Babylon, king of kings, against Tyre from the north with horses, chariots, cavalry, and a huge assembly of troops. ⁸He will slaughter your villages on the mainland with the sword. He will set up siege works, build a ramp, and raise a wall of shields against you. ⁹He will direct the blows of his battering rams against your walls and tear down your towers with his iron tools. ¹⁰His horses will be so numerous that their dust will cover you. When he enters your gates as an army entering a breached city, your walls will shake from the noise of cavalry, wagons, and chariots. ¹¹He will trample all your streets with the hooves of his horses. He will slaughter your people with the sword, and your mighty pillars will fall to the ground. ¹²They will take your wealth as spoil and plunder your merchandise. They will also demolish your walls and tear down your beautiful homes. Then they will throw your stones, timber, and soil into the water. ¹³I will put an end to the noise of your songs, and the sound of your lyres will no longer be heard. ¹⁴I will turn you into a bare rock, and you will be a place to spread nets. You will never be rebuilt, for I, the Lord, have spoken." This is the declaration of the Lord God. . . .

²¹"I will make you an object of horror, and you will no longer exist. You will be sought but will never be found again." This is the declaration of the Lord God.

(The verses have been numbered for easier reference.)

Ezekiel began his prophetic ministry in 593 BC, shortly after the Babylonian captivity began, and continued until at least 571 BC.[1] When Ezekiel gave this particular prophecy is not known with certainty. The future tense of the prophecy indicates the events described had not yet happened. Skeptics will point out that Ezekiel or some later editor of his material could have simply written past events as future events for his own glorification or some other reason. However, although some of the prophecies came true during his lifetime, many did not.

Tyre in the time of Ezekiel existed in two parts, one on the coast of the mainland in what is modern-day Lebanon, and the other on an island about half a mile from shore. In 585 BC, Nebuchadnezzar, king of Babylon, was on a campaign to conquer the region. Other cities such as Jerusalem and Sidon had fallen earlier, but Tyre put up a valiant fight. So strongly did the people of Tyre resist that Nebuchadnezzar laid siege to the city—a siege that lasted until 572 when Tyre finally fell. After thirteen years, the soldiers entered the city to find most of its treasure and wealth missing. It seems it had been smuggled out to the island city. *The fall of mainland Tyre fulfilled the prophecies of verses 7 and 8.*

In 332 BC, long after Ezekiel's death, Alexander the Great undertook the task of defeating the island city of Tyre. He decided to take the city not by sea, but by linking the island to the mainland. It seems he was inspired by the debris of the old city still lying where it fell. And since the water between the island and the mainland was around twenty feet deep, the Greeks used debris to build a causeway 200 feet wide that led to the island. This plan fulfilled the prophecies of verses 4 and 12. The clearing away of this debris created a flat place that fishermen still use today to dry their nets. *This fulfilled the first part of the prophecy of verse 14.* Following Alexander's conquest of Tyre, it fell to Antigonus ca. 314 BC. In AD 1291, Muslims took control of the island. *This succession of invaders fulfills the prophecy in verse 3.*

Though today there is a tiny fishing village on the spot of ancient Tyre, the great city has never been rebuilt, *fulfilling the prophecy of the second half of verse 14.* Josh McDowell suggests the phrase "will never be found again" means that though men attempt to rebuild Tyre, she will never be elevated "to her former position of wealth and splendor."[2]

Thus the prophecies of Ezekiel concerning Tyre have all been fulfilled. Mathematician and astronomer Peter Stoner calculated the odds of all these prophecies being fulfilled as 1 in 75,000,000.[3] To be fair, some of these events, such as Nebuchadnezzar's attack of Tyre, could be reasonably guessed by Ezekiel or are just so vague, such as many nations coming against Tyre in waves, that history makes it fairly possible. But note that the Old Testament canon was closed for all practical purposes 100 years or so before Alexander's conquests, making it highly unlikely any editing after the fact was done to make Ezekiel more accurate.

If such were the case, we would expect to find variants in the texts, some with the accurate prophecies and some without. But that is just not the case. And even if the

Satellite photo of the Middle East. Note how Alexander's causeway silted in the bay creating an isthmus. (photo by NASA)

prophecies were added in or altered after Alexander's time or even later, it remains that the ancient city of Tyre, which was prosperous and thriving in Ezekiel's time, has never been rebuilt, a prophecy that was fulfilled regardless of when the writing of Ezekiel is fixed.

The Kingdom of Edom
Jeremiah 49:17-18

> 17 "Edom will become a desolation. Everyone who passes by her will be appalled and scoff because of all her wounds. 18 As when Sodom and Gomorrah were overthrown along with their neighbors," says the LORD, "no one will live there; no human being will stay in it even temporarily."

By the time of Jeremiah's prophetic ministry (627–587/586 BC),[4] Edom was a long-established kingdom south of the Dead Sea. Petra, its capital, was formerly on a major trade route and was surrounded by mountains on all sides. The main entrance into Petra is through a very narrow cleft in cliffs 500 feet tall and over a mile long. It may be best known for its buildings, some of which were hewn directly into the face of the sandstone cliffs.

By the time the Muslims gained control of the area in AD 636 (fulfilling the prophecy of the first part of verse 18), Edom was already in decline because of changing trade routes due to Roman occupation and a devastating earthquake in AD 363. By the time the crusaders built a castle near Petra in the 1200s, they found it was a desolate place. From their time until Petra's rediscovery in the early nineteenth century, nothing is known of the place. The area in general is desolate and remains uninhabited to this day, fulfilling the prophecy of verse 17 and the last part of verse 18.

By the time the Crusaders built a castle near Petra (the capital of Edom) in the 1200s, they found it was a desolate place.

According to John Urquhart:

> The desolation is appalling. Its commerce has utterly passed away. We do not know the story, but the great market of Petra has long since ceased to exist. Edom is no longer sought by those who desire to sell or by those who desire to buy. None go forth from it laden with the merchandise which once made its name famous in the Earth.[5]

Jeremiah was not alone in his prophecies of Edom. Isaiah (ca. second half of the eighth century BC)[6] made similar prophecies of Edom's abandonment and desolation (Isa. 34:10–15). Ezekiel prophesied that Edom would be conquered by Israel at some point (which it briefly was), would become desolate wasteland, and that it would be cut off from travelers (which was fulfilled by the changing of the trade route) (Ezek. 25:13–14; 35:4–7).

Castle near Petra.

Alexander the Great
Daniel 11:2-4

[2] "Now I will tell you the truth. Three more kings will arise in Persia, and the fourth will be far richer than the others. By the power he gains through his riches, he will stir up everyone against the kingdom of Greece. [3] Then a warrior king will arise; he will rule a vast realm and do whatever he wants. [4] But as soon as he is established, his kingdom will be broken up and divided to the four winds of heaven, but not to his descendants; it will not be the same kingdom that he ruled, because his kingdom will be uprooted and will go to others besides them."

A bust of Alexander the Great from the British Museum.

Daniel wrote his prophecy in Persia toward the end of the sixth century BC, almost 200 years before the birth of Alexander the Great in 356. Alexander ascended the throne at the age of twenty and immediately embarked on a campaign of vengeance to conquer Persia in retaliation for an attempted invasion by King Xerxes more than a century earlier. After vanquishing Persia, Alexander conquered most of the rest of the Mediterranean world, creating a vast empire.[7] This fulfilled verse 3 of the prophecy. After Alexander's sudden death in 323 BC, his empire was divided among his generals, not his heirs. Generals Ptolemy, Seleucus, Lysimachus, Cassander, and Antigonids wran-

Daniel wrote his prophecy in Persia toward the end of the sixth century BC, almost 200 years before the birth of Alexander the Great in 356.

gled and conspired against one another until ultimately solidifying into four different kingdoms (Antigonids's territory having been taken over by Seleucus).[8] This fulfilled verse 4 of Daniel's prophecy.

Like the prophecy of Tyre, this prophecy could not have been written back into Daniel after the events because the canon of the Tanak, the Jewish Scriptures, had closed more

This mosaic of the battle of Issus dates from first-century Pompeii and shows Alexander at the far left.

A detail of Pilate presenting Jesus to his accusers as painted by Daumier.

than 100 years before the death of Alexander, and by this time the text had been firmly established. There are no alternate versions of Daniel that have a different chapter 11.

One of the interesting features of these and other biblical prophecies is that the prophets may not have had a clear picture of what they were foretelling or predicting. How these prophecies came to pass, the time between the stages, and even the order of the stages are not necessarily known by the prophets themselves. The pictures of future things to the prophets were often without a sense of the proper relationship between the different elements involved. Only in hindsight can such things be discerned.

Prophecies of the Coming of Christ

The authenticating nature of prophecy exerts even more force in the context of the messianic prophecies. We see frequently in the New Testament how people asked whether Jesus was the Messiah[9] but not what a Messiah was in the first place. No education was needed about what the Messiah was because there were so many prophecies in the Tanak about a Messiah who would come to rescue Israel. Certainly there were a number of misconceptions about what the Messiah would look like in terms of function and role, but a Messiah was expected nonetheless. This was a notion found in Jewish Scriptures and not an innovation of the followers of Jesus.

The importance of these prophecies is hard to underestimate. If these prophecies have been fulfilled, then we find confirmation for the claim of the Bible that it is the Word of God. We also find confirmation of a personal, involved, benevolent, all-powerful God who has chosen to reveal himself in a particular way. Last, we find the person that these predictions were written about, the person whom God has sent to bring

> *We see frequently in the New Testament how people asked whether Jesus was the Messiah but not what a Messiah was in the first place.*

about salvation, the person through whom God has chosen to reveal himself in the most clear and unambiguous way. If such a person has fulfilled the prophecies, then we must listen to him and take his teaching seriously.

But how many messianic prophecies are we talking about? Three or four, like our earlier examples? Surely the odds are that more than one person who has ever lived could fulfill three or four prophecies or even double or triple that many prophecies. Fortunately, the Old Testament prevents such an argument. By some counts, there are 300 to 400 messianic prophecies in the Old Testament. Other scholars believe that this number is a bit high. They certainly see that number of allusions to the Messiah, but count the major prophecies as fewer than 100. *The Holman Illustrated Bible Dictionary* lists 121 fulfilled messianic prophecies.[10] Josh McDowell has made an excellent study of the major prophecies and numbers them at 61.[11] He rightly characterizes these prophecies as credentials that anyone claiming to be the Messiah had to have.

In McDowell's list is a group of prophecies concerning the genealogy of the Messiah. If we consider only these genealogical prophecies, we begin to see just how narrow the list of candidates for the Messiah actually is. The Messiah will be of the seed of Abraham (Gen. 22:18), the son of Isaac (Gen. 21:12), the son of Jacob (Num. 24:17), of the tribe of Judah (Gen. 49:10; Mic. 5:2), in the family line of Jesse (Isa. 11:1,10), of the house of David (Jer. 23:5).

To explore in further detail, we first notice that these prophecies use a male pronoun when referring to the Messiah's gender. This excludes half of everyone who has ever lived (the women) from the pool of candidates. Abraham had two sons, one of whom was Isaac (Gen. 16:16; 21:2–3). Thus half the men who have ever lived are descended from Abraham are excluded from the pool. Isaac also had two sons, one of whom was Jacob (Gen. 25:24). This eliminates half the male descendants of Isaac from the pool. Jacob had twelve sons, one of whom was Judah (Gen. 29:32–30:24), which eliminates eleven out of every twelve of his male descendants from the pool. Judah had five sons (Gen. 38:3–5,27–30), which eliminates four out of five of all his male descendants. Jesse fathered eight sons, one of whom was David (1 Sam. 17:12). This eliminates seven out of eight male descendants of Jesse from the pool. Last, David had ten sons, eliminating nine out of ten male descendants of David. It is obvious that the Messiah was someone extremely specific and that the pool of candidates is incredibly small. Not just anyone could make that claim and be taken seriously.

The Messiah will be of the seed of Abraham, the son of Isaac, the son of Jacob, of the tribe of Judah, in the family line of Jesse, of the house of David.

But the prophecies further provide credentials that must be met by the Messiah. In his book *Science Speaks*, Peter Stoner took just eight of these prophecies and calculated the odds of all them being fulfilled. The eight he used were

1. Messiah would be born in Bethlehem (Mic. 5:2).
2. Messiah will be preceded by a messenger (Mal. 3:1).
3. Messiah will come to Jerusalem riding on a colt (Zech. 9:9).
4. Messiah will be betrayed by a friend (Zech. 13:6).
5. Messiah will be betrayed for thirty silver pieces (Zech. 11:2).
6. Messiah's betrayer will try to return the thirty silver pieces but they will be refused. The betrayer will then throw them on the floor of the temple (Zech. 11:13).
7. Messiah will not speak in his own defense (Isa. 53:7).
8. Messiah's hands and feet would be pierced (Ps. 22:16).[12]

Most scholars do not agree that Zech. 13:6 refers to the Messiah, so we will discount Stoner's odds regarding that point. The numbers Stoner used to calculate the odds were arrived at by himself and more than 600 of his students over the course of ten years or so. When Stoner found reason for the numbers to be revised, he made them more conservative. Stoner and his students found that in considering these eight prophecies, the odds that they would be fulfilled by any man who has lived between the writing of the prophecies (no later than 400 BC) and today is 1 in

All people who ever lived

Men → Women

Abraham's sons

Isaac → Ishmael

Isaac's sons

Jacob → Esau

Jacob's sons

Reuben Simeon Levi Zebulun Gad Issachar Dan Asher Naphtali Joseph **Judah** Benjamin ↓

Judah's sons

Er Onan Shelah Perez Zerah

Jesse's sons

Eliab Abinadab Shimea Nethanel Raddai Ozem Elihu **David** ↓

David's sons

Amnon Daniel Absalom Adonijah Shephaitah Ithream Shimea Shobab Nathan Solomon

Messiah

100,000,000,000,000,000 (or 100 quadrillion, expressed as 100^{17}). The odds assigned to the fulfillment of Zech. 13:6 were 1 in 1,000. [13] If we remove this number from the equation, we are still left with an astronomically high number.

To understand how big this number is, Stone gave the following illustration:

> Suppose that we take 10^{17} silver dollars and lay them on the face of Texas. They will cover all of the state two feet deep. Now mark one of these silver dollars and stir the whole mass thoroughly, all over the state. Blindfold a man and tell him that he can travel as far as he wishes, but he must pick up one silver dollar and say that this is the right one. What chance would he have of getting the right one? Just the same chance that the prophets would have had of writing these eight prophecies and having them all come true in any one man, from their day to the present time, providing they wrote using their own wisdom. [14]

According to the New Testament, each of the above prophecies was indeed fulfilled.

1   Messiah would be born in Bethlehem (Matt. 2:1; Luke 2:15; John 7:24).
2   Messiah will be preceded by a messenger (Matt. 3:1-13; Mark 1:1-11; Luke 3:1-22; John 1:6-36).
3   Messiah will come to Jerusalem riding on a colt (Matt. 21:1-11; Mark 11:1-10; Luke 19:28-38; John 12:14-16).
4   (Most scholars don't interpret this as a prophecy; see number 4 on p. 252 [in Stoner's book].)
5   Messiah will be betrayed for thirty silver pieces (Matt. 26:15).
6   Messiah's betrayer will try to return the thirty silver pieces but they will be refused. The betrayer will then throw them on the floor of the temple (Matt. 27:3-5).
7   Messiah will not speak in his own defense (Matt. 26:57–27:22; Mark 14:55–15:15; Luke 22:54–23:24; John 18:13–19:16).
8   Messiah's hands and feet would be pierced (Matt. 27:35; Mark 15:25; Luke 23:33; John 19:18).

Stoner then calculated the odds of fulfilling forty-eight prophecies. Assuming the forty additional prophecies have similar odds as the first set of prophecies, the chances that any one man would fulfill all forty-eight is 1 in 100 quadrillion (or 10^{17}). Stoner tried to convey this staggering number in this way:

> Let us make a solid ball of electrons, extending in all directions from the earth to the distance of six billion light-years. Have we used up our 10^{157} electrons? No, we have made such a small hole in the mass that we cannot see it. We can make this solid ball of electrons, extending in all directions to the distance of six billion light-years 6×10^{28} times. [15]

As incredibly large as this number is, it must be remembered that there are at least sixty-one major messianic prophecies. If the odds of forty-eight prophecies being fulfilled are statistically close to zero, how much greater are the odds of the sixty-one prophecies? The improbability is overwhelming.

There are, of course, some prophecies that can be fulfilled intentionally, like entering Jerusalem on a donkey. But it must be understood that most of the prophecies cannot be

discounted in such a way. The Messiah could not contrive his place of birth, time of birth, descendants, the actions of others (such as his betrayer), or manner of death.[16] Also, the intentional fulfillment of some of the prophecies, as mentioned above, would be a tacit declaration that that person fulfilled all of the prophecies—a claim that could be investigated. It must also be understood that these prophecies were not added into the text later to fit the life of Jesus. Remember that Jewish interpreters used the exact same text that these prophecies came from. They never argued against the Christians by saying the prophecies were inserted. Rather, they argued against the interpretation and fulfillment of the prophecies.

Daniel's Seventy Weeks

One of the best known and astounding prophecies regarding the Messiah is found in Daniel. This passage, Dan. 9:24–27, often referred to as "Daniel's Seventy Weeks," gives a very narrow window of time during which the Messiah would appear.

> [24] Seventy weeks are decreed about your people and your holy city—to bring the rebellion to an end, to put a stop to sin, to atone for iniquity, to bring in everlasting righteousness, to seal up vision and prophecy, and to anoint the most holy place. [25] Know and understand this: From the issuing of the decree to restore and rebuild Jerusalem until an Anointed One, the ruler, will be seven weeks and sixty-two weeks. It will be rebuilt with a plaza and a moat, but in difficult times. [26] After those sixty-two weeks the Anointed One will be cut off and will have nothing. The people of the coming ruler will destroy the city and the sanctuary. The end will come with a flood, and until the end there will be war; desolations are decreed. [27] He will make a firm covenant with many for one week, but in the middle of the week he will put a stop to sacrifice and offering. And the abomination of desolation will be on a wing of the temple until the decreed destruction is poured out on the desolator.

To understand the timetable given, it must be noted that the word translated "week" is the Hebrew word for seven as it refers to a duration of time, a "period of sevens."[17] Throughout the Tanak, it has been used to mean a period of seven days or years. In this case, it is believed to refer to weeks of years: 70 weeks = 490 years.

The window of time given for the Messiah to appear within closes with the destruction of Jerusalem. ("The people of the coming ruler will destroy the city and the sanctuary.") At the time Daniel wrote this, about 530 BC, Jerusalem lay in ruins already. His prophecy said that the city would be rebuilt before it was destroyed. It also said that the decree that ordered Jerusalem's restoration was the beginning of the seventy weeks. After sixty-nine weeks of years pass, the Messiah will appear. This is when the window opens. And the window shut in AD 70 with the destruction of Jerusalem. No one appearing in history outside this window could be the promised Messiah.

Daniel as portrayed by Michelangelo.

The question now becomes, when did the window open? Do we know of a decree that ordered the rebuilding of Jerusalem and, if so, when was the decree issued? If we did know of such a decree, then we would know the start of the seventy weeks, the end sixty-ninth week that would mark the opening of the Messiah's window.

Several decrees mentioned in Scripture have been pointed to as the start date for the seventy weeks. One of these decrees, Neh. 2:1–8, mentions the restoration of the city (as stated in the prophecy), not just the temple. Another decree often used is found in Ezra 7:11–16. Although this decree does not meet the criteria mentioned in the prophecy, Ezra does give a prayer of thanks in 9:6–15 that mentions that the decree allows for the rebuilding of Jerusalem and its temple. We will look at both of these.

Those who argue for using the decree of Artaxerxes in Ezra 7:11–16 begin in 457 BC, the year the decree was issued: sixty-nine weeks of years = 483 years; 457 BC + 483 years = AD 27 (there is no year "0"). According to Luke 3:1, John the Baptist began his ministry in the fifteenth year of the rule of Tiberius. Although Tiberius ascended the throne in AD 14, he began a coregency in AD 12 making his fifteenth year of rule AD 26.[18] Thus the Messiah appeared in AD 27. This fits the life of Jesus quite well and puts his crucifixion in AD 30.

The other view is that the decree of Artaxerxes in Nehemiah is the proper starting point; this decree is the only one that specifies the rebuilding of the city according to the prophecy. The decree is dated in the month of Nisan during the twentieth year of the reign of Artaxerxes. Artaxerxes ascended the throne in 465 BC, giving us a 444 BC start date for the year. Traditionally, if the day of the month was not mentioned in a writing, ancient Hebrews intended the first day of the month to be understood as the day in question. Thus the start date for the seventy weeks would be Nisan 1, 444 BC, which is the equivalent of March 4, 444 BC, on our calendar.

Advocates of this start date also point out that years in the time of the prophecy were reckoned differently. Though we use 365.25-day years (solar years), the prophetic literature of the ancient world used 360-day years.[19] To understand weeks of years correctly, we must convert the sixty-nine weeks, 483 years, to days: 483 x 360 = 173,880 days. Beginning at March 4, 444 BC and counting forward 173,880 days on the current calendar, if we account for leap years and the lack of a year 0, we arrive at Sunday, March 29, AD 33.[20] This would be Palm Sunday, the day Jesus presented himself to Israel as Messiah, making April 3, AD 33 the date of the crucifixion.

Carson, Moo, and Morris make the observation that Jesus was crucified quite likely on either Nisan 14 or 15. They make this claim not based on Daniel's prophecy but on astronomical data and suggestions in the Gospels. They found that in the general time frame in question, the best candidates in terms of exact dates for the crucifixion are Friday, Nisan 14, AD 30, and Friday, Nisan 15, AD 33.[21] Each of these dates corresponds to one of the two ways of reckoning the end of Daniel's sixty-nine weeks.

Again, this astonishing prophecy could not have been added into the Scripture to make it fit the life of Jesus because the Tanak was reverently preserved by Jews and Christians alike. The text itself has never been an issue, only its interpretation.

Conclusion

Prophecy is important because it is a miracle that is testable. We have only to see whether such events have come to pass to verify or reject a prophet. As we have seen, there are prophecies that have indeed come true and can be demonstrated. These verifiable prophecies have an extremely small probability of being fulfilled by chance. Also, these prophecies could not have been written into the text at a later date. Thus having shown authentic credentials as ones who speak the very words of God, we have good reason to treat the messages of the biblical prophets as authoritative.

> *Prophecy is important because it is a miracle that is testable.*

More than that, we find a large number of prophecies pertaining to the identity of one man, the Messiah. All indications are that the Messiah did appear as prophesied and fulfilled further prophecies written about him. This man was Jesus of Nazareth. But Jesus of Nazareth himself made prophetic statements and so his authority should be able to be tested as well. There are many miracles attributed to Jesus, but one in particular is the event on which Christianity itself stands or falls—the resurrection of Jesus.

Notable Quote

The seeker after certainty in religion will be grateful for the multiplicity, as well as for the minuteness and distinctness, of Scripture prophecy. One or two lights in a chamber may not entirely sweep away its gloom. But the remedy is simple. The lights have only to be multiplied and the place will at last be brighter than the day could make it.[22] —*John Urquhart*

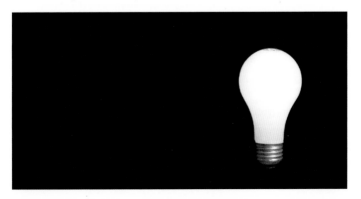

Notes

1 Charles F. Fensham, *The Oxford Companion to the Bible*, ed. Bruce M. Metzger and Michael D. Coogan (Oxford: Oxford University Press, 1993), 217.

2 Josh McDowell, *Evidence That Demands a Verdict* (San Bernardino: Here's Life, 1972, 1992), 279.

3 Peter Stoner, *Science Speaks* (Chicago: Moody Press, 1969), 72–79.

4 Robert Davidson, *The Oxford Companion to the Bible*, ed. Bruce M. Metzger and Michael D. Coogan (Oxford: Oxford University Press, 1993), 343.

5 John Urquhart, *The Wonders of Prophecy* (Harrisburg, PA: Christian Alliance, 1925), 98.

6 Joan Comay and Ronald Brownrigg, *Who's Who in the Bible* (New York: Wings, 1971), 163.

7 Guy MacLean Rogers, *The Oxford Companion to the Bible*, ed. Bruce M. Metzger and Michael D. Coogan (Oxford: Oxford University Press, 1993), 19–20.

8 Merrill C. Tenney, *New Testament Survey* (Grand Rapids: Zondervan, 1953, 1961, 1985), 17.

9 Cp. Matt. 16:16; Luke 2:26; John 1:41; 4:25,29; 20:31, et al.

10 *Holman Illustrated Bible Dictionary* (Nashville: Broadman & Holman, 2003), 1112–14.

11 McDowell, *Evidence That Demands a Verdict*, vol. 1 (San Bernardino: Here's Life, 1972, 1992), 144–66.

12 Stoner, *Science Speaks*, 101–5.

13 Ibid., 101.

14 Ibid., 106–7.

15 Ibid., 111.

16 In fact, crucifixion did not even exist at the time Ps. 22 was written; cp. *The Zondervan Pictorial Encyclopedia of the Bible*, vol. 1, ed. Merrill C. Tenny (Grand Rapids: Zondervan), s.v. "crucifixion."

17 *Zondervan Pictorial Encyclopedia of the Bible*, vol . 5, s.v. "seventy weeks."

18 D. A. Carson, Douglas J. Moo, and Leon Morris, *An Introduction to the New Testament* (Grand Rapids: Zondervan, 1992), 54.

19 See Rev. 11:2–3 for an example of the Bible using thirty-day months.

20 This calculation is taken from a seminary lecture by Bruce K. Waltke and is based on work by Harold Hoehner. Others, such as Josh McDowell, have used Hoehner's work to arrive at the same crucifixion date but fix the beginning of the calculation at March 5, 444 BC and thus the terminus on Monday, March 30, AD 33 (see McDowell, *Evidence That Demands a Verdict*, 173).

21 Carson, Moo, and Morris, *An Introduction to the New Testament*, 55–56.

22 Urquhart, *Wonders of Prophecy*, 93.

CHAPTER 11
THE RESURRECTION?

What Is at Stake?

In the first chapter of this book, it was mentioned that the apostle Paul appealed to the resurrection of Jesus as the central claim of Christianity. According to Paul in 1 Cor. 15:12–19, if Jesus was not resurrected from the dead, then the entire Christian faith is worthless, a waste of time.

This is such an important passage that it bears to be repeated here.

> Now if Christ is proclaimed as raised from the dead, how can some of you say, "There is no resurrection of the dead"? If there is no resurrection of the dead, then not even Christ has been raised; and if Christ has not been raised, then our proclamation is in vain, and so is your faith. Moreover, we are found to be false witnesses about God, because we have testified wrongly about God that he raised up Christ—whom he did not raise up, if in fact the dead are not raised. For if the dead are not raised, not even Christ has been raised. And if Christ has not been raised, your faith is worthless; you are still in your sins. Those, then, who have fallen asleep in Christ have also perished. If we have put our hope in Christ for this life only, we should be pitied more than anyone.

If Jesus was not resurrected from the dead, then the entire Christian faith is worthless, a waste of time.

The reason the resurrection is so important to the case for Christianity is that if it is true, it confirms the teaching of Jesus as having the authority of God. The teaching of Jesus is often about his own identity, not just ethical and moral issues. At stake is the ability to know who Jesus was and thus how we should respond to him.

A first-century tomb in Jerusalem.

Detail of the resurrection by Pino, 1555.

1433 painting of the burial and resurrection of Jesus by Memling.

The previous two chapters dealt with miracles and prophecy. It was shown that both of these kinds of things are to be dealt with seriously and cannot be dismissed out of hand. In the case of the resurrection, it would certainly be a miraculous event.

If it is true, the resurrection confirms the teaching of Jesus as having the authority of God.

It was also prophesied by Jesus himself several times (see Mark 8:31; 9:31; 10:34; John 2:19). But is resurrection the best explanation for what happened three days after the execution of Jesus? What are the other options? We will take a look at nine options: swoon theory, twin theory, stolen body, hallucination, the wrong tomb, the alien theory, legend, the Quranic account, and the biblical account of resurrection. Before we can turn our attention to the various theories, however, we must first discuss what resurrection is and what facts the theories need to account for.

What Is Resurrection?

To make sure we understand each argument correctly, we need to define what resurrection is and what it is not. Resurrection is not resuscitation. We are not talking about a body brought back to its former life, a body that needs food, can get sick, can age, and must eventually die again. When Jesus raised Lazarus from the dead, he did not resurrect him; he resuscitated him. A resurrected state, however, is a body that is physical yet incorruptible; it cannot die, age, or become ill. This is the body anticipated by Pharisees at the end times.[1] N. T. Wright defines resurrection as being when "the *present* state of those who had died would be replaced by a *future* state in which they would be alive once more"[2] (emphasis in the original).

Just the Facts

According to the Gospels, Jesus was crucified, died on the cross, and was buried in a tomb. Three days later, the tomb was found empty, and many of his followers claimed to have seen his physical body risen from the dead over the following forty days. There are non-Christian sources that corroborate at least some of these claims. Josephus, writing in the first century, mentions Jesus's crucifixion.[3] Pliny the Younger records that Christians met on a fixed day to corporately worship Jesus (presumably the day they believe he rose from the dead—Sunday—judging from writings of the early church fathers).[4] The Talmud, a book of Jewish oral tradition and commentary dating from the second century AD, mentions the crucifixion of Jesus.[5]

The Toledoth Jeshu, an anti-Christian Jewish document, tells of a plot by Jesus's disciples to steal the body of Jesus, thus explaining why the tomb was empty. According to Gary Habermas:

> It is true that the Toledoth Jesu was not compiled until the fifth century AD, although it does reflect early Jewish tradition. Even though Jewish scholars scorn the reliability of this source, the teaching that the disciples were the ones who removed the dead body of Jesus persisted in the early centuries after Jesus's death.[6]

Talmud from the fifteenth century.

These are the things that must be accounted for by any theory that hopes to make sense of Jesus's death and the events of the following Sunday. Now let us look at each of the theories and their explanatory power.

Swoon Theory

The swoon theory posits that Jesus fainted on the cross and only appeared to be dead. Jesus then awoke and recuperated in the damp coolness of the tomb and subsequently fully recovered. To appreciate this argument fully, we must first understand what was involved in the torture and crucifixion of Jesus.

Before Jesus was crucified, Pontius Pilate ordered that Jesus be scourged (Matt. 27:26;

Mark 15:15; Luke 23:16; John 19:1). A Roman scourging was done with a whip called a flagrum or a flagellum that comprised a handle about eight inches long with twelve-inch- to twenty-four-inch-long leather straps attached to one end. At the other end, the straps were tied to lead balls (that looked something like barbells), sharp pieces of metal, bone shards, broken glass, or sharp rock. Whatever was on the end of the whip quickly broke the skin, allowing the flagrum to deeply penetrate the tissue and pull away the flesh, often exposing the bowels, ribs, or spine. Eusebius, writing in the fourth century, preserves this description of a scourging from the second century:

Roman scourge

The traditional spot of Jesus's scourging.

> Those standing around were struck with amazement, at seeing them lacerated with scourges, to their very blood and arteries, so that no flesh concealed in the very inmost parts of the body, and the bowels themselves were exposed to view.[7]

So vicious was this torture that victims often did not survive a scourging.

So vicious was this torture that victims often did not survive a scourging.[8] Victims lost so much blood that they went into hypovolemic shock. This means that the heart would speed up trying to compensate for the loss of blood; the blood pressure would drop, making the victim faint or collapse; the kidneys would shut down to keep as much blood volume as possible; and because the body needs fluids so badly to replace the lost blood, the victim would become extremely thirsty.[9]

Following this was Jesus's crucifixion, miscellaneous beatings aside. In crucifixion, the victim was laid down with his arms perpendicular to the torso. Nails five to nine inches long would then be driven through both wrists, crushing the median nerve (the largest nerve going to the hand) and creating extraordinary pain. Nails would also be driven through the ankles with the legs in a bent position. When the victim was raised to a vertical position, his shoulders (and sometimes elbows and wrists) would become dislocated from the weight, making them useless to alleviate the pressure on his chest.

At this point the nailing of the wrists kept the position of the body so that the pressure on the chest was relentless and kept the victim from flopping forward. With the pressure on the chest, the victim could not exhale. To lessen the pressure, the victim had to straighten his legs, using the nail through his ankles as leverage. Having exhaled, the victim then sank back down to his original position. The wood from which the cross was made was rough, making the sliding of the victim's back, whose flesh was exposed from scourging, very painful. As the victim's strength was slowly worn down, breathing would become less

First-century Roman nail.

frequent, increasing the acidity in the blood. This acidity would cause an irregular heartbeat that was already rapid because of the hypovolemic shock. This would have caused fluid to build up in the membranes surrounding the heart and lungs. Death would ultimately come in the form of asphyxiation or heart failure. Depending on a victim's condition upon being put on the cross, death could sometimes take days. If the executioner wanted to speed up the process, he would break the legs of the crucified man with a club; death would come within minutes.

In the case of Jesus, the executioner was preparing to do just that—break his legs—but Jesus appeared to be dead already (John 19:31–37). To make sure, the executioner took his spear and thrust it into Jesus's side, piercing his heart and a lung. If Jesus had not already died, he surely would have as a result of the wound caused by the spear. There was no question whatsoever in the mind of the professional executioner that Jesus was dead.

If Jesus had not already died, he surely would have as a result of the wound caused by the spear.

With this in mind, let us now return to the swoon theory. For the swoon theory to be true, Jesus would have had to have not only survived the spear piercing his heart and one of his lungs, but he would have had to control how much blood flowed out of the wound by sheer willpower. After all, if the wound bled too much, it would have betrayed a beating heart that would have led to the breaking of his legs and inevitable death. Thus the professional executioner was apparently fooled by Jesus's act and then Jesus was buried in the tomb. After 36 hours or so, Jesus had sufficiently recovered from his wounds to rise. After getting up on his feet, which had been so recently impaled, Jesus would then have had to pop his shoulders back into place and possibly his arms and wrists as well. Using these hands, which have now lost most of their ability to function because of the nails through the wrists, Jesus would then have had to roll away an extremely heavy stone. Upon exiting the tomb, using no weapons whatsoever he then would have to overpower a number of Roman guards. Then Jesus, who would have been easily recognizable, would have had to walk unrecognized and unnoticed through Jerusalem in broad daylight, not clothed properly and with strips of flesh hanging from his body, exposing his bowels and bones, and proceed several miles down the road to Emmaus. After the evening meal, he would have then returned to Jerusalem, discovered where the apostles were hiding out, and broken into a locked room leaving no clue as to how he got in. Having gotten into the room, Jesus then presented himself as having risen from the dead and convinced his followers that all was well despite the fact that he looked like someone who had fallen into a meat grinder and needed immediate, intense, and prolonged medical attention. To top it off, he then performed the illusion of vanishing into thin air.

Although this does account for the empty tomb (however implausibly), the theory does not account for anything else. In fact, it raises more questions given that the colossal fraud that would have to be committed by Jesus to accommodate the swoon theory is completely contradictory to everything we know of Jesus's character and teaching. The foolishness of the swoon theory is self-evident.

For the swoon theory to be true, Jesus would have had to have not only survived the spear piercing his heart and one of his lungs, but he would have had to control how much blood flowed out of the wound by sheer willpower.

Twin Theory

The twin theory suggests that Jesus had an identical twin brother nobody knew about who took Jesus's place on the cross.

As with the swoon theory, a major weakness in this theory is that Jesus would have to have behaved completely contrary to his teachings to make the fraud a success. For this theory to work, Jesus would somehow have had to convince or coerce the twin to spend his life in hiding and to die for Jesus's own self-aggrandizing plan, a plan of deceit and manipulation. In fact, if this theory is true, then Jesus is not only not worthy of worship, but he deserves to be punished severely.

Another problem with the twin theory is that there is simply no reason to believe it. There is no evidence that supports its claim. The facts we do have about Jesus's family mention brothers and sisters but no twin (Matt. 12:47–48; 13:55–56; Mark 3:31–34). Luke, who many scholars believe may have received his information about Jesus's birth from Mary herself, makes no mention of a twin in this birth narrative. Especially considering this was Mary's first pregnancy, it would be an odd detail to leave out. Even more preposterous is that for the twin theory to stand, it would require Jesus's mother not to recognize the difference between her own sons. She was at the foot of the cross and had a close-up view of the man hanging there, yet we see no indication that she believed this was not Jesus but his twin (John 19:25–26).

> *The twin theory suggests that Jesus had an identical twin brother nobody knew about who took Jesus's place on the cross.*

Also problematic is that the theory does not explain the empty tomb. If it was Jesus's twin who was executed and buried, then what happened to the body? If a contemporary of Jesus wanted to shut up the early Christians and discount the claims that Jesus had risen from the dead, they had to do one of two things—produce the body or prove the body was stolen. The fact that a body was not produced and that an empty tomb is traditionally attested to by both Christians and by those antagonistic to Christianity is a very powerful point. The possibility of the body being stolen by Jesus's followers will be dealt with below. In short, there is simply no reason whatsoever to hold this position.

> *The facts we do have about Jesus's family mention brothers and sisters but no twin. Luke, who many scholars believe may have received his information about Jesus's birth from Mary herself, makes no mention of a twin in this birth narrative. Especially considering this was Mary's first pregnancy, it would be an odd detail to leave out.*

Stolen Body

The stolen body theory says that Jesus's followers stole his body from the tomb. This particular theory has a great advantage over all other nonresurrection theories: it is the only alternate theory that dates from the first century, the time when the event in question took place. This theory is actually recorded by the Bible itself in Matt. 28:11–15 as well as by Jewish tradition including the above mentioned Toledoth Jeshu.

> *The weakness of the stolen body theory is that it does not account for the behavior of the disciples.*

The weakness of the stolen body theory is that it does not account for the behavior of the disciples. Though Jesus spoke of his death and resurrection to his disciples, they had no expectation that he would physically rise again three days later. His appearances were news to them. In fact, the picture of the disciples after Jesus's arrest until his first appearance is not at all flattering. The Gospels say that when Jesus was arrested, all the disciples deserted him (Matt. 26:56; Mark 14:50) despite their pledge earlier that night to die with him (Mark 14:31). Peter, leader of the disciples, denied he even knew Jesus three times the night of the arrest (Matt. 26:69–75; Mark 14:66–72; Luke 22:54–62; John 18:25–27). The Sunday morning after the crucifixion, Mary returned from the tomb to discover the other disciples mourning and weeping (Mark 16:10). They even refused to believe her story (Mark 16:11). Sunday evening, the disciples are described as hiding behind locked doors because they feared the Jews (John 20:19). When Jesus then appeared in the room, they were terrified, not expectant (John 24:38).

Fifty days later, we see the apostles suddenly preaching publicly and performing miracles in Jerusalem (Acts 2:1–11,43). Peter, rather than denying Jesus, is now preaching the resurrection of Jesus boldly (Acts 2:14–42). It seems very odd that if they stole the body, they would then, within a matter of weeks, turn around and proclaim the resurrection of Jesus so unabashedly and with such uniform passion and commitment. In fact, their passion seemed to grow, and they became more emboldened as their lives unfolded. So committed were they to the resurrection of Jesus that most likely all of the disciples except John paid for the claim with their lives.

James, brother of John, was beheaded in Jerusalem by Herod ca. AD 44.[10]

Philip was scourged and crucified in Hieropolis, Greece, AD 54.[11]

Andrew was crucified on an "X"-shaped cross in Greece ca. AD 60.[12]

Matthew was pinned to the ground and beheaded in Ethiopia ca. AD 60.[13]

Peter was crucified upside down in Rome ca. AD 64.[14]

Thomas was executed with spears in India ca. AD 70.[15]

Bartholomew (Nathaniel) was flayed alive in Armenia.[16]

Matthias, Judas Iscariot's replacement, was stoned and beheaded in Jerusalem.[17]

Judas (Thaddeus) was crucified in Edessa, Greece ca. AD 72.[18]

Simon was martyred in Persia.[19]

Last, most biblical references have no information on the death of *James*, son of Alphaeus. Some references believe James, son of Alphaeus, is the same person as James, the brother of Jesus, but the evidence is against this position.[20] According to tradition, James, the brother of Jesus, was thrown from the temple tower in Jerusalem and then beaten until he died.[21]

It must be admitted that many of the sources for this information are late and that sometimes there are competing traditions regarding the method, time, and/or place of martyrdom. However, there are no competing traditions that contend that any of the apostles apart from John and James, son of Alphaeus, died natural deaths, only different forms of martyrdom.

The point is that these men scattered around the known world for the sole reason of proclaiming the physical, historical resurrection of Jesus. For the stolen body theory to be true, we would have to believe that these eleven nonmilitary men overpowered a number of Roman soldiers guarding the tomb (Matt. 27:63-66), disposed of the body, and fabricated a story that they all fanatically stuck to even as they were being crucified, stoned, scourged, beheaded, thrown from buildings, and flayed. Not only that, but they did it for no personal gain whatsoever. Thus the lives of the eleven apostles show absolutely no motive for stealing the body or perpetuating the lie of Jesus's resurrection.

Hallucination Theory

The hallucination theory claims that in the midst of their profound grief, the disciples and other followers of Jesus experienced hallucinations in which they saw him raised from the dead. These hallucinations were private in some cases yet corporate in others. In these corporate hallucinations, Jesus imparted the same information to everyone having the experience.

The *Merriam-Webster 11th Collegiate Dictionary* defines hallucination as:

    1a: perception of objects with no reality usually arising from disorder of the nervous system or in response to drugs (as LSD) b: the object so perceived.

    2: an unfounded or mistaken impression or notion: DELUSION.

Clearly the object and source of hallucinations are not external to the mind. The mind is not witnessing a strange event in the real world that it then struggles to interpret. Rather, hallucinations are entirely internal events created by the mind. The possibility of several different people having the exact same hallucination in the exact same way at the exact

same time is extremely unlikely to say the least—let alone twelve or even 500 people at once (see 1 Cor. 15:5–7).

Like the twin theory, the hallucination theory also has the problem of the empty tomb. If the followers of Jesus were simply experiencing hallucinations, then his body must still be in the tomb. All that would be required to extinguish Christianity would be to produce the body. Yet the earliest accounts all say the tomb was empty. Thus there is no reason to take the hallucination theory seriously.

The hallucination theory claims that in the midst of their profound grief, the disciples and other followers of Jesus experienced hallucinations in which they saw him raised from the dead.

The oldest argument against the resurrection is that the tomb was empty, which presumes the correct tomb was visited.

Wrong Tomb

The wrong tomb theory states that the followers of Jesus discovered the tomb to be empty because they went to the wrong tomb. This theory has a number of problems. First, Mary Magdalene and "the other Mary" were at the tomb when Jesus was buried, so they knew which tomb to go to (Matt. 27:61; Mark 15:46–47; Luke 23:55). Second, as if they needed a landmark, Pilate placed a number of Roman soldiers outside the tomb to prevent the body's theft (Matt. 27:63–66). Third, as mentioned above, the oldest argument against the resurrection is that the tomb was empty, which presumes the correct tomb was visited. Again we find a theory for which there is no evidence and therefore, no reason to believe.

This first-century tomb is an excellent example of a rolling stone tomb. It is not Jesus's tomb, however, since it is in Midras, not Jerusalem. (HolyLandPhotos.org)

The Alien Theory

The alien theory says that Jesus was an alien from another planet. According to the theory, because he was from another planet he was very advanced in his knowledge of medicine and science. He also had highly developed psychic abilities, and many things that were natural to him looked miraculous to people in the first century. Thus he had the ability to heal himself in the tomb, exit the tomb unnoticed by guards, was able to locate the disciples' hideout telepathically, and transport himself into their presence. There are many different takes on how this works out, but this is the general idea.

The problem with this theory is that it actually proves too much.

The problem with this theory is that it actually proves too much. Any objection that can be offered against the theory is too easily dismissed by invoking Jesus's alien nature. This nature is presumed to include abilities that look supernatural to humans and that are sufficient for Jesus to pull off this charade. The result is that there is no possible way to prove the theory right or wrong; there is no test that can be performed to determine the truth of the claim. Philosophers dismiss this type of flawed argument as unfalsifiable.

Another weakness of this claim is that instead of weighing all the evidence and being led to this conclusion, adherents start with this conclusion and try to conform all the facts to the theory in a favorable way. This is also a fallacy known as "confirmation bias." This leaves us with an argument that proves so much that it actually proves nothing.

Legend

The legend theory is probably the most popular nonresurrection theory in the list. It says Jesus was either never taken down from the cross and was left to rot and be eaten by birds of prey,[22] or his body was thrown in a common grave and eaten by scavenging dogs.[23] Several months later, Peter and the other apostles came to the realization that what happened to Jesus's body was irrelevant. The apostles could still carry on the ministry of Jesus and spread his teaching no matter whether he was buried properly or rotted away and left for carrion. In this way, the apostles considered Jesus still to be alive and present in the world. The epiphany that they could carry on Jesus's ministry is what came to be known as the resurrection. Because these things were so difficult to convey, especially by uneducated men to an uneducated audience, the apostles did what Jesus would have done; they spoke in parables and symbols. Therefore, everything recorded in the Gospels about the burial and resurrection of Jesus was a fiction invented by his followers to convey greater spiritual truths and vindicate their beloved, slain leader.

The Crucifixion by Velasquez.

For legend theorists, history stops here.

The first problem with this story is that it does not account for the claim of the Jews that Jesus's body was stolen. Again, this first-century claim presupposes that Jesus was buried and that the tomb was found empty. The legend theory ignores both of these pieces of evidence.

The second problem is that the legendary story is full of historical details that could be investigated by anyone interested and was proclaimed publicly in the very city where these events took place to people who were quite likely witnesses of at least some part of the story. If the apostles put a spin on their story or invented elements of what they preached, there were plenty of people in a position to correct or refute them. Public memory of the execution of someone who caused such commotion and on whom such high hopes were hung could not fade so quickly. If it was truly the plan to spread a legendary tale, why do it in the very place it could be easily exposed as false? It would have been much more sensible to begin the ministry in Galilee or somewhere else remote that wasn't full of witnesses.

The Resurrection of Christ by Meister von Hohenfurth ca. 1350.

Third, if one were to invent a legendary account that was to be taken as actual history, one would include the most reliable witnesses of the event. The account would exclude as much suspicion as possible. Yet this is not the case with the resurrection of Jesus. One of the most difficult and puzzling elements in the resurrection accounts, if the resurrection is a legend, is the discovery of the tomb by women. In first-century Palestine, women were considered untrustworthy and were not even allowed to testify in a court of law. According to Josephus, a Jewish historian writing in the first century, "Put not trust in a single witness. Let there be three or at least two whose evidence shall be accredited by their past lives. From women let no evidence be accepted because of the levity and temerity of their sex."[24]

If this legend was to be truly convincing, why would the apostles have the very discovery of the empty tomb rest on witnesses whose testimony would be highly suspect and perhaps dismissed out-of-hand?

If this legend was to be truly convincing, why would the apostles have the very discovery of the empty tomb rest on witnesses whose testimony would be highly suspect and perhaps dismissed out of hand? Why not skip the discovery of the tomb by the women and just rely on the discovery by respected men who were known to be trustworthy, such as Peter and John?

Many advocates of the legend theory believe there is a discernible development of legend in the Gospels. One example is found in the accounts regarding Joseph of Arimathea. This is a particularly important example, since if there was no Joseph of Arimathea, then there was no acquisition of Jesus's body, no tomb in which to bury him, no tomb to be found empty, and therefore no resurrection. The relevant passages that reveal this developing legend are as follows.

Mark 15:42–46

When it was already evening, because it was the day of preparation (that is, the day before the Sabbath), Joseph of Arimathea, a prominent member of the Sanhedrin who was himself looking forward to the kingdom of God, came and boldly went to Pilate and asked for Jesus's body. Pilate was surprised that he was already dead. Summoning the centurion, he asked him whether he had already died. When he found out from the centurion, he gave the corpse to Joseph. After he bought some linen cloth, Joseph

took him down and wrapped him in the linen. Then he laid him in a tomb
cut out of the rock and rolled a stone against the entrance to the tomb.

Matthew 27:57–60

When it was evening, a rich man from Arimathea named Joseph came,
who himself had also become a disciple of Jesus. He approached Pilate and
asked for Jesus's body. Then Pilate ordered that it be released. So Joseph
took the body, wrapped it in clean, fine linen, and placed it in his new
tomb, which he had cut into the rock. He left after rolling a great stone
against the entrance of the tomb.

Luke 23:50–53

There was a good and righteous man named Joseph, a member of the
Sanhedrin, who had not agreed with their plan and action. He was from
Arimathea, a Judean town, and was looking forward to the kingdom of
God. He approached Pilate and asked for Jesus's body. Taking it down, he
wrapped it in fine linen and placed it in a tomb cut into the rock, where no
one had ever been placed.

John 19:38-42

After this, Joseph of Arimathea, who was a disciple of Jesus—but secretly
because of his fear of the Jews—asked Pilate that he might remove Jesus's
body. Pilate gave him permission; so he came and took his body away.
Nicodemus (who had previously come to him at night) also came, bringing
a mixture of about seventy-five pounds of myrrh and aloes. They took
Jesus's body and wrapped it in linen cloths with the fragrant spices,
according to the burial custom of the Jews. There was a garden in the

Detail of a fifteenth-century altarpiece.

place where he was crucified. A new tomb was in the garden; no one had yet been placed in it. They placed Jesus there because of the Jewish day of preparation and since the tomb was nearby.

Assuming Mark was written before Matthew, we see that at first Joseph was part of the Sanhedrin and therefore implicated in Jesus's death. Matthew adds that Joseph was a disciple of Jesus. Luke adds that Joseph was a good man and a member of the Sanhedrin who did not agree with their verdict. John then adds that Joseph feared the Jews and was a secret disciple.

The development of legend is also said to be evident in the descriptions of the tomb, the burial shroud, and the stone in front of the tomb.

The development of legend is also said to be evident in the descriptions of the tomb, the burial shroud, and the stone in front of the tomb. Mark says simply that Joseph had a tomb. Matthew says the tomb was new. Luke says it had never been used. John says the tomb had not only never been used but was in a garden. Mark says the burial cloth was fine linen. Matthew says the linen was not only fine but clean. Luke repeats Mark and adds nothing. John says the linen cloth was accompanied by aromatic spices. Mark says a stone was rolled against the tomb. Matthew says the stone was a "great stone."

To the proponents of this theory, these passages provide justification for believing that a legend had developed and that the resurrection of Jesus has no historical basis.[25] But surely this is a counterintuitive interpretation of the facts. Just because Mark says "a stone" was rolled in front of the tomb and Matthew calls it a "great stone" is no cause to dismiss the account as legend. Likewise, the descriptions of the burial shroud as linen, fine linen, or clean linen is not contradictory, nor does it indicate the development of legend. The absence of the detail from the Synoptic Gospels that the tomb was in a garden is no reason to suspect John invented it. That Joseph was a member of the council and feared the council's reprisals, if it were known he was a follower of Jesus and therefore kept his conviction secret, seems the most obvious reading of the texts. These details do not contradict one another. Rather, it seems far more likely that the details are coming from different accounts of the same event and thus have a corroborative and complementary quality. Indeed, imagine if all the accounts were identical. One can easily hear the argument that the authors conspired to invent the story. The claim that Joseph of Arimathea is legendary can therefore be dismissed for lack of evidence.

Other details of the burial of Jesus are dismissed in a similar fashion. Were there one, two, or three women who discovered the tomb? Was there one angel or two at the tomb? Was Jesus recognizable at the tomb appearance or was he not? Some scholars see in these diverse accounts the making of legends.

Detail of a 1404 painting by Monaco.

But as we have shown above, this argumentation is not the best reading of the accounts. The better explanation is that the accounts are complementary and corroborative. And this reading brings with it the problem of the empty tomb and the discovery of the empty tomb by women.

A variation of the legend theory has enthusiastic followers of Jesus other than the apostles begin to tell exaggerated tales of his deeds that developed over the years into the story we now know. There are three major flaws in this version of the legend theory.

> *The better explanation is that the accounts are complementary and corroborative.*

- *The first is the ever-present problem of the empty tomb being attested to very early on by enemies of Christianity.*
- *The second is the behavior of the apostles, detailed in the stolen body theory.*
- *The third is that the apostles would have corrected errors in the false teaching about Jesus. Indeed, this is exactly why some of the New Testament books were written—to combat false teaching about Jesus.*

Finally, legend theorists reject the idea that the apostles claimed Jesus was resurrected in bodily form.[26] Marcus Borg puts it this way: "Are we to think of these stories as reporting the kinds of events that anybody could have witnessed if they had been there, that is, video-cam kinds of events?"[27] Luke 1:1–4 seems to directly answer Borg:

> Many have undertaken to compile a narrative about the events that have been fulfilled among us, just as the original eyewitnesses and servants of the word handed them down to us. It also seemed good to me, since I have carefully investigated everything from the very first, to write to you in an orderly sequence, most honorable Theophilus, so that you may know the certainty of the things about which you have been instructed.

Paul defended what must have been similar challenges he faced. He writes, "Have nothing to do with pointless and silly myths" (1 Tim. 4:7). And in 1 Tim. 1:3–4, he instructs "not to teach false doctrine or to pay attention to myths."

According to N. T. Wright:

> Paul not only believed that Jesus had been bodily raised from the dead; he believed he knew how it was done, both in the sense of where the power came from (the Spirit of the creator God), and in the sense that he knew what the difference was (corruptibility and noncorruptibility) between the body which died on the cross and the body that rose.[28]

The understanding the apostles had of resurrection came from the tradition of the Pharisees. The Pharisees believed in the resurrection of the physical body to an incorruptible state at the end of time. The apostles' claim of Jesus's resurrection differed with their expectation only on the point of timing; they did not expect the resurrection of Jesus three days after his death. But they did recognize what they experienced as a physical, bodily resurrection.

The Quranic Account of the Resurrection

The New Testament is not the only sacred book that gives an account of the resurrection. The Quran, Islam's holy scripture, tells of the arrest, crucifixion, and resurrection, but it differs in no small way from the biblical account. In Surah 4:157–158, the Quran states:

> And for saying, "We killed (the Messiah) Jesus, son of Mary," the messenger of GOD. They never killed him, they never crucified him—they were made to think that they did.

All factions are full of doubt concerning this issue. They possess no knowledge; they only conjecture. For certain, they never killed him.

Instead, GOD raised him to Him; GOD is Almighty, Most Wise. (Authorized English Version)

The Quranic account of the resurrection.

Islam teaches that Jesus never died but was assumed into heaven. There are a couple of variations explaining the mechanics of this. One version has the soul of Jesus departing from the body before the torture and execution. According to the footnote in the Authorized English Version of the Quran quoted above, "his enemies tortured and crucified his living, but empty body."[29]

Thus Jesus was assumed into heaven, but his soulless body was left on earth to be tortured.

Islam teaches that Jesus never died but was assumed into heaven.

Another, more popular tradition explains that Judas, unbeknownst to the disciples, made his way to Jesus's prison cell and took Jesus's place, allowing Jesus to escape. God then made Judas to look and sound like Jesus. The executioners of Jesus only thought they had crucified Jesus when in reality he was in hiding. Three days later, he appeared to his followers, passing himself off as having been resurrected. This view is based on the Gospel of Barnabas, which gives a similar account in verses 216–219.

There are, however, a number of problems with this account. The first problem is that the Quran dates from the seventh century. Its account, therefore, is almost 600 years removed from the event it claims to correctly document. Compare that with the New Testament that makes claims of Jesus's death by crucifixion, burial, resurrection on the third day, and resurrection sightings that date back within one to three years of the crucifixion itself.[30] Given the choice between believing an account one to three years removed from the event that is confirmed repeatedly by eyewitnesses and an account 600 years removed from the event

The Gospel of Barnabas is a very poor source to cite in corroboration of the Quranic claims since it is an apocryphal document written as late as the Middle Ages.

that has no corroboration, the burden is very heavily placed on the latter. Chapter 9's dealing with miracles demonstrated why there is no reason to take the claims of Muhammad or the Quran seriously. Muhammad was simply not in a position to speak with authority against the New Testament account. And if he was in that position, he was not able to demonstrate his prophetic office in a way that was consistent with how God authenticated every previous prophet in history. Either way, the Quranic account deserves dismissal.

The Gospel of Barnabas is a very poor source to cite in corroboration of the Quranic claims since it is an apocryphal document[31] written as late as the Middle Ages.[32] As such, it was not only written too late to even be considered for inclusion in the canon, but it may be removed from the crucifixion by up to twice the amount of time as the Quran. It also suffers from being the only source besides the Quran making such a claim, as opposed to the twenty-seven books of the New Testament, all of which date within the first century, and not counting the multitude of writings by the early church fathers and non-Christian first-century sources such as Josephus.

Also, according to the Gospel of Barnabas, the body laid in the tomb was stolen by Jesus's disciples. As shown above, this objection does not stand. Also as shown above, it means that Jesus was nothing more than a fraud, a conclusion radically inconsistent with his character. And again, the behavior of the disciples argues against the possibility of such a scenario.

The Biblical Account of Resurrection

Resurrection is the claim that on the third day after he was crucified and buried, Jesus was resurrected from the dead by the power of God for the purpose of testifying to Jesus's authority to say and do the things he did. There are many points of support for this claim, some of which have already been mentioned, including the empty tomb being attested to by very early and hostile sources, the discovery of the empty tomb by witnesses whose testimony would not be allowed in court, the testimony of Gospels (which are eyewitness accounts),[33] and the radical change in the disciples after that Sunday.

In addition to these points, we must add the conversion of Saul of Tarsus who became known as the apostle Paul. Saul was a Jew trained in religious studies by the most respected of Pharisees (Acts 22:3), learned in Greek culture and language, and a Roman citizen. This was a privileged and uncommon combination. According to his own account, he was extremely devoted to the religion of the Jews and to the tradition of the Pharisees (Gal. 1:14; Phil. 3:5). So devoted was he that he enthusiastically persecuted the early Christians, who were to his mind heretics worthy of prison and even death (see Acts 8:1–3; 9:1–2; 26:9–11; Phil. 3:6; Gal. 1:13).

On one such mission of persecution, Paul was on the road to Damascus when he was thrown to the ground in the face of a brilliant, heavenly light. A voice asked him, "Saul, Saul, why are you persecuting me?" Paul asked who was speaking, to which the voice replied, "I am Jesus, whom you are persecuting." The voice of Jesus then explained he was appointing Paul to the purpose of preaching to the Gentiles.

Those with Paul heard a sound but did not discern a voice and saw no one (Acts 9:3–19; 22:6–11; 26:13–23). From that moment on, Paul became the most indus-

The apostle Paul

The traditional spot in Damascus from which Paul was lowered in a basket to escape as recorded in Acts 9:23–25.

trious, tenacious, and fearless of all Christian evangelists. He had almost no concern for his personal well-being. He was beaten, jailed, flogged, and shipwrecked on numerous occasions. He forfeited his position of privilege, and probably wealth, as a student of Gamaliel. Indeed the heretic hunter himself became a hunted heretic. Ultimately his preaching that Jesus had been resurrected physically from the dead in keeping with the messianic prophecies made in the Tanak cost him his life. He was beheaded in Rome by Nero ca. AD 64 or 65.[34]

Several things are clear from this account. Paul was not predisposed to believe in Jesus. In fact, he was predisposed *not* to believe in Jesus. Paul was not converted to a belief that if he just believed in Jesus's teaching, then it would be just like Jesus had come back from the dead. Paul was not converted by a hallucination, because those with him at the conversion could testify to Paul's state of mind, the light that appeared, and that a sound they could not discern came from the light. Hallucinations are internal to the mind, not externally verifiable like this event. If the tomb had not been empty, someone as radically devoted to the cause of defeating Christianity as Paul would have had Jesus's tomb open at once to expose the body and extinguish the movement. In addition to this, the apostles did not believe Paul's conversion. Paul had to work to gain their trust. When Paul did finally meet the apostles, they approved him and endorsed the message he claimed was personally given to him by Jesus to spread to the Gentile world (Acts 9:26–30; Gal. 1:18–19). And, as a Pharisee, Paul believed in a physical, bodily resurrection, not an apparition, hallucination, or fanatical remembrance of someone's life. Thus the best explanation for Paul's embracing the very thing he hated most in the world is that he had a real, historical encounter with the resurrected person of Jesus. Only a radical event such as this could explain so radical a conversion in so passionate a person.

Finally, consider Paul's writing in 1 Cor. 15:3–8. As mentioned in chapter 6, this is most likely the oldest part of the New Testament because it is a creed that Paul says he received after his conversion. This, of course, means it existed before his conversion. Because of reasons given in chapter 6, it is widely held by scholars of all stripes that Paul's conversion happened around three years after the crucifixion. This also means the creed came into existence no later than three years after the crucifixion. This creed is as follows:

> For I passed on to you as most important what I also received: that Christ
> died for our sins according to the Scriptures, that he was buried, that he
> was raised on the third day according to the Scriptures, and that he
> appeared to Cephas, then to the Twelve. Then he appeared to over five
> hundred brothers and sisters at one time; most of them are still alive, but
> some have fallen asleep. Then he appeared to James, then to all the apostles.
> Last of all, as to one born at the wrong time, he also appeared to me.

In this ancient creed, we see that the earliest Christians believed that Jesus was buried, rose on the third day in fulfillment of messianic prophecy in the Tanak, and then appeared to numerous people, most of whom, according to Paul, were still alive at the time of his writing. The information about Jesus's appearances in his resurrected state implies that

these people could be questioned. There is no doubt that the earliest Christians believed that Jesus died and was resurrected in bodily form. And this belief remains the best explanation for the events surrounding Jesus's death. As N. T. Wright puts it:

> The truly extraordinary thing is that this belief was held by a tiny group who, for the first two or three generations at least, could hardly have mounted a riot in a village, let alone a revolution in an empire. And yet they persisted against all the odds, attracting the unwelcome notice of the authorities because of the power of the message and the worldview and lifestyle it generated and sustained. And whenever we go back to the key texts for evidence of why they persisted in such an improbable and dangerous belief they answer: it is because Jesus of Nazareth was raised from the dead.[35]

Conclusion

The resurrection of Jesus from the dead, taken in complete isolation, is admittedly difficult to accept at face value. However, to investigate the resurrection in isolation is to discount not just a large amount of information that contributes to what we can know about the event, but it discounts the resurrection's context entirely. The previous ten chapters give us excellent reason for thinking that the God of the Bible exists, that he has communicated with humanity very specifically, and that he is involved in our world. Because we have shown miracles are possible, the claim of Jesus's resurrection cannot be discarded out of hand.

The tomb of Jesus in the Church of the Holy Sepulchre. The original tomb was probably covered with dirt to make way for a temple of Venus in the early second century. Constantine recovered the original tomb and enshrined it in a church in the fourth century. Muslims then took control of the city. Initially they left the Christian sites undisturbed, but in 1009 they destroyed the tomb. At most, the two side walls remain of the original. A number of renovations have taken place over the years due to fire and neglect. The current rotunda and exterior of the tomb are from the early–mid nineteenth century. (HolyLandPhotos.org)

Because the resurrection, the time of its occurrence, and the person being resurrected were foretold, it becomes both more difficult to construct alternate explanations and provides more criteria that a claim of resurrection must meet. When the events of the Sunday after the crucifixion are studied in context, we see that the resurrection alone makes sense of the facts and falls prey to none of the objections.

As a result, the resurrection has real meaning. It is the event that authenticated Jesus as someone who spoke the very words of God. His teaching is divinely authoritative. But what exactly did he teach? Jesus's moral and ethical teaching is revered not just by Christians but also by many who confess other religions and even by many atheists. However, Jesus also taught about who he was and what he was here for. He taught about himself, his identity and nature.

> *When the events of the Sunday after the crucifixion are studied in context, we see that the resurrection alone makes sense of the facts and falls prey to none of the objections.*

The big question is this: Did Jesus claim to be God?

Notable Quote

Without the historical resurrection, Jesus would have been at best just another prophet who met the same unfortunate fate as others before him, and faith in him as Messiah, Lord, or Son of God would have been stupid. It would be no use trying to save the situation by interpreting the resurrection as a symbol. The cold, hard facts would remain: Jesus was dead, and that's it.[36]   —*William Lane Craig*

Notes

1 John Riches, "Pharisees," *The Oxford Companion to the Bible,* ed. Bruce M. Metzger and Michael D. Coogan (Oxford: Oxford University Press, 1993), 588–89.

2 N. T. Wright, *The Resurrection of the Son of Man* (Minneapolis: Fortress, 2003), 201.

3 Josephus, *Antiquities,* 33.3.

4 Pliny the Younger, *Epistles,* 10.96.

5 Babylonian Talmud, Sanhedrin 43a.

6 Gary R. Habermas, *The Historical Jesus* (Joplin, MO: College Press, 1996), 205.

7 Eusebius, *Ecclesiastical History* (Grand Rapids: Baker, 1955), 143.

8 *Holman Illustrated Bible Dictionary* (Nashville: Broadman & Holman, 2003), 1452–53.

9 Dr. Mark Eastman's lecture "The Agony of Love" provides a graphic medical description of the body's response to both scourging and crucifixion. Much of this book's description is indebted to his work. His lecture can be heard online at http://www.marshill.org/, accessed June 22, 2005.

10 This event is mentioned in Acts 12:2. Eusebius preserves Clement's late first-century account in his *Ecclesiastical History,* 2,9. The date is mentioned in the *Holman Illustrated Bible Dictionary,* 866.

11 Joan Comay and Ronald Brownrigg, *Who's Who in the Bible* (New York: Random House, 1971, 1993), 2:346; John Foxe and Harold J. Chadwick, *The New Foxe's Book of Martyrs* (1563; Gainesville, FL: Bridge-Logos, 2001), 6.

12 Comay and Brownrigg, *Who's Who in the Bible,* 2:27.

13 Ibid., 2:294; John Foxe, *Foxe's Book of Martyrs* (1563; repr., New Kensington, PA: Whitaker House, 1981), 7–9.

14 Comay and Brownrigg, *Who's Who in the Bible,* 2:337; 1 Clement 5; Eusebius, *Ecclesiastical History,* 2.1.

15 Alexander Roberts and James Donaldson, eds., *Ante-Nicene Fathers,* vol. 8, *The Consummation of Thomas the Apostle* (1886; Peabody, MA: Hendrickson, 2004), 551; Foxe and Chadwick, *New Foxe's Book of Martyrs,* 8.

16 Comay and Brownrigg, *Who's Who in the Bible,* 2:42.

17 Foxe and Chadwick, *New Foxe's Book of Martyrs,* 6.

18 Comay and Brownrigg, *Who's Who in the Bible,* 2:243; Foxe and Chadwick, *New Foxe's Book of Martyrs,* 8.

19 Comay and Brownrigg, *Who's Who in the Bible,* 2:397; Foxe and Chadwick, *New Foxe's Book of Martyrs,* 6–7.

20 Cp. Eusebius, *Ecclesiastical History*, 2.1 (Nashville: Thomas Nelson, 1897), 386.

21 *Holman Illustrated Bible Dictionary*, 867.

22 Marcus Borg and N. T. Wright, *The Meaning of Jesus—Two Visions* (San Francisco: HarperSanFrancisco, 1999), 89. This is the position put forth by Borg and argued against Wright.

23 Robert W. Funk, *Honest to Jesus* (San Francisco: HarperSanFrancisco, 1996), 220–21.

24 Josephus, *Antiquities of the Jews*, 4.13.

25 John Dominic Crossan, *Who Killed Jesus?* (San Francisco: HarperSanFrancisco, 1995), 172.

26 Funk, *Honest to Jesus*, 259.

27 Borg and Wright, *The Meaning of Jesus*, 134.

28 N. T. Wright, *The Resurrection of the Son of Man* (Minneapolis: Fortress, 2003), 360.

29 *Quran, Authorized English Version*, trans. Rashad Khalifa (Tucson: Islamic Productions, 1989), 103.

30 See the discussion of 1 Cor. 15:3–8 in chap. 6.

31 Craig A. Evans, *Noncanonical Writings and New Testament Interpretation* (Peabody, MA: Hendrickson, 1992), 149.

32 Norman L. Geisler and Abdul Saleeb, *Answering Islam* (Grand Rapids: Baker, 1994), 304.

33 See chaps. 6 and 7.

34 Eusebius, *Ecclesiastical History*, 2.25.

35 Wright, *Resurrection of the Son of Man*, 570.

36 William Lane Craig, "Did Jesus Rise from the Dead?," in *Jesus under Fire*, ed. Michael J. Wilkins et al. (Grand Rapids: Zondervan, 1995), 165.

CHAPTER 12
DID JESUS CLAIM TO BE GOD?
IS JESUS THE ONLY WAY?

God or Fraud?

Many people think of Jesus as a great teacher, an itinerant sage. Some say he was an example of realizing the divinity that is within us all. Others say he was a sorcerer and a heretic. Christianity says he was God incarnate, the Word made flesh.

Having shown good arguments for God's existence, the Bible's trustworthiness, the possibility of miracles, the occurrence of prophecy, and the historicity of the resurrection, the question now becomes, who did Jesus claim to be? If he indeed performed miracles, fulfilled prophecy, and was truly resurrected, then it was not without purpose. Those events were done to establish his authority to make certain claims, claims that primarily had to do with his identity. So who did Jesus say he was?

> The word "messiah" comes from the Hebrew word for "anointed one."

The Messiah Question

The word "messiah" comes from the Hebrew word for "anointed one." The word "Christ" is derived from the translation of "messiah" into Greek. The word had two uses in the Old Testament. One is a general term, and the other is specific. The first had to do with "installing a person in an office in a way that the person will be regarded as accredited by Yahweh, Israel's God."[1] The second use of the word came to indicate a specific person spoken of in the prophecies.

Palastkapelle's triumphal entry of Christ.

This Messiah was to be a savior for the nation of Israel who would overthrow Gentile rule and establish an eternal reign. And yet the prophecies also predicted the Messiah would suffer. These were two different descriptions difficult to envision in one particular person. But it was this specific, narrower sense that Jesus claimed to fulfill.

When Jesus arrived on the scene, many Jews wondered whether he was the Messiah promised in the prophecies of the Old Testament, the person who would come to build a house in the name of Yahweh and would "establish the throne of his kingdom forever" (2 Sam. 7:13). But by the time Jesus was born, expectations of what the Messiah would be like and what he would do had changed. Most believed only in a political Messiah who would free Israel from the heavy hand of Rome, not bring to bear the image of the coming one as a suffering servant. The era between Malachi and John the Baptist even produced literature about such a political Messiah. As Merrill C. Tenney observes, "In all of this literature the Messiah is nowhere represented as suffering for men or as redeeming them by his personal sacrifice."[2] Albert H. Baylis adds, "That Messiah would come without restoring Israel to nationhood was unthinkable."[3]

Michelangelo's *Pieta*.

Thus Jesus was viewed by his audiences through a lens distorted by misunderstood prophecies and unwarranted expectations.

In fact, Jesus appeared, in the end, to be completely disqualified from being considered Messiah. N. T. Wright puts it this way:

The prophecies also predicted the Messiah would suffer.

> What nobody expected the Messiah to do was to die at the hands of the pagans instead of defeating them; to mount a symbolic attack on the Temple, warning it of imminent judgment, instead of rebuilding or cleansing it; and to suffer unjust violence at the hands of the pagans instead of bringing them justice and peace. The crucifixion of Jesus, understood from the point of view of any onlooker, whether sympathetic or not, was bound to have appeared as the complete destruction of any messianic pretensions or possibilities he or his followers might have hinted at.[4]

The Jews at that time simply had no concept that the Messiah might actually be God incarnate. Even if they did, they were completely unprepared for Jesus's apparent failure. As a result, although Jesus spoke about his being Messiah, this was not necessarily taken by his audiences to be a claim of divinity.

Jesus Never Said, "I Am God"

It is true that in Scripture we never see Jesus say the words, "I am God." But this does not mean that Jesus did not claim to be God. In the first century, much like today, to say "I am God" would be almost meaningless. Even Roman emperors were ascribed deity or claimed deity for themselves.[5] What Jesus did do was claim to be a very specific God to a specific people in a very specific way. And the way in which he made his claims was unambiguous and unmistakable to those people.

Jesus claimed to be the God of the ancient Hebrews as described in the Old Testament.

In making this claim, Jesus spoke idiomatically, meaning he spoke in a way that was peculiar to his audience, first-century Jews. To understand this more fully, consider the sentence: "That cat can wail." If you heard a veterinarian say that sentence, it would mean something completely different than if you heard it from an old jazz musician. Though the words are the same, the idiom provides the framework for the proper interpretation.

With this in mind, we see that Jesus claimed to be the God of the ancient Hebrews as described in the Old Testament. He made this claim explicitly in ways that would have rightly been considered blasphemous if he were, in fact, not God. He also made this claim in more implicit ways by exercising prerogatives that belong solely to God himself, such as forgiving sins and accepting worship. Each of these ways is worth looking at more closely.

Blasphemy (?)

One of the best indicators of who Jesus claimed to be is the response of his audiences. Their reaction to his words is very helpful in understanding the content of his words. In John 8:52–59, we see the following scene:

> Then the Jews said, "Now we know you have a demon. Abraham died and so did the prophets. You say, 'If anyone keeps my word, he will never taste death.' Are you greater than our father Abraham who died? And the prophets died. Who do you claim to be?"

Julius Caesar, AD 44, the first Roman emperor to be worshiped as deity.

"If I glorify myself," Jesus answered, "my glory is nothing. My Father—about whom you say, 'He is our God'—he is the one who glorifies me. You do not know him, but I know him. If I were to say I don't know him, I would be a liar like you. But I do know him, and I keep his word. Your father Abraham rejoiced to see my day; he saw it and was glad."

The Jews replied, "You aren't fifty years old yet, and you've seen Abraham?"

Jesus said to them, "Truly I tell you, before Abraham was, I am."

So they picked up stones to throw at him. But Jesus was hidden and went out of the temple.

A detail of *Jesus* by Caravaggio.

Why did the Jews respond with such violence toward Jesus? The first thing to notice is the oddly structured sentence of Jesus's last statement, "Truly I tell you, before Abraham was, I am." When Jesus said, "I am," he was not being grammatically incorrect. He was claiming the personal name God gave himself when he spoke to Moses from the burning bush (Exod. 3:13-14). His audience understood this but did not believe it. Not just that, but they immediately tried to execute Jesus because of the proscription found in Lev. 24:16: "Whoever blasphemes the name of the LORD must be put to death; the whole community is to stone him."

Death by stoning is the punishment for breaking the fourth commandment, "Do not misuse the name of the LORD your God" (Exod. 20:7).

But this is not the only instance of such an explicit claim. Other examples include:

John 10:30-33

[Jesus said,] "I and the Father are one."

Again the Jews picked up rocks to stone him.

Jesus replied, "I have shown you many good works from the Father. For which of these works are you stoning me?"

"We aren't stoning you for a good work," the Jews answered, "but for blasphemy, because you—being a man—make yourself God."

John 5:16-18

Therefore, the Jews began persecuting Jesus because he was doing these things on the Sabbath.

Jesus responded to them, "My Father is still working, and I am working also." This is why the Jews began trying all the more to kill him: Not only

was he breaking the Sabbath, but he was even calling God his own Father, making himself equal to God.

Matthew 26:63–66

But Jesus kept silent. The high priest said to him, "I charge you under oath by the living God: Tell us if you are the Messiah, the Son of God."

"You have said it," Jesus told him. "But I tell you, in the future you will see the Son of Man seated at the right hand of Power and coming on the clouds of heaven."

Then the high priest tore his robes and said, "He has blasphemed! Why do we still need witnesses? See, now you've heard the blasphemy. What is your decision?"

They answered, "He deserves death!"[6]

John M. Frame notes:

If Jesus' claims were false, he certainly was a blasphemer, and we can well understand why the strongly monotheistic Jews would be quick to accuse any man who claimed to be God. On this matter, they did understand him rightly.[7]

Thus the very specific words Jesus used and the reaction of his audience confirm that Jesus claimed to be the God of the Bible. Jesus did not correct their misunderstanding of the law which declared that blasphemers must be executed. Rather, he tried to correct their misunderstanding of his identity.

The Forgiving of Sins

Jesus also claimed to be the God of the Bible in implicit ways. These ways have to do with Jesus's claiming rights, privileges, and powers that belong exclusively to God alone. One of the divine prerogatives that Jesus claimed was the ability to forgive sins. We find an example of this in Mark 2:3–12:

They came to him bringing a paralytic, carried by four of them. Since they were not able to bring him to Jesus because of the crowd, they removed the roof above him, and after digging through it, they lowered the mat on which the paralytic was lying. Seeing their faith, Jesus told the paralytic, "Son, your sins are forgiven."

But some of the scribes were sitting there, questioning in their hearts: "Why does he speak like this? He's blaspheming! Who can forgive sins but God alone?"

Right away Jesus perceived in his spirit that they were thinking like

Giotto's rendition of Caiaphas tearing his robes in response to Jesus's claims.

Ruins of homes from the first century in Capernaum, the town where the paralytic was lowered through the roof. (HolyLandPhotos.com)

this within themselves and said to them, "Why are you thinking these things in your hearts? Which is easier: to say to the paralytic, 'Your sins are forgiven,' or to say, 'Get up, take your mat, and walk'? But so that you may know that the Son of Man has authority on earth to forgive sins"— he told the paralytic— "I tell you: get up, take your mat, and go home."

Immediately he got up, took the mat, and went out in front of everyone. As a result, they were all astounded and gave glory to God, saying, "We have never seen anything like this!"

Jesus's audience understood that forgiving sins is an exclusive right of God, and they rightfully objected to the claim. After all, it is easy to say, "Your sins are forgiven," but how could anyone actually verify such an outrageous claim? Jesus did just that by performing a miracle to authenticate his claim and thus establish his identity. The miracle confirmed the claim that Jesus is God and, as such, can forgive sins.

In another example, found in Luke 7:36–50, Jesus was dining at a Pharisee's house when a woman identified as a sinner washed Jesus's feet with her tears and fragrant oil. The Pharisee reacted quite judgmentally, to which Jesus replied:

"Do you see this woman? I entered your house; you gave me no water for my feet, but she, with her tears, has washed my feet and wiped them with her hair. You gave me no kiss, but she hasn't stopped kissing my feet since I came in. You didn't anoint my head with olive oil, but she has anointed my feet with perfume. Therefore I tell you, her many sins have been forgiven; that's why she loved much. But the one who is forgiven little, loves little." Then he said to her, "Your sins are forgiven."

A Galilean landscape. It was in Galilee that Jesus's feet were washed by the woman's tears.

The west coast of the Sea of Galilee, where Jesus walked on water. (HolyLandPhotos.org)

> Those who were at the table with him began to say among themselves, "Who is this man who even forgives sins?" (vv. 44b–49)

Again, the audience understood that Jesus was claiming for himself a right that belongs to God alone. And again, they were unwilling to accept the implications of the claim. But they did understand the claim was a claim of being the Hebrew God incarnate. Though the claim is implicit, it is a bold and unambiguous statement made in such a way that Jesus's hearers would not misunderstand his meaning.

Acceptance of Worship

Another way Jesus claimed to be God is by accepting worship. If Jesus were simply a good teacher living an exemplary moral life, then he would surely rebuke such behavior as misguided or inappropriate. Otherwise, his teaching would not be good, and we would find him acting immorally by accepting that which was not his. Jesus, however, taught and reacted in the opposite way, a way that indicated that it was right and proper for him to receive worship.

Consider Matt. 14:22–33, the famous story of Jesus walking on water. According to verse 33, when the disciples realized Jesus was not a ghost and saw him calm the wind, "those in the boat worshiped him and said, 'Truly you are the Son of God.'"

Though Jesus had just rebuked Peter's lack of faith in verse 31, he did not rebuke the disciples when they reacted to his works with worship. In Jesus's view, this was the proper response.

Another way Jesus claimed to be God is by accepting worship.

This acceptance of worship is found again in John 9:35–38 after Jesus had healed a blind man.

> Jesus heard that they had thrown the man out, and when he found him, he asked, "Do you believe in the Son of Man?"
>
> "Who is he, Sir, that I may believe in him?" he asked.
>
> Jesus answered, "You have seen him; in fact, he is the one speaking with you."
>
> "I believe, Lord!" he said, and he worshiped him.

Here we see Jesus making two claims. By accepting worship, he is tacitly claiming to be God incarnate—one to whom worship is rightly offered. And by identifying himself as the Son of Man, he is claiming to be the promised Messiah prophesied in Dan. 7:13.

A detail of a painting by Giotto showing Jesus accepting worship.

This implicit claim was not lost on Jesus's audience. In fact, the Jewish leaders complained about Jesus's acceptance of worship.

A good example of this is found in Matt. 21:14–16.

> The blind and the lame came to him in the temple, and he healed them. When the chief priests and the scribes saw the wonders that he did and the children shouting in the temple, "Hosanna to the Son of David!" they were indignant and said to him, "Do you hear what these children are saying?"
>
> Jesus replied, "Yes, have you never read: You have prepared praise from the mouths of infants and nursing babies?"

It was Jesus who had prompted the praise from the children, praise that he did not rebuke. The quote referenced by Jesus is from Ps. 8, which was written in praise of the glory of God. And the fact that he quoted that psalm to give a correct understanding of the situation indicates that Jesus believed himself to be the "you" of the psalm—God himself. Again we find Jesus making the claim to be a specific God to a specific audience in a specific way.

But Jesus goes even further in his claim. He does not simply accept worship. He teaches us to pray to God in his name, an absolutely outlandish thing to do if he were not, in fact, God. John 16:23–24 records Jesus as saying: "Truly I tell you, anything you ask the Father in my name, he will give you. Until now you have asked for nothing in my name. Ask and you will receive, so that your joy may be complete."

This is also seen in verses such as John 14:12–14; 15:16. This is surely more than a recommendation such as, "Tell God, 'Jesus sent ya!'" This is a claim of divine authority and access to the very throne of God.

Is Jesus the Only Way to God?

But it is more than that. By teaching us to pray in his name, Jesus is claiming to be in the position of mediator or reconciler between humans and God. It is only through praying in Jesus's name that believers can have access to God. We see this in John 14:6, when Jesus says, "I am the way, the truth, and the life. No one comes to the Father except through me." This is not to say that invoking the name of Jesus itself is some inherently magical incantation that obliges God to hear and answer prayer. Rather, it is belief in the work and person of Jesus that allows believers to come before a righteous and holy God. Jesus explicitly says this in John 3:16-18.

Jesus does not simply accept worship. He teaches us to pray to God in his name, an absolutely outlandish thing to do if he were not, in fact, God.

For God loved the world in this way: He gave his one and only Son, so that everyone who believes in him will not perish but have eternal life. For God did not send his Son into the world to condemn the world, but to save the world through him. Anyone who believes in him is not condemned, but anyone who does not believe is already condemned, because he has not believed in the name of the one and only Son of God.

This is also seen in Matt. 11:27: "All things have been entrusted to me by my Father. No one knows the Son except the Father, and no one knows the Father except the Son and anyone to whom the Son desires to reveal him."

As William Lane Craig points out, the second verse "tells us that Jesus claimed to be the Son of God in an exclusive and absolute sense." He goes on to note, "[Jesus] also claims to be the only one who can reveal the Father to men."[8] The claims of Jesus and his self-understanding are also accurately preserved by his followers in the New Testament. Peter, for example, testifies, "There is salvation in no one else, for there is no other name under heaven given to people by which we must be saved" (Acts 4:12; cp. 1 Cor. 8:5–6). Jesus, being fully human and fully God, is uniquely qualified for this position of mediator. It is because the death of Jesus paid for the sins of those who

> *"Jesus claimed to be the Son of God in an exclusive and absolute sense."*

believe in him and because the perfect obedience of his life is credited to those same believers that Jesus can provide reconciliation between individuals and God. This is the gospel, the good news that proclaims the possibility and the certainty of salvation through Jesus Christ.

Jesus's exclusive and absolute claims of being the sole avenue of access to God as well as God incarnate are not just an important part of his teaching; they are the foundation on which all his teachings rest. They are the reasons so many conversations Jesus had with the Jewish leaders quickly turned to his identity and authority. They are the primary distinctions between him and other religious leaders such as the Buddha, Muhammad, and Moses. Paul Copan notes:

> *"The founders of the world's great religions made no claims as extravagant as Jesus of Nazareth did: to forgive sins, to be the judge of all, to always be present with his followers throughout the ages, to hear their prayers."[9] Because of Jesus's claims the earliest believers were even referred to as being members of the Way."[10]*

The exclusivist claims of Jesus to be the only way humans can access God and be saved is extremely unpopular and far from politically correct. But the criticism leveled against Christianity on this count

The Ascension (detail) by Tintoretto.

is quite unjustified. Every religion makes exclusive claims. That is what makes them distinct religions. The answers to who Jesus is and what must be done to attain salvation differ from religion to religion.

Some believe that each religion is like a different road leading to the same place.

It may be that Hinduism is perfectly open to accepting Jesus into its pantheon of gods. It may also be that Buddhists are willing to allow that Jesus is someone who attained enlightenment. And it is true that Islam is willing to admit Jesus was a great prophet. But the acceptance of Jesus by other religions does not reveal Christianity to be a chauvinistic enterprise that is uniquely exclusivist. For Hinduism, Buddhism, or Islam to accept Jesus, they must reject much or all of what he taught about himself and the world. In other words, Jesus is fine with Hinduism as long as Jesus is Hindu; Jesus is fine with Buddhism as long as he is Buddhist; Jesus is fine with Islam as long as he is Muslim. The same follows for every religion including Universalism and Bahaism. And, similarly, Christianity would welcome the Buddha or Muhammad or any other religion's founder into the fold if that person were to renounce his exclusive teachings and accept the work and person of Jesus for his salvation.

Another way of thinking about this is by considering the saying, "All roads lead to Rome." Some believe that each religion is like a different road leading to the same place. This quickly falls apart when we look at each road's directions. One says Rome is everywhere. One says Rome is in oneself. One says Rome is unknowable. One says Rome doesn't even exist. But one says Rome is in a specific place and can only be gotten to in a very specific way. Really, instead of all roads leading to Rome, all roads lead to their own exclusive destinations and do not even intersect. They may even each call their destination "Rome," but they do not mean the same things by it. Either all the roads are wrong, or only one is right. There are no other options.

Really, instead of all roads leading to Rome, all roads lead to their own exclusive destinations and do not even intersect.

This exclusive nature is what we mean when we say something is true. All truth is exclusive by definition. Contradictory statements cannot each be true at the same time and in the same way. This is why people do not adhere to more than one religion simultaneously. There are no Islamic Christians. Rather, they convert their thinking about God, themselves, and the world from one way to another.

One last thing to consider is this: If Jesus is not the exclusive avenue to salvation, but just one way, then why did he die? Why did he live at all? For what possible reason

The Crucifixion by Fra Angelico.

would God become incarnate in the person of Jesus of Nazareth, live a life of perfect obedience, service, and self-denial, and suffer torture and then execution in one of the most horrible ways imaginable if there were plenty of other avenues to God? Only a cruel and sadistic God, a God far from being worthy of worship by any religion, would perpetrate such a gratuitous and evil act. For those who say there is no fundamental difference between religions, this is the God they are left with.

But this cruel God contradicts the God demonstrated by the existence of morality in chapter 4. If our moral intuitions were rooted in and informed by the character of our Creator, God, then we would not be able to recognize the evil in his behavior. In fact, we would agree with it, approve of it, and call it good instead. But we clearly cannot do this. And as chapter 4 has shown, we are not left with the option of an objective moral standard that exists outside of God's character and to which he, as well as we, are obliged. As a result, we arrive back at exclusivity, a feature of all religions, not just Christianity.

Conclusion

It is clear, then, that Jesus thought of himself not just as God, but as the God of the Jews—the God of Abraham, Moses, Isaiah, David, and so on. He did this in a way that would be easily understood, though not necessarily accepted, by his culture. Jesus also taught that belief in him was the only way by which we may access God.

It is imperative to understand that these things deal with the content of faith, not the sincerity of the believer. Many people sincerely believe false things, but that does not prove the truthfulness of what they believe. The object of faith, the content, is what determines whether a religion is true or false, not the sincerity of its adherents.

Many people sincerely believe false things, but that does not prove the truthfulness of what they believe. The object of faith, the content, is what determines whether a religion is true or false, not the sincerity of its adherents.

Notable Quote

Plenty of great teachers, mystics, martyrs and saints have made their appearance at different times in the world, and lived lives and spoken words full of grace and truth, for which we have every reason to be

grateful. Of none of them, however, has the claim been made, and accepted, that they were Incarnate God. In the case of Jesus alone the belief has persisted that when he came into the world God deigned to take on the likeness of a man in order that thenceforth men might be encouraged to aspire after the likeness of God; reaching out from their mortality to His immortality, from their imperfection to His perfection.[11]

—*Malcolm Muggeridge*

Notes

1   *Holman Illustrated Bible Dictionary* (Nashville: Broadman & Holman, 2003), 1111.

2   Merrill C. Tenney, *New Testament Survey* (Grand Rapids: Eerdmans, 1953, 1961, 1985), 87.

3   Albert H. Baylis, *From Creation to the Cross* (Grand Rapids: Zondervan, 1996), 372.

4   N. T. Wright, *The Resurrection of the Son of God* (Minneapolis: Fortress, 2003), 557–58.

5   Bruce Shelley, *Church History in Plain Language* (Nashville: Thomas Nelson, 1982, 1995), 43–45; *Eerdmans Handbook to the World's Religions* (Grand Rapids: Eerdmans, 1982, 1994), 108–9.

6   This account of Jesus's trial is also found in Mark 14:61–64.

7   John M. Frame, *Apologetics to the Glory of God* (Phillipsburg, NJ: Presbyterian & Reformed, 1994), 141.

8   William Lane Craig, *Reasonable Faith* (Wheaton, IL: Crossway, 1984), 246.

9   Paul Copan, *True for You, but Not for Me* (Minneapolis: Bethany, 1998), 108.

10 Acts 9:2; 19:9,23

11 Malcolm Muggeridge, *Jesus* (New York: Harper & Row, 1975), 16.

CHAPTER 13

HOW COULD GOD ALLOW EVIL?

What Is Evil?

No matter where we live, no matter the circumstances of our lives, no matter how much money or worldly success we may have, we all experience evil. Presidents and preschoolers, criminals and clerics, the famous and the fan—no one is left untouched. And there are a great many people throughout history who have considered the existence of evil, the amount of evil, and the nature of evil as excellent evidence that there is no God—especially not one who has the will and the power to do anything about it. But although it seems we all recognize evil when we see it in the Holocaust, murder, a tsunami, or cancer, what exactly is evil?

Augustine defined evil as "a privation of a good, even to the point of complete nonentity."[1] In other words, evil is where good should be but is not. This definition also specifies that evil is not a thing; it has no substance. This does not imply evil does not exist. Rather, it means that evil exists in the same way as dark or cold does. Dark and cold are very real things that are ways of speaking of the absence of light or heat. Both dark and cold are parasites, in a way, of light and heat since light and heat can exist without dark and cold, but dark and cold cannot exist without the existence of

No matter where we live, no matter the circumstances of our lives, no matter how much money or worldly success we may have, we all experience evil.

Think of the phrase, "Elvis has left the building." There can be no absence of Elvis unless Elvis exists and is somewhere other than here.

light and heat. Think of the phrase, "Elvis has left the building." There can be no absence of Elvis unless Elvis exists and is somewhere other than here. This would be a privation of Elvis. But when Elvis is here, we do not speak of an absence of Elvis.

Another way of defining evil is "a departure from the way things ought to be."[2] The importance of thinking about evil is that although evil is real it was not created by God, but it was made possible by God.

John M. Frame is quick to point out, however, that the Bible says all things are subject to his will (see Gen. 50:20; Acts 4:28; Rom. 9:11–22; Eph. 1:11). According to Frame, "The problem is simply that God is sovereign over all events, good and evil, and however one analyzes evil metaphysically, it is a part of God's plan."[3] Here again, God is not directly responsible for creating evil but rules over it and uses it to accomplish his good purposes. This idea of God and evil coexisting is extremely difficult to reconcile at times even for the staunchest believer. And this is precisely the rub that is so often exploited to show that God does not exist.

There are two kinds of arguments against God that spring from the existence of evil. One argument holds that evil could not exist at the same time as a morally perfect, all-powerful, all-knowing God. This is called the logical argument from evil. The other kind of argument says the amount and quality of evil make it extremely unlikely that a morally perfect, all-powerful, all-knowing God exists. This is known as the evidential or probabilistic argument.

A hurricane as seen from the International Space Station. (photo by NASA)

Theodicy and Defense

The attempt to justify the actions of God, especially as it explains the reality of evil, is called a "theodicy." A theodicy endeavors to show God's actual reasons for allowing evil. This is a difficult task given the paucity of information on the subject in the Bible. It is true that the Bible has a significant amount of material dealing with the nature of evil and its remedy, but it does not explicitly reveal why God allows it (nor does it have to, as we shall see).

A more modest approach is to justify God by giving reasons that are possible but not necessarily actual. This way of arguing is known as a defense. Its advantage lies in its being able to demonstrate the bankruptcy of a challenge without the burden of making a case for the actual reasons God has for permitting evil.

The Logical Argument from Evil

Epicurus (341–270 BC) was one of the earliest philosophers to articulate an argument against the existence of God from the problem of evil. He famously stated:

> God . . . either wishes to take away evils, and is
> unable; or He is able, and is unwilling; or He is neither willing nor able, or
> He is both willing and able. If He is willing and is unable, He is feeble,
> which is not in accordance with the character of God; if He is able and
> unwilling, He is envious, which is equally at variance with God; if He is
> neither willing nor able, He is both envious and feeble, and therefore not
> God; if He is both willing and able, which alone is suitable to God, from
> what source then are evils? or why does He not remove them?[4]

Epicurus is not alone. Throughout history the most commonly articulated objection to belief in God has been the inability to reconcile a perfectly benevolent, all-powerful, omniscient God with the existence of evil. Indeed, more than two thousand years later, the complaint of Epicurus can be heard in an interview with popular rock musician Dave Matthews: "If there is a God, a caring God, then we have to figure he's done an extraordinary job of making a very cruel world."[5]

> *"If there is a God, a
> caring God, then we
> have to figure he's done
> an extraordinary job of
> making a very cruel
> world." —Dave Matthews*

As evidenced by the above quotes, in the logical argument from evil one of two things must be mistaken; either there is no such God or there is no evil. There are certainly those who have tried to solve the problem by denying the existence of evil (e.g., Christian Science[6]), but this response is clearly inadequate. It is extremely difficult to imagine a person who knows about and could prevent the Holocaust, a rape, or murder but instead does nothing simply because they do not believe in the reality of evil. One could certainly imagine callous and hateful excuses, such as "It wasn't any of my business" or "I didn't want to get hurt," but not "Evil doesn't exist so there was nothing to actually stop." For people concerned with truth—beliefs that correspond with reality—evil is undeniable and cannot be solved by merely defining it out of existence. Those who deny the existence of evil still get cancer, are raped, murdered, and suffer in natural disasters. They may call it something else or try to ignore it, but they still experience evil.

That leaves the existence of God to be dealt with. The logical argument then takes the following form:

- *If God were truly all-powerful, he could prevent evil.*
- *If God were omniscient, he would know when evil was about to take place and therefore could act to stop it.*
- *If God were morally perfect and benevolent, he would want to prevent evil.*
- *Evil exists.*
- *Therefore, God, at least with those characteristics, does not exist.*

This puts the case developed in the preceding twelve chapters of this book in a difficult place. Using both the general revelation of nature and the special revelation of the Bible, we have seen there is excellent reason to believe that the God objected to by the logical argument from evil does in fact exist. But is it actually the case that God and evil are incompatible and that to hold that both exist is inconsistent?

This question was taken up by Alvin Plantinga in his landmark book, *God, Freedom, and Evil,* in which he makes what he calls a free will defense. According to Plantinga, "the aim [of a free will defense] is not to say what God's reason is, but at most what God's reason might possibly be."[7] The idea is that if there is merely a possible reason for God's permission of evil then the existence of God and evil, simultaneously, is not incompatible or inconsistent and the logical argument from evil fails.

Very simply stated, the free will defense suggests the possibility that

The Expulsion of Adam and Eve by Gustave Doré.

- An all-knowing, all-powerful, all-benevolent God created human beings as free moral agents. This entails the ability to choose evil as well as good.
- Because God is all-knowing, he knew evil would result; because he is

The Creation of Adam, a detail from the Sistine Chapel painting by Michelangelo.

all-powerful, he could create the world in alternate ways; and because he is all-benevolent and morally perfect, he could only have good reasons for making the world in this way.

- As a result, God may have created the potential for evil, but human beings, because they have chosen evil things, made it actual. But this actualizing of evil was not news to God. Thus ultimately, there is evil in the world because God has a good reason for its existence.

According to the Bible, neither humankind nor the world was made in a state corrupted by evil. God created all things and called them "very good" (Gen. 1:31). God also provided in abundance for everything that Adam and Eve, creatures made in his image, could ever need. As creatures made in God's image, they were endowed with moral ability, the freedom to choose between good (adhering to God's will) and evil (violating God's will). How long this good state lasted is unknown, but at some point Adam and Eve freely disobeyed God by violating God's one commandment (which was designed to preserve and perpetuate the good state of the world). Thus evil was introduced into the world by the free choice of morally accountable creatures. God made evil possible, but people made evil actual.

Of course, if God is omniscient, then he knew all along that people would sometimes choose evil. But if God is morally perfect and benevolent, then he must have a good reason for permitting evil, and this is all we need to know. The specific reasons God allows evil are not given, nor are they required for Christianity to be logically consistent.

The free will defense demonstrates that it is not incompatible for both the God of the Bible and evil to exist.

The free will defense, then, demonstrates that it is not incompatible for both the God of the Bible and evil to exist. One does not negate the other. And since there is a possible explanation as to how God and evil can both exist, the logical argument from evil, which says they cannot coexist, fails. It must be reiterated that the free will defense merely suggests a possible state of affairs and does not claim to explain the world as it really is. However, the argument has no less force regardless of whether it is actually true.

The Evidential Argument from Evil

Another way of arguing against the existence of God from evil is to take the enormous amount of evil and the egregiousness of evil and weigh those factors against the proposition that God exists. More simply stated, which do we see more of—evil or evidence of God? Unlike the logical argument from evil, which is a compatibility argument, this argument is based on probability. The probabilistic (or evidential) argument from evil does not say unequivocally that God does not exist, only that it is very likely or even probable that God does not exist.

Which do we see more of—evil or evidence of God?

For people who hold this view, it is a justification to not believe in God. This form of the argument also has a long history and has been articulated many different ways by many kinds of thinkers. One example is found in the stand-up routine of George Carlin.

> Something is wrong here. War, disease, death, destruction, hunger, filth, poverty, torture, crime, corruption, and the Ice Capades. Something is definitely wrong. This is not good work. If this is the best God can do, I am not impressed. Results like these do not belong on the résumé of a Supreme Being.[8]

Philosopher William L. Rowe mentions two examples of evil in his version of this argument. One is hypothetical: the slow, painful death of a fawn that was burned in a forest fire started by lightning. The other is an actual incident: the beating, rape, and murder of a five-year-old girl in Flint, Michigan. Rowe uses these illustrations to show cases where no known

World Trade Center carnage, slaves being transported, and a medieval mask used in torture.

good results from evil.[9] For him, this apparent lack of goodness is reason enough to reject the God of the Bible.

Some people who use the evidential argument do not deny that some amount of evil might be necessary for God to achieve his purpose. However, they do believe that there is more evil than necessary for God's plan to succeed. But how could anyone know such a thing? Plantinga points out the flaw in this kind of reasoning when he notes, "Of course, there doesn't seem to be any way to measure moral evil—that is we don't have units like volts or pounds or kilowatts so that we could say 'this situation contains exactly 35 turps of moral evil.'"[10] Ronald N. Nash sharpens this point further:

> One final point is worth noting: what properties must a being possess in order to know that some evils really are gratuitous? It certainly appears as though one such property must be omniscience. It would seem then that the only kind of being who could know whether some gratuitous evils exist would be God. But if the only being who could know whether such evils exist is God, there surely are problems in arguing that the existence of gratuitous evils are a defeater for the existence of God.[11]

In short, there is just no way of knowing how much evil is required to bring about a perceived good.

One problem with both these flavors of the evidential argument is that they are based on arrogance. Both put finite, flawed human beings in the place of an infinite, perfect God and then declare that nothing makes sense. But just because we cannot see the good in a given situation does not mean that there is no good. Human beings do not have an exhaustive knowledge of all the workings of the universe and therefore cannot determine how much evil is required to bring about a particular good. Human beings do not have purpose for the whole of creation, a greater good that they drive all things toward. Humans are selfish and myopic, and the evidential argument is an outworking of this state.

Human beings do not have an exhaustive knowledge of all the workings of the universe and therefore cannot determine how much evil is required to bring about a particular good.

Another problem that the evidential argument faces is that it loads the question to be answered a certain way. If someone makes the claim that all the evil we see in the world (genocide, rape, torture, slavery, disease, injustice, terrorism, etc.) makes it likely that God does not exist, then that person has a thumb on the scale. Taken as a statement in isolation, this argument might have some force. But to cache out the evidence for evil and leave the evidence for God unstated is disingenuous at best. Probability is calculated by the relevant background information. We all know quite a lot about evil and can easily compile our own catalogs like the one above. Our personal experience and observation of the world make up the background information we use to be able to speak about evil. But the same consideration must be given to the arguments for the existence of God. We cannot just plop the idea of God unexamined on the other side of the scale. The background information that is relevant to this question contains much more than evidence for evil. And in this background information we find the cosmological, teleological, and axiological arguments for the existence of God; that the God described by those arguments is the God of the Bible; that the Bible is a trustworthy document both in terms of its manuscript authority, authorship, and content; that God reveals himself to humans through prophecy verified by miracles; that the resurrection of Jesus was an actual historical event that authenticated Jesus's claim of divinity, his message of salvation, and his ability to reveal the will of God. It is against this list that genocide, rape, torture, slavery, disease, injustice, terrorism, and so forth, must be weighed. Given all this background information, the weight of evil is shown to be no match for the overwhelming evidence for the existence of the God of the Bible.

Given all this background information, the weight of evil is shown to be no match for the overwhelming evidence for the existence of the God of the Bible.

The Problem of Evil Redefined

The most powerful way to respond to the problem of evil is not, however, to argue facts. Rather, the issue can best be settled by trying to define our terms. When someone speaks of evil, what are they actually saying? For anything to be called "good" or "evil," we must first recognize that we are not talking about preferences. What is personally appealing or appalling to us is not in view here. When things are declared to be evil, we mean that something ought to be a certain way but is not. We mean that there is a violation of an intended order and that its purpose is not being achieved. But where do things like intention, order, purpose, and oughtness come from? They come from a person, of course. And since we are talking about intentions and purposes that are universal and transcend individual human beings, cultures, and times, these intentions and purposes must come from a transcendent source. This source must be a personality that has the power to impose his will on the world and has the ability to enforce it. This person is the one whom we call God. Good and evil therefore find their reference point in the person of God. If an act or event is evil, it is because it diverges from God's intention or purpose.

But this claim is often challenged. From the dilemma in Plato's *Euthyphro* to the present day, critics point out that either God is conforming to a standard of goodness outside of himself or that something is good just because God says it is.

> *When things are declared to be evil, we mean that something ought to be a certain way but is not.*

Either way, we see a God who does not deserve our obedience and worship. For if a thing is good just because God says it is, then we are saying that might makes right. And if there is a standard of goodness to which God is obliged, then it is to that standard that we are also obliged. This apparent flaw in the logic of Christianity has given shade to a good many people wishing to avoid the God of the Bible. But are these two solutions the only ways to make sense of the God of the Bible? The answer is no, there is a third possibility. According to Gregory Koukl:

> The third option is that an objective standard exists (this avoids the first horn of the dilemma). However, the standard is not external to God, but internal (avoiding the second horn). Morality is grounded in the immutable character of God, who is perfectly good. His commands are not whims, but rooted in His holiness.[12]

The source of goodness is not arbitrary or based on moods or preferences that can change. Nor is the standard for goodness a law outside of God. Goodness finds its source in God's character, and the standard of goodness is God's character itself. Things

Detail of Plato as painted by Raphael.

are not good just because God says they are; they are good because they correspond to his perfectly good character. God's intentions and purposes are strictly informed by his character. The degree to which something does not correspond to God's omnibenevolent character is the degree to which that thing is evil.

Goodness finds its source in God's character, and the standard of goodness is God's character itself.

The point is that to say something is evil is to say that there is an objective, transcendent, personal being whose will is being violated or whose order is being disturbed. In short, to say something is evil is to claim there is a God. In fact, the existence of evil is one of the most powerful evidences for God. Without the existence of God, the idea of evil becomes unintelligible. As a result, the problem of evil is not a problem for the Christian. Rather, the problem of evil is a problem for unbelievers.

Why Doesn't God Destroy Evil?

We have seen how God could allow evil and that the existence of evil is compatible with God's character. But if God is all-powerful, omnibenevolent, and omniscient, why doesn't he destroy evil? The answer may have to do with our moral character. Because we are made in the image of God, human beings have the ability to make choices that have a moral dimension to them. We can choose to do or say things that would be right or wrong. This ability, of course, allows that we can choose the wrong thing and as a result introduce evil. For God to destroy evil, he must take away the ability of his creatures to introduce evil into the world. But to do that God would also be destroying the ability to do the greatest moral good as well, and that is to be able to love. Thus for God to destroy evil would ultimately be evil itself, since it would take away the greatest good—the ability to love God. Norman Geisler and Ron Brooks note, "If evil is to be overcome we need to talk about it being defeated, not destroyed."[13]

For God to destroy evil would ultimately be evil itself, since it would take away the greatest good—the ability to love God.

"If evil is to be overcome we need to talk about it being defeated, not destroyed."

The Solution to the Problem of Evil

Perhaps the greatest difficulty of the answer to evil given above is that it does not provide a great deal of comfort for those in the midst of evil and suffering who have never thought deeply on the issue before. Although the answer may be intellectually satisfying, it often fails to provide real pastoral comfort to the grieving and afflicted who are asking why such things happen to them. In fact, to give this answer to those in crisis can come off quite cold and uncaring; it can be completely inappropriate to respond with this answer at certain times. The proper time to explore the reason for evil is not while in a season of evil. This question is best answered before such situations arise—and they will arise. If the answer is understood beforehand, then it provides a framework to understand, at least to some degree, why things are the way they are. It also gives assurance to believers and buoys them for their journey. It strengthens faith and can be used to magnify God to unbelievers brought in contact with suffering believers.

The main answer, however, to the problem of evil is the person of Jesus. If moral evil that you have committed is what plagues you, then Jesus takes the punishment that you deserve and pays for it himself by his death. If you are a victim of some-

> *The main answer to the problem of evil is the person of Jesus.*

one else's moral evil, then either Jesus pays for it with his death or he sits as judge and punishes the person responsible. Whether Jesus pays for or punishes moral evil depends on the response of the person. Either way, moral evil finds its remedy in the perfect obedience of the life of Jesus and his death on behalf of those who believe in him for the payment of sin. He will either judge or justify every person who ever lived.

Jesus is also the solution for natural evil. In his resurrection, we see him not merely restored to his physical body but to a glorified state. His resurrected body cannot die, get sick, or be corrupted in any way. This indicates a fulfillment of the way things were intended to be, an achievement of the goal to which all things are moving according to God's good purpose. This demonstration gives an answer to those who are suffering from physical or natural evil. The blind shall have their sight restored, the deaf shall hear, the crippled shall walk, the mentally handicapped shall think clearly. More than that, there will be no more tsunamis to kill thousands of people,

> *All things will be not merely restored to their state before the fall, but will attain the good purpose for which they were created.*

no more hurricanes, tornados, floods, sickness, disease. All things will be not merely restored to their state before the fall, but will attain the good purpose for which they were created. Jesus overcame both moral and physical/natural evil. He alone is the solution. Evil is only a problem for those who refuse him.

It is only when we stop viewing the world in a self-centered way and see the world as it really is, centered on God, that we can make sense of evil. And not just evil, but the whole of our experience finds its answer and meaning in a God-centered universe. Let us glorify him and enjoy him forever.

> *Moral evil finds its remedy in the perfect obedience of the life of Jesus and his death on behalf of those who believe in him for the payment of sin.*

Notable Quote

Then Job replied to the LORD:
I know that you can do anything and no plan of yours can be thwarted. You asked, "Who is this who conceals my counsel with ignorance?" Surely I spoke about things I did not understand, things too wondrous for me to know. You said, "Listen now, and I will speak. When I question you, you will inform me." I had heard reports about you, but now my eyes have seen you. Therefore, I reject my words and am sorry for them; I am dust and ashes. —*Job 42:1–6*

Notes

1 Augustine, Confessions, 3.7.

2 This definition of evil was given by philosopher Doug Geivett during a lecture on theodicy at Biola University.

3 John M. Frame, *Apologetics to the Glory of God* (Phillipsburg, NJ: Presbyterian & Reformed, 1994), 156–57.

4 Alexander Roberts and James Donaldson, eds., *Ante-Nicene Fathers*, vol. 7, *A Treatise on the Anger of God*, by Lactantius (Grand Rapids: Eerdmans, 1965), 271. Lactantius (AD 260–330) preserved this quotation of Epicurus, whose works have been lost.

5 Tracey Pepper, "Dave Matthews Band," Treatise on the Anger of God, Lactantius (June 1998): 102.

6 Walter Martin, *The Kingdom of the Cults* (Minneapolis: Bethany House, 1965, 1982), 122–23.

7 Alvin Plantinga, *God, Freedom, and Evil* (1974; Grand Rapids: Eerdmans, 1977), 28.

8 George Carlin, "There Is No God," on *You Are All Diseased*, Atlantic Records, 1999, compact disc.

9 William L. Rowe, "Reply to Plantinga," *Noûs* 32, no. 4 (December 1998): 545–46.

10 Plantinga, *God, Freedom, and Evil*, 55.

11 Ronald N. Nash, "The Problem of Evil," in *To Everyone an Answer*, ed. Francis J. Beckwith, William Lane Craig, and J. P. Moreland (Downers Grove, IL: InterVarsity, 2004), 220.

12 Gregory Koukl, *Solid Ground* (July–August 2003), 1–4.

13 Norman Geisler and Ron Brooks, *When Skeptics Ask* (Grand Rapids: Baker, 1996), 64.

CHAPTER 14
METHODOLOGY

The Toolbox

As we have seen in the previous thirteen chapters, apologetics is a multifaceted enterprise. It covers a number of disciplines in a way that is defensive, offensive, reasonable, factual, intellectual, and pastoral. Because of its broad application, a number of different apologetic methods have developed over the course of Christian history. Most of these methods use the arguments of this book (as well as others not mentioned) to make their cases. The differences in methodology are distinguished largely by which kinds of arguments are emphasized. The apologetic arguments are somewhat like ingredients; methodology is like what you choose to bake using these ingredients. The various results may look or taste a bit different from each other, but all have the same purpose: to justify the Christian faith.

Apologetic method has four basic camps: classical apologetics, evidentialism, presuppositionalism, and fideism (although most would classify fideism as more of an anti- or nonapologetic). A fifth camp seeks to employ the strengths of all the methods or at least the first three. Each of these methods developed at different times and in response to different circumstances, challenges, and opportunities. Although these formal names draw hard lines between the different approaches, it is fair to say that most apologists probably do not fall exclusively into one camp. They often favor one but draw from others as well.

> *Differences in methodology are distinguished largely by which kinds of arguments are emphasized.*

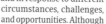

Classical Apologetics

The emphasis of classical apologetics is on reason. Christianity's logical soundness and internal coherence is exploited in this method. As a result, tests are developed and proofs are given that demonstrate the truthfulness of Christianity and the irrationality of competing worldviews.

According to classical apologist Norman L. Geisler, "If no test for truth is sufficient, then truth cannot be established

and tested; and if truth cannot be established, then the Christian apologist is out of business."[1] These tests and proofs take many forms but are most often philosophical in nature. Kenneth D. Boa and Robert M. Bowman Jr. note that "the classical apologists

The emphasis of classical apologetics is on reason.

lay great emphasis on the examples of apologetic argument found in the New Testament (especially Paul's apologetic speech in Athens in Acts 17)."[2] The cosmological and teleological arguments are staples of the classical apologist's case.

The classical method is so called because it traces its roots back to the second century and the earliest apologists. As such, it has been the most widely held approach in apologetics, though its popularity has waned somewhat in more recent times, particularly with those who are Reformed in their theology. Classical apologists count among their number Justin Martyr, Thomas Aquinas, B. B. Warfield, and C. S. Lewis. Current adherents include R. C. Sproul, William Lane Craig, Alister McGrath, J. P. Moreland, and Ravi Zacharias.

Evidentialism

Evidentialism, as its name suggests, focuses on the factual verification of the Christian claims. If the Bible is to be taken seriously, its factual claims must be able to be investigated and found to agree with history, archaeology, anthropology, geography, and the findings of

A view of the Areopagus, or Mars Hill, as seen from the Acropolis. It was here that Paul gave his apologetic to the people of Athens. (HolyLandPhotos.org)

other relevant disciplines. Evidentialist cases are often presented like legal cases and appeal to legal standards of evidence. Like classical apologetics, evidentialism is an approach that hinges on probability. All of the facts of the matter are weighed and arguments are made to best explain all the facts. John Warwick Montgomery explains,

> Historians, and indeed all of us, must make decisions constantly, and the only adequate guide is probability—since absolute certainty lies only in the realms of pure logic and mathematics, where, by definition, one encounters no matters of fact at all. . . . If probability does in fact support these claims . . . then we must act in behalf of them.[3]

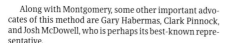

Along with Montgomery, some other important advocates of this method are Gary Habermas, Clark Pinnock, and Josh McDowell, who is perhaps its best-known representative.

Evidentialism focuses on the factual verification of the Christian claims.

Evidentialism's value as a substantial tool to defend the faith rose in the nineteenth and early twentieth centuries as archaeology in particular developed as a science and turned its attention to the Mediterranean world and the Middle East. The findings of ancient manuscripts contributed immensely to our ability to know the original text of the Bible. Inscriptions recovered in archaeological digs corroborated historical claims found in Scripture, and locations of some biblical events were discovered. The investigation of the resurrection has been of particular interest, for obvious reasons. New discoveries continue to be made, adding to the wealth of facts at the evidentialist's disposal.

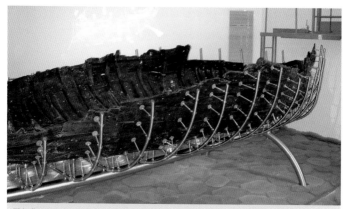

This first-century boat was found on the northwest shore of the Sea of Galilee in 1986. At more than twenty-five feet long, it could carry around fifteen people. (HolyLandPhotos.org)

Presuppositionalism

Presuppositionalism is a method that is deeply rooted in epistemology, our theory of knowledge, or how we can know what we know. Rather than arguing from evidences or the traditional philosophical proofs for Christianity, presuppositionalists employ transcendental arguments to make their case. A transcendental argument is a deductive argument that seeks to explain the necessary conditions for some fact or phenomenon. The premises of a transcendental argument assert the existence of that fact and the conclusion specifies what must be the case for that fact or phenomenon to exist.

Presuppositionalists are more concerned with what makes evidence evidential and what makes reason reasonable. Because the God of the Bible is the creator of all things, we know that he is not the source only of all physical things, but also of all laws whether they be scientific laws, moral laws, or logical laws. Therefore there can be no reason or logic, for example, apart from God.

In fact, according to Cornelius Van Til,

According to presuppositionalism, there can be no reason or logic apart from God.

> The best and only possible proof for the existence of such a God is that his existence is required for the uniformity of nature and for the coherence of all things in the world. . . . Thus there is absolutely certain proof for the existence of God and the truth of Christian theism.[4]

There can be no fact that does not ultimately point back to God.

Greg Bahnsen puts it this way:

> Upon analysis, all truth drives one to Christ. From beginning to end, man's reasoning about anything whatsoever (even reasoning about reason itself) is unintelligible or incoherent unless the truth of the Christian Scriptures is presupposed. Any position contrary to the Christian one, therefore, must be seen as philosophically impossible. It cannot justify its beliefs or offer a worldview whose various elements comport with each other. . . . In short, presuppositional apologetics argues for the truth of Christianity from the "impossibility of the contrary."[5]

According to Van Til, "revelation in Scripture must be made our starting point."[6] Presuppositionalism does not reject the classic philosophical arguments or the evidences by any means. Instead, it provides a grounding that gives the other approaches meaning and shows how competing worldviews have insufficient grounding. Bahnsen states, "Van Til's presuppositionalism explicitly aims to provide rational and objective proof of the inescapable and certain truth of Christianity."[7]

Van Til was the pioneer of this apologetic and began developing his approach in the 1920s as a student at Princeton and as a professor at Westminster Seminary in Philadelphia. His influence in the world of Reformed theology in particular has been enormous. He is considered by many to be one of the most original apologetic thinkers in the history of Christianity and one of the most important of the twentieth century. Along with Bahnsen, Van Til's students include John Frame and Francis Schaeffer.[8] Philosopher Alvin Plantinga is also an advocate of the presuppositional method, though he is not strictly Van Tilian.

Fideism

In sharp contrast to these three methods, fideism rejects reason, evidence, and transcendental arguments as sufficient ways to justify the Christian faith (*fide* is Latin for faith). Faith and faith alone is the only proper way to understand the truth of Christianity. Boa and Bowman provide the insight that "fideists answer ... apologetic challenges by explaining why reason is incompetent to provide a satisfactory answer and then showing that faith does provide a way to deal with the problem."[9] For the fideist, reasoning is a strictly intellectual pursuit that reaches its limits when it tries to deal with the things of God. A sermon by Martin Luther on the Gospel of John illustrates this well:

Martin Luther

According to fideism, faith and faith alone is the only proper way to understand the truth of Christianity.

> Any attempt to fathom and comprehend such statements with human reason and understanding will avail nothing, for none of this has its source in the reason: that there was a Word in God before the world's creation, and that this Word was God; that, as John says further on, this same Word, the Only-begotten of the Father, full of grace and truth, rested in the Father's bosom or heart and became flesh; and that no one else had ever seen or known God, because the Word, who is God's only-begotten Son, rested in the bosom of the Father and revealed Him to us. Nothing but faith can comprehend this. Whoever refuses to accept it in faith, to believe it before he understands it, but insists on exploring it with his reason and his five senses, let him persist in this if he will. But our mind will never master this doctrine; it is far too lofty for our reason.[10]

The Reason has brought the God as near as possible, and yet he is as far away as ever.
–Søren Kierkegaard

Elsewhere in the sermon, Luther says that the knowledge of God "is as impossible of comprehension by reason as it is inaccessible to the touch of the hand."[11]

Søren Kierkegaard agreed, saying, "The Reason has brought the God as near as possible, and yet he is as far away as ever."[12] In more recent times, Karl Barth, a man who is often named as the most important theologian of the twentieth century, espoused fideism.

Interaction and Critique

The way these different schools of thought see one another is a good way to understand their strengths and weaknesses. For just as each method emphasizes different aspects, each is also critical of the others' emphasis to some degree (the exceptions being classical apologetics and evidentialism; they are very much cousins without a critique of each other). Looking at their interaction is necessary for a proper evaluation of each approach. It must also be remembered that this is a family quarrel that can be passionate but should never be contentious.

> *Just as each method emphasizes different aspects, each is also critical of the others' emphasis to some degree.*

Classical apologists, evidentialists, and presuppositionalists all reject fideism as a legitimate apologetic, seeing it as an irrational declaration of truth that is not supported by arguments. There is an enormous ideological gulf isolating fideism from the other approaches. One of the main discussions in the world of apologetics is on the nature of presuppositionalism—which side of the gulf does it belong on? Classical and evidential apologists criticize presuppositionalists for arguing in a circle. They point out that presuppositionalism assumes God exists in order to prove that he exists.

Thus, they say, the presuppositional approach amounts to little more than a proclamation, a form of fideism. Even if it is not a full-blown fideism, it is a big step on a slippery slope to fideism. Some classical apologists have even contended that "presuppositional principles, carried out consistently, undermine the Christian religion itself."[13]

In response, presuppositionalists give a most unexpected reply by admitting to circular reasoning. Van Til wrote,

> To admit one's own presuppositions and to point out the presuppositions of others is therefore to maintain that all reasoning is, in the nature of the case, circular reasoning. The starting point, the method, and the conclusion are always involved in one another."[14]

John Frame notes, "You can't question logic without presupposing it; you can't argue against the primacy of logic without presupposing it as primary."[15]

Because all arguments are ultimately circular, the question becomes one of grounding. What makes one's starting point the starting point? And on this issue presuppositionalism finds great strength. Presuppositionalism begins with presupposing God because if God is the author of all creation, as the Bible says, then everything—including reason itself—is grounded in his person. In other words, what makes reason reasonable is that it is grounded in God's ordered character, just as morality is grounded in God's good character. Therefore, the starting point for our ability to know anything must be God, and reason is the first step out from the starting point in our thinking. Classicalists and evidentialists begin with reason, not God. Presuppositionalists strongly criticize this approach. After all, what reason do they have for using reason? Presuppositionalists accuse the classicalists and evidentialists of treating reason as if it were some inde-

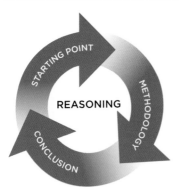

REASONING

STARTING POINT

METHODOLOGY

CONCLUSION

> *Because all arguments are ultimately circular, the question becomes one of grounding.*

pendent, objective standard outside of God. But if we are to have a robust biblical apologetic, then such independent standards must be rejected. Van Til's goal was to have a relentlessly biblical apologetic method.

Presuppositionalists do not reject reason as an appropriate apologetic tool, as the fideists do. Rather, their argument is extremely reasonable, given that it emphasizes the foundation of reason. This necessary grounding justifies Van Til's position: "The only 'proof' of the Christian position is that unless its truth is presupposed there is no possibility of 'proving' anything at all."[16]

To do otherwise is to act autonomously, without God. Van Til was fond of illustrating this concept with a scene he once saw on a train:

> A little girl was sitting on her daddy's lap and was playfully slapping his face. She could only slap his face because he allowed her to sit on his lap; she was not capable of this on her own. She had to be supported by him in order to slap him. God is like the father and unbelieving thought, is like the little girl. It uses reason to attack the source of reason. It operates on borrowed capital, as it were.

Presuppositionalists hold that classical apologists and evidentialists are guilty of this same autonomous approach to some degree and therefore reject their approaches as acquiescing to unbelieving thought.

Classical apologists and evidentialists reply to this charge with a simple question: In presuppositionalism, just who does the presupposing? Isn't the act of presupposing an autonomous act itself the very thing presuppositionalism eschews?[17] Presuppositionalists would say that the act is justified because it calibrates and grounds our epistemology correctly, in the God of the Bible. Classical apologists and evidentialists do not buy this excuse and see an egregious flaw in the method.

In presuppositionalism, just who does the presupposing?

At issue also is the language of probability. When dealing with evidence and philosophical proofs, the result is always expressed in a degree of probability. No matter how high the degree of probability, the presuppositionalist, by and large, takes exception. Because the presuppositional method employs a transcendental argument (an argument based on the impossibility of the contrary), it speaks in the language of certainty. Probability, in the presuppositionalist view, always gives an excuse to those who refuse to believe because there is always a chance that the proof is wrong.

Some presuppositionalists, Bahnsen, for example, take this opportunity to turn the tables on the classical apologists and evidentialists by claiming that their view is actually closer to fideism than presuppositionalism is.[18] This position is based on the fact that proofs and evidences can only offer probability. At some point, they hit their limit of explanatory power and persuasion that is shy of the mark of the certain existence of the God of the Bible. So how is one to bridge the gap?

When dealing with evidence and philosophical proofs, the result is always expressed in a degree of probability.

Apparently by a leap of faith—the very thing that classical apologists and evidentialists eschew. Classical apologists and evidentialists no doubt take exception to this characterization, just as presuppositionalists do when the name is hung on them.

Integrative Apologetics

As was noted at the beginning of this chapter, most apologists do not fall strictly into one camp or another. But there are some who self-consciously draw from the strengths of all the approaches. The idea is to let each individual person's concerns drive what method is used rather than apply a particular method of apologetics to all encounters. As such, there is no formal method in the integrative approach. This is well expressed by Francis Schaeffer:

> I do not believe that there is any one system of apologetics that meets the need of all the people, any more than I think there is any one form of evangelism that meets the need of all the people. It is to be shaped on the basis of love for the person as a person.[19]

More recently, in their book *Faith Has Its Reasons,* Boa and Bowman make a case for an integrative approach and examine ways in which this can be accomplished. They conclude:

> Just as the four Gospels present complementary portraits of Jesus Christ, so the four approaches emphasize complementary truths about Jesus that can be used to persuade people to believe.[20]

Conclusion

In the end, each apologist develops his own method according to felt needs and the needs he sees in those around him. How that method is developed, what it emphasizes, and how it is articulated vary from apologist to apologist. But in the end, the goal is the same for all: to give an answer to those who ask and to be light and salt in a dark and decaying world.

> *In the end, the goal is the same for all: to give an answer to those who ask and to be light and salt in a dark and decaying world.*

Notable Quote

> If these people understood who God really is, his wrath and his love, what he demands and what he offers, they would (or should) break down the doors to worship him.[21]
>
> —*John M. Frame*

Notes

1 Norman L. Geisler, *Christian Apologetics* (Grand Rapids: Baker, 1976), 141.

2 Kenneth D. Boa and Robert M. Bowman Jr., *Faith Has Its Reasons* (Colorado Springs: NavPress, 2001), 71.

3 John Warwick Montgomery, *History, Law and Christianity* (Edmonton, AB: Canadian Institute for Law, Theology & Public Policy, 2002), 64.

4 Greg L. Bahnsen, *Van Til's Apologetics* (Phillipsburg, NJ: Presbyterian & Reformed, 1998), 78. Bahnsen here quotes Van Til from his *Defense of the Faith*.

5 Ibid., 6.

6 Cornelius Van Til, *Christian Apologetics* (Phillipsburg, NJ: Presbyterian & Reformed, 1976, 2003), 64.

7 Bahnsen, *Van Til's Apologetics*, 76.

8 Frame disagreed in some areas with Van Til and is known for a slightly different flavor of presuppositionalism than taught by Van Til. Though Schaeffer was a student of Van Til, he did not strictly follow his professor's thinking. He is considered by some to be a presuppositionalist but is, by his own declaration, more correctly classified as one who integrates all the approaches (save fideism).

9 Boa and Bowman, *Faith Has Its Reasons*, 364.

10 Martin Luther, *Luther's Works*, vol. 22, *Sermons on the Gospel of St. John*, ed. Jaroslav Pelikan (St. Louis, MO: Concordia House, 1957), 8.

11 Ibid.

12 Soren Kierkegaard, *Philosophical Fragments*, trans. David Swenson and Howard V. Hong (Princeton, NJ: Princeton University Press, 1936, 1974), 57.

13 R. C. Sproul, John Gerstner, and Arthur Lindsley, *Classical Apologetics* (Grand Rapids: Zondervan, 1984), 184.

14 Van Til, *Christian Apologetics*, 130.

15 John Frame, *Apologetics to the Glory of God* (Phillipsburg, NJ: Presbyterian & Reformed, 1994), 226.

16 Cornelius Van Til, "My Credo," in *Jerusalem and Athens*, ed. E. R. Geehan (Philadelphia: Presbyterian & Reformed, 1971), 21. As quoted by Bahnsen, *Van Til's Apologetics*, 113.

17 A fictitious dialogue of this sort between Van Til and a classical apologist appears in Sproul, Gerstner, and Lindsley, *Classical Apologetics*, 234–39.

18 Bahnsen, *Van Til's Apologetics*, 77.

19 Francis A. Schaeffer, *The Complete Works of Francis Schaeffer*, vol. 1, *A Christian View of Philosophy and Culture* (Wheaton, IL: Crossway, 1982), 177. This appears in Appendix A to his book *The God Who Is There*.

20 Boa and Bowman, *Faith Has Its Reasons*, 532.

21 John M. Frame, *Contemporary Worship Music: A Biblical Defense* (Phillipsburg, NJ: Presbyterian & Reformed, 1997), 95.

TIMELINE OF APOLOGISTS AND NOTABLE WORKS

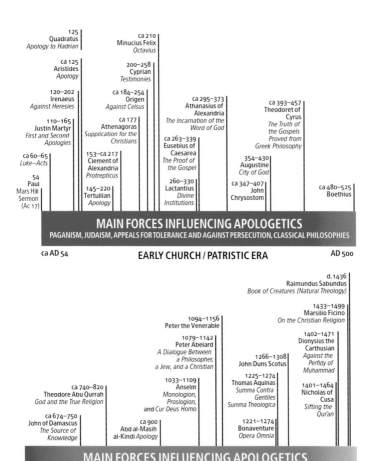

125
Quadratus
Apology to Hadrian

ca 125
Aristides
Apology

120–202
Irenaeus
Against Heresies

110–165
Justin Martyr
First and Second Apologies

ca 60–65
Luke–Acts

54
Paul
Mars Hill Sermon
(Ac 17)

ca 210
Minucius Felix
Octavius

200–258
Cyprian
Testimonies

ca 184–254
Origen
Against Celsus

ca 177
Athenagoras
Supplication for the Christians

153–ca 217
Clement of Alexandria
Protrepticus

145–220
Tertullian
Apology

ca 295–373
Athanasius of Alexandria
The Incarnation of the Word of God

ca 263–339
Eusebius of Caesarea
The Proof of the Gospel

260–330
Lactantius
Divine Institutions

ca 393–457
Theodoret of Cyrus
The Truth of the Gospels Proved from Greek Philosophy

354–430
Augustine
City of God

ca 347–407
John Chrysostom

ca 480–525
Boethius

MAIN FORCES INFLUENCING APOLOGETICS
PAGANISM, JUDAISM, APPEALS FOR TOLERANCE AND AGAINST PERSECUTION, CLASSICAL PHILOSOPHIES

ca AD 54

EARLY CHURCH / PATRISTIC ERA

AD 500

---

d.1436
Raimundus Sabundus
Book of Creatures (Natural Theology)

1433–1499
Marsilio Ficino
On the Christian Religion

1094–1156
Peter the Venerable

1079–1142
Peter Abelard
A Dialogue Between a Philosopher, a Jew, and a Christian

1402–1471
Dionysius the Carthusian
Against the Perfidy of Muhammad

1266–1308
John Duns Scotus

1033–1109
Anselm
Monologion, Proslogion, and Cur Deus Homo

1225–1274
Thomas Aquinas
Summa Contra Gentiles
Summa Theologica

1401–1464
Nicholas of Cusa
Sifting the Qur'an

ca 740–820
Theodore Abu Qurrah
God and the True Religion

ca 674–750
John of Damascus
The Source of Knowledge

ca 900
Abd al-Masih al-Kindi *Apology*

1221–1274
Bonaventure
Opera Omnia

MAIN FORCES INFLUENCING APOLOGETICS
ISLAM, JUDAISM, SCHOLASTICISM, OTHER CULTURAL HERITAGES

AD 500

MIDDLE AGES

AD 1500

TIMELINE OF APOLOGISTS AND NOTABLE WORKS

1718–1790
Nicolas
Sylvestre
Bergier
*The Certainty of
the Proofs of
Christianity*

1710–1796
Thomas Reid
*Inquiry into
the Human Mind*

1632–1704
John Locke
*The Reasonableness of Christianity
as Delivered in the Scriptures*

1692–1752
Joseph Butler
*The Analogy of Religion, Natural
and Revealed, to the Constitution
and Course of Nature*

1627–1705
John Ray
*The Wisdom of God in
the Creation*

1549–1623
Philippe de Mornay
*On the Truth of the
Christian Religion*

1686–1742
Claude François
Alexandre Houtteville
*The Christian Religion
Proved by Facts*

1627–1691
Robert Boyle
*The Christian
Virtuoso*

1509–1564
John Calvin
*Institutes
of the
Christian
Religion*

1623–1662
Blaise Pascal
Pensées

1685–1753
Bishop George Berkeley
Minute Philosopher

1743–1805
William Paley
*Natural
Theology,
A View of the
Evidences of
Christianity*

1596–1650
René Descartes
Meditations

1675–1729
Samuel Clarke
*The Unchangeable
Obligations of
Natural Religion and the
Truth and Certainty of the
Christian Revelation*

1483–1546
Martin
Luther

1583–1645
Hugo Grotius
*The Truth of the
Christian Religion*

MAIN FORCES INFLUENCING APOLOGETICS
PROTESTANT REFORMATION, HUMANISM, THE RISE OF SCIENCE

AD 1500   REFORMATION / RENAISSANCE / ENLIGHTENMENT   AD 1750

TIMELINE OF APOLOGISTS AND NOTABLE WORKS

1801–1890
John Henry Newman
Essays on Miracles

1799–1877
August Tholuck
The Credibility of the Evangelical History

1787–1863
Richard Whately
Introductory Lessons on Christian Evidence

1783–1853
Simon Greenleaf
The Testimony of the Evangelists

1782–1860
Abbé Félicité de Lamennais
Essay on Indifference in Matters of Religion

1780–1847
Thomas Chalmers
Miraculous and Internal Evidences of the Christian Revelation

1777–1853
Johann Sebastian von Drey
Apologetics as a Scientific Demonstration of the Divinity of Christianity

1768–1848
François René de Chateaubriand
The Genius of Christianity; or, Beauties of the Christian Religion

1759–1844
Bruno Liebermann
Theological Intstitutions

1753–1821
Joseph de Maistre
St. Petersburg Dialogues

1797–1878
Charles Hodge
What is Darwinism and *Systematic Theology*

1796–1867
Abbé Louis-Eugène Bautain
Philosophy of Christianity

1796–1865
Carl Ullmann
The Sinlessness of Jesus

1794–1876
Giovanni Perrone, S.J.
Lectures on Dogmatics

1818–1888
August Ebrard
Apologetics; or the Scientific Vindication of Christianity

1813–1855
Søren Kierkegaard
Philosophical Fragments

1810–1848
Jaime Balmes
Criterion and *Letters to a Skeptic on Religious Matters*

1807–1888
C.F. Keil
Commentary on the Old Testament

1844–1913
James Orr
The Bible Under Trial

1837–1920
Abraham Kuyper
Principles of Sacred Theology

1837–1915
Fulcran Vigouroux
The Bible and Modern Discoveries in Egypt and Assyria

1834–1895
Paul de Broglie
Positivism and Experimental Science

1831–1899
Alexander B. Bruce
Apologetics; or Christianity Defensively Stated

MAIN FORCES INFLUENCING APOLOGETICS
HUMANISM, DARWINISM, SCIENTIFIC ADVANCES, AND THE DEVELOPMENT OF ARCHAEOLOGY AND HISTORICAL METHODS

AD 1750

NINETEENTH CENTURY

AD 1850

TIMELINE OF APOLOGISTS AND
NOTABLE WORKS

TWENTIETH CENTURY

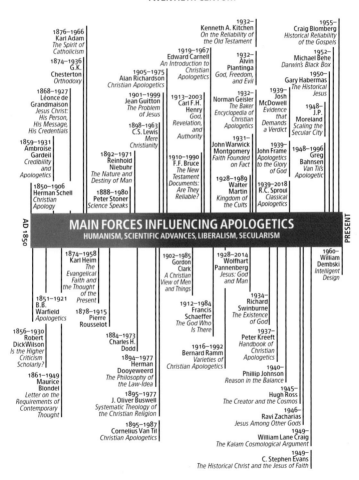

1876–1966
Karl Adam
The Spirit of Catholicism

1874–1936
G.K. Chesterton
Orthodoxy

1868–1927
Léonce de Grandmaison
Jesus Christ: His Person, His Message, His Credentials

1859–1931
Ambroise Gardeil
Credibility and Apologetics

1850–1906
Herman Schell
Christian Apology

1892–1971
Reinhold Niebuhr
The Nature and Destiny of Man

1888–1980
Peter Stoner
Science Speaks

1905–1975
Alan Richardson
Christian Apologetics

1901–1999
Jean Guitton
The Problem of Jesus

1898–1963
C.S. Lewis
Mere Christianity

1919–1967
Edward Carnell
An Introduction to Christian Apologetics

1913–2003
Carl F.H. Henry
God, Revelation, and Authority

1910–1990
F.F. Bruce
The New Testament Documents: Are They Reliable?

1932–
Kenneth A. Kitchen
On the Reliability of the Old Testament

1932–
Alvin Plantinga
God, Freedom, and Evil

1932–
Norman Geisler
The Baker Encyclopedia of Christian Apologetics

1931–
John Warwick Montgomery
Faith Founded on Fact

1928–1989
Walter Martin
Kingdom of the Cults

1955–
Craig Blomberg
Historical Reliability of the Gospels

1952–
Michael Behe
Darwin's Black Box

1950–
Gary Habermas
The Historical Jesus

1939–
Josh McDowell
Evidence that Demands a Verdict

1939–
John Frame
Apologetics to the Glory of God

1939–2018
R.C. Sproul
Classical Apologetics

1948–
J.P. Moreland
Scaling the Secular City

1948–1996
Greg Bahnsen
Van Til's Apologetic

MAIN FORCES INFLUENCING APOLOGETICS
HUMANISM, SCIENTIFIC ADVANCES, LIBERALISM, SECULARISM

AD 1850

PRESENT

1874–1958
Karl Heim
The Evangelical Faith and the Thought of the Present

1851–1921
B.B. Warfield
Apologetics

1878–1915
Pierre Rousselot

1856–1930
Robert Dick Wilson
Is the Higher Criticism Scholarly?

1884–1973
Charles H. Dodd

1861–1949
Maurice Blondel
Letter on the Requirements of Contemporary Thought

1894–1977
Herman Dooyeweerd
The Philosophy of the Law-Idea

1895–1977
J. Oliver Buswell
Systematic Theology of the Christian Religion

1895–1987
Cornelius Van Til
Christian Apologetics

1902–1985
Gordon Clark
A Christian View of Men and Things

1912–1984
Francis Schaeffer
The God Who Is There

1916–1992
Bernard Ramm
Varieties of Christian Apologetics

1928–2014
Wolfhart Pannenberg
Jesus: God and Man

1934–
Richard Swinburne
The Existence of God

1937–
Peter Kreeft
Handbook of Christian Apologetics

1940–
Phillip Johnson
Reason in the Balance

1945–
Hugh Ross
The Creator and the Cosmos

1946–
Ravi Zacharias
Jesus Among Other Gods

1949–
William Lane Craig
The Kalam Cosmological Argument

1949–
C. Stephen Evans
The Historical Christ and the Jesus of Faith

1960–
William Dembski
Intelligent Design

Bibliography: Avery Dulles, *A History of Christian Apologetics*, (Corpus Instrumentorum, 1971; San Francisco: Ignatius Press, 2005).
Kenneth D. Boa and Robert M. Bowman, JR., *Faith Has Its Reasons*, (Colorado Springs: Navpress, 2001).

SELECTED IMPORTANT OLD TESTAMENT
ARCHAEOLOGICAL FINDS

FIND	DISCOVERED	IMPORTANCE
Dead Sea Scrolls	1947-56, Qumran, Israel	Provided our oldest copies of almost all books of the Old Testament and confirmed reliability of the transmission process
Taylor Prism	1830, Nineveh, Iraq	Corroborates the campaigns of Sennacherib found in 2 Kings 18:13–19:37; 2 Chron. 32:1-12; Isa. 36:1–37:38
House of David Inscriptions	1993-4, Tel Dan, Israel	Earliest mention outside the Bible of King David, whom some scholars have held to be a fictional character
Cylinder of Nabonidus	1854, Ur, Iraq	Corroborates Belshazzar as last king of Babylon as recorded in Daniel 5:1-30; 7:1; 8:1
Sargon Inscriptions	1843, Khorsabad, Iraq	Confirms the existence of Sargon, King of Assyria, Isaiah 20:1, as well as his conquering of Samaria (2 Kings 17:23-24)
Tiglath-Pileser III Inscriptions	1845-9, Nimrud, Iraq	Corroborates 2 Kings 15:29
Cyrus Cylinder	1879, Babylon, Iraq	Contains a decree from Cyrus that corroborates Ezra 1:1-3; 6:3; 2 Chronicles 36:23; Isaiah 44:28
Black Obelisk of Shalmaneser	1846, Nimrud, Iraq	Depicts Jehu, son of Omri, oldest known picture of an ancient Israelite
Moabite Stone	1868, Palestine	Corroborates 2 Kings 3
Ketef Hinnom Amulets	1779, Jerusalem	Contain the Hebrew text of Numbers 6:24-26 and Deuteronomy 9:7. This is the oldest instance to date of Hebrew text of the Old Testament, 7th–6th century BC.
Seal of Baruch	early-mid 1970's, Jerusalem	Contains the phrase "belonging to Beruch son of Neriah," Jeremiah's scribe, 6th century BC.
Epic of Gilgamesh	1853, Nineveh, Iraq	First extra-biblical find that appears to reference the great flood of Gen. 7–8
Weld-Blundell Prism	1922, Babylon, Iraq	Contains a list of Sumerian Kings that ruled before and after the great flood; the kings that pre-dated the flood are attributed enormous life spans reminiscent of, though greater than, the lifespans of pre-flood inhabitants of the Bible
Siloam Inscription	1880, Jerusalem	One of the few extant ancient Hebrew writings from the eight century BC or earlier.
Gedaliah Seal	1935, Lachish, Israel	Corroborates 2 Kings 25:22

BIBLIOGRAPHY
E.M. Blaiklock and R.K. Harrison, *The New International Dictionary of Biblical Archaeology*, (Grand Rapids: Zondervan, 1983).
Walter C. Kaiser Jr., "Top 15 Finds from Biblical Archaeology," *Contact*, Winter 2005–2006.
Josh McDowell, *Evidence that Demands a Verdict*, (San Bernadino: Here's Life, 1972, 1979).
Randal Price, *Secrets of the Dead Sea Scroll*, (Eugene, OR.: Harvest House, 1996).
Hershel Shanks, *Understanding the Dead Sea Scrolls*, (New York: Random House, 1992).
Keith N. Schoville, "Top Ten Archaeological Discoveries of the Twentieth Century Relating to the Biblical World," http://biblicalstudies.info
Merrill F. Unger, *Archaeology and the Old Testament*, (Grand Rapids: Zondervan, 1954, 1975).
Howard F. Vos, *Archaeology in Bible Lands*, (Chicago: Moody Press, 1977, 1982).

SELECTED IMPORTANT NEW TESTAMENT ARCHAEOLOGICAL FINDS

FIND	DISCOVERED	IMPORTANCE
The Pilate Stone Inscription	1961, Caesarea Maritima	Confirmed the existence and office of Pilate
The Delphi, or Gallio, Inscription	1905	Fixed the date of Gallio's proconsulship at AD 51–52, providing a way of dating Acts 18:12-17, and as a result, much of the rest of Paul's ministry
Caiaphas Ossuary	1990, near Jerusalem	Confirmed the existence of Caiaphas
Sergius Paulus Inscription	1877, Paphos, Cyprus	Confirms the existence of Sergius Paulus, proconsul of Cyprus encountered by Paul and Barnabas in Acts 13:7
Pool of Siloam	2004, Jerusalem	Site of Jesus' miracle recorded in John 9:1-11
Skeleton of Yohanan	1968, Jerusalem	Only known remains of crucifixion victim; corroborates the Bible's description of crucifixion
Rylands Papyrus P52	1920	Oldest universally accepted manuscript of the New Testament, a small fragment of John's Gospel dated by papyrologists to AD 125
Bodmer Papyrus II	1952, Pabau, Egypt	Contains most of John's Gospel and dates from AD 150–200
Magdalene Papyrus	1901, Luxor, Egypt	Contains framents of Matthew and has been dated as being earlier than AD 70, though there is debateconcerning the date
Chester Beatty Papyri	acquired 1931–35, Cairo, Egypt	Three papyri dating from AD 200 that contain most of the New Testament
Codex Vaticanus	In the Vatican Library's earliest	Dated AD 325–50 and contains a nearly complete Bible inventory (1481)
Codex Sinaiticus	1859, Mt Sinai, Egypt	Codex containing nearly complete New Testament and over half of the Old Testament (the books at the beginning of the Bible appear to have been lost to damage), dated at AD 350
7Q5	1955, Qumran, Israel	Possible fragment of Mark that can be dated no later than AD 68 which would make it the oldest extantNew Testament fragment if confirmed
Galilee Boat	1986, near Tiberias, Israel	The boat, 30' x 8', held approximately 15 passengers and would be like the boats Jesus' disciples used in crossing the Sea of Galilee. Carbon 14 dating places the boat between 120 BC and AD 40.

BIBLIOGRAPHY

Craig Blomberg, "The Historical Reliability of the New Testament," in William Lane Craig, *Reasonable Faith*, (Wheaton: Crossway, 1994).
Norman Geisler, *Christian Apologetics*, (Grand Rapids: Baker, 1976).
Gary Habermas, *The Historical Jesus*, (Joplin, MO: College Press, 1996).
Walter C. Kaiser Jr., "Top 15 Finds from Biblical Archaeology," *Contact*, Winter 2005–2006.
Josh McDowell, *Evidence that Demands a Verdict*, (San Bernadino: Here's Life, 1972, 1979).
Bruce M. Metzger, *The New Testament, Its Background, Growth, and Content*, (Nashville: Abingdon, 1965, 1983).
Randal Price, *Secrets of the Dead Sea Scroll*, (Eugene, OR: Harvest House, 1996).
Keith N. Schoville, "Top Ten Archaeological Discoveries of the Twentieth Century Relating to the Biblical World," http://biblicalstudies.info
Richard N. Soulen, *Handbook of Biblical Criticism*, (Atlanta: John Knox, 1976, 1982).

NUMBER OF ORIGINAL

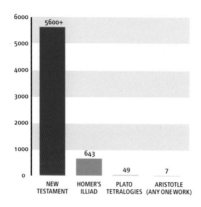

SPAN OF YEARS BETWEEN

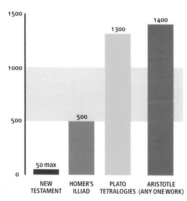

Note: Homer's *Illiad* is the best attested ancient work after the New Testament.
Plato and Aristotle are used in the graph for how well known they are.

Bibliography: Josh McDowell, *Evidence that Demands a Verdict*, (San Bernadino, CA: Here's Life, 1972, 1992).

NATURALISM VS. THEISM: WHICH CONTEXT BEST EXPLAINS THE PHENOMENA WE OBSERVE?

PHENOMENA WE OBSERVE	THEISTIC CONTEXT	NATURALISTIC CONTEXT
(Self-)consciousness exists.	God is supremely self-aware/-conscious.	The universe was produced by mindless, non-conscious processes.
Personal beings exist.	God is a personal Being.	The universe was produced by impersonal processes.
We believe we make free personal decisions/choices, assuming humans are accountable for their actions.	God is spirit and a free Being, who can freely choose to act (e.g., to create or not).	We have emerged by material, deterministic processes and forces beyond our control.
Secondary qualities (colors, smells, sounds, tastes, textures) exist throughout the world.	God is joyful, and secondary qualities make the world pleasurable and joyful to his creatures.	The universe was produced from colorless, odorless, soundless, tasteless, textureless particles and processes.
We trust our senses and rational faculties as generally reliable in producing true beliefs.	A God of truth and rationality exists.	Because of our impulse to survive and reproduce, our beliefs would only help us survive, but a number of these could be completely false.
Human beings have intrinsic value/dignity and rights.	God is the supremely valuable Being.	Human beings were produced by valueless processes.
Objective moral values exist.	God's character is the source of goodness/moral values.	The universe was produced by non-moral processes.
The universe began to exist a finite time ago—without previously existing matter, energy, space or time.	A powerful, previously-existing God brought the universe into being without any pre-existing material. (Here, something emerges from something.)	The universe came into existence from nothing by nothing—or was, perhaps, self-caused. (Here, something comes from nothing.)
The universe is finely-tuned for human life (known as "the Goldilocks effect"—the universe is "just right" for life).	God is a wise, intelligent Designer.	All the cosmic constants just happened to be right; given enough time and/or many possible worlds, a finely-tuned world eventually emerged.
First life emerged.	God is a living, active Being.	Life somehow emerged from non-living matter.
Beauty exists (e.g., not only in landscapes and sunsets but also in "elegant" or "beautiful" scientific theories).	God is beautiful (Ps. 27:4) and capable of creating beautiful things according to his pleasure.	Beauty in the natural world is superabundant and in many cases superfluous (often not linked to survival).
We (tend to) believe that life has purpose and meaning. For most of us, life is worth living.	God has created/designed us for certain purposes (to love him, others, etc.); when we live them out, our lives find meaning/enrichment.	There is no cosmic purpose, blueprint, or goal for human existence.
Real evils—both moral and natural—exist/take place in the world.	Evil's definition assumes a design plan (how things ought to be, but are not) or standard of goodness (a corruption or absence of goodness), by which we judge something to be evil. God is a good Designer; his existence supplies the crucial moral context to make sense of evil.	Atrocities, pain, and suffering just happen. This is just how things are —with no "plan" or standard of goodness to which things ought to conform.

COMPARISONS OF WORLD RELIGIONS

	DOCTRINE OF GOD	HUMAN PREDICAMENT	WAY OF DELIVERANCE	ULTIMATE GOAL
BUDDHISM	Essentially atheistic at core, Buddha himself did not emphasize the gods, though some forms of Buddhism practice devotion to specific deities; in some cases the "deities" are departed Bodhisattvas—great figures of Buddhist history.	Release from suffering by entering a state of nonexistence (moksha) as an individuated human being (nirvana); to cease to exist as an individual is the highest goal.	Follow the "Eight-fold path"; it includes right understanding, right speech, right effort, and right mindfulness (meditation and concentration); this practiced over a lifetime with the right intensity leads to elimination of desire, which is the key to deliverance (moksha); there are variations in different Buddhist traditions, but this was the teaching of Gautama.	Humanity is in state of suffering; this suffering arises from a desire, any kind of desire, even the desire for good things; desire is the root of all human problems.
HINDUISM	Many gods, but the most important are Brahma (impersonal reality), Shiva (death and reproduction), Vishnu (love and play); gods not sovereign over events in the world, but subject to the same cosmic forces as humans are, such as karma; along with the common gods recognized by most Hindus, many locations have their own unique deities; at the same time, "Atman (humanity) is Brahman (ultimate reality)"—all is One.	Release from existence by achieving nonexistence (moksha) and an entering into oneness with the One (Brahman) ceasing to exist as an individuated human being (nirvana); one becomes like a drop of water that falls into the ocean; this can be achieved quickly for those who achieve enlightenment, though eventually it will be the experience of all.	Understanding the human predicament through disciplines such as yoga, devotion to one of the gods (especially Shiva), and through a flash of knowledge; knowledge brings release from karmic cycle of reincarnation (samsara); often, men leave their families in their later years to become hermits, working off their karma by ascetic practices.	The human predicament is existence itself; humanity lives with the illusion (maya) of perceiving the world as it seems to be rather than as it really is (Brahman, or the One); moral retribution (karma) follows us through multiple incarnations (samsara).
ISLAM	"No God but Allah"; a unitarian, monotheistic faith which sees Allah as determining every specific event that happens in the world; Allah is virtually coterminous with his word, part of which is found in the Koran.	Future resurrection of the righteous unto eternal bliss in a heavenly Paradise; all of the physical pleasures that one may not have access to in this life will be available in Paradise; infidels spend eternity in a most torturous hell.	Embrace the Five Pillars (daily recitation of creed, prayer, giving aims, pilgrimage to Mecca, fasting during Ramadan); complete and utter devotion to Allah; final salvation is reserved only for the most diligent of Muslims.	Humans are finite in contrast to the infinite sovereignty of Allah; they are foolish and need instruction, which comes from the Koran; they are also sinners, such sin being especially seen in violations of Muslim taboos or prohibited behavior and failure to do the will of Allah perfectly.

COMPARISONS OF WORLD RELIGIONS

	DOCTRINE OF GOD	HUMAN PREDICAMENT	WAY OF DELIVERANCE	ULTIMATE GOAL
JUDAISM	"The Lord is God, the Lord is One"; monotheistic faith in which God is maker of all things and the Lord of heaven and Earth; contemporary (Conservative and Reform) Judaism tends to see God as not exercising dominant sovereignty over the world.	Future state of resurrection in an earthly Paradise centered in the Holy Land (Orthodox); or a state of spiritual bliss after death (Reform); most Jews have no clear doctrine of eternal punishment, though some hold to the annihilation of the wicked.	Follow the teachings of Torah, especially as it relates to Sabbath, food laws, and holy days (among the Conservative and Orthodox); practice the faith with its traditions; many contemporary Jews (especially in the Reform and Conservative synagogues) are inclusivists, believing that salvation can be found in many religions; Kabalistic Judaism (mysticism) calls for a series of spiritual experiences that eventually allows one to see God.	Humanity is sinful, but not so blinded by sin that they cannot be instructed in the way of righteousness.
CHRISTIANITY	Monotheistic, trinitarian belief; Father, Son and Spirit are equal and eternal and sovereign over all; God is love and is also holy; he is both transcendent and immanent, but is never dependent upon the world; his true nature is most easily seen in the person of his Incarnate Son, Jesus.	Immediate entering into the spiritual presence of God at death for believers; future resurrection of the body at the second coming of Christ; new heavens and new earth in an eternal realm of peace and righteousness for believers; eternal punishment in hell for the finally impenitent.	Receive the gift of God's grace by trusting in Jesus Christ alone for salvation, which he purchased with his shed blood; this initial experience of justification is followed by a life of fellowship with other Christians and faithfulness to the Lord.	In their natural condition, humans are dead in trespasses and sins; they require a specific work of the Holy Spirit to rescue them; they cannot be saved by their own goodness and efforts.

COMPARISONS OF NEW RELIGIOUS MOVEMENTS

	AUTHORITY	GOD	MAN	CHRIST	SALVATION	FUTURE HOPE
LDS	The Church of Jesus Christ of Latter-day Saints (Mormons) has four primary works (the "Standard Works") which are authoritative: *The Bible* (preferably the KJV), *The Book of Mormon*, *Doctrine and Covenants*, and *The Pearl of Great Price*. Joseph Smith is considered to be the latter-day prophet who has reestablished the true church with his teachings.	There are many gods and the Trinity is comprised of three separate beings, two with physical bodies and one with a spirit body. The Father is an exalted man who was granted rule over our world. He himself has a father and mother and also has a wife. He is the creator of all the spirits of those who will eventually be born on earth.	The Fall of Adam and Eve was not actually a serious sin, since it was necessary for opening the way to perfection. Humans do commit sins, but they can overcome that tendency and live lives that please the Father.	Jesus was the eldest of the Father's spirit children before being born into this world. He was conceived through physical union between the Father and the virgin Mary. He was a man who lived a perfect life, was married and had children, and was exalted to god-hood in his resurrection.	Christ's death canceled the penalty of death, but did not actually purchase salvation. Though grace plays a role in salvation, it only comes into play after we do all we can to merit eternal life.	The future life is made up of three realms, plus hell, though it is not clear that many besides the devil and his angels will spend eternity in hell. Some hold that hell also includes anyone who has specifically rejected LDS teaching, as well as LDS apostates. The other realms include the telestial kingdom, the terrestrial kingdom, and the celestial kingdom. Only the celestial kingdom is actually "heaven," open only to Mormons.
WATCHTOWER SOCIETY (JEHOVAH'S WITNESSES)	*The New World Translation of the Bible*, a translation produced by the JW organization, deliberately reinforces certain doctrinal beliefs of the organization. The organization also teaches that one cannot understand the *Bible* without its help.	God is unitarian, not trinitarian, and is creator of the earth. The doctrine of the Trinity, according to this group, is a satanic doctrine.	Humans are made in God's image, and they are a combination of a body and the "life force" given by Jehovah. Humans do not "have" souls as something distinct from the body, and at death they simply go to sleep until the resurrection.	Before becoming a man, Jesus was Michael the archangel, the first creation of Jehovah. Christ is "a god," but not God, and in his earthly life was merely a perfect man. He was made immortal in his resurrection.	Jesus' death did not pay for humans' sin, but only opened the way to salvation. Salvation is merited by following the teachings of the JW organization.	Three possible destinies await human beings. Those who are finally unrepentant will be destroyed in the lake of fire—hell is thus a temporary flash of punishment after which the wicked cease to exist. The redeemed are divided into two groups. The "little flock" (144,000) will live in heaven, sharing the divine nature of Christ and, in effect, becoming gods. The "other sheep" live on a redeemed earth (Paradise) forever.

COMPARISONS OF NEW RELIGIOUS MOVEMENTS

	AUTHORITY	GOD	MAN	CHRIST	SALVATION	FUTURE HOPE
CHRISTIAN SCIENCE (CHURCH OF JESUS CHRIST, SCIENTIST)	*The Bible* is authoritative, but only as interpreted by Mary Baker Eddy, especially through her book, *Science and Health with Key to Scriptures*.	God is infinite Mind. God is the Father-Mother. The Trinity is only a trinity of attributes, not of persons.	Humans, like God, are also mind. Matter, sin, disease, and death are unreal.	"Christ" is the divine or spiritual element of God. The man Jesus was possessed of the Christ spirit. He came to show us the way to attain the Christ spirit for ourselves.	Salvation is gained through enlightenment as to the true nature of humans. All are eventually saved, but it is good to attain that enlightenment during their earthly sojourn.	There is no actual heaven or hell, but humans will progress even after this earthly sojourn to a higher form of spiritual consciousness. Only mind and spirit are good, and in fact, it will become clear that they are all that really exists.
SCIENTOLOGY	Spiritual authority is found in the writings of L. Ron Hubbard, especially *Dianetics*. Hubbard claimed that the sources for this book included various eastern traditions as well as Native American shamanism.	Scientology claims to have no dogma and claims that God is what God is to each person. Hubbard's own discussions about God are essentially a combination of Judeo-Christian monotheism with Hindu polytheism and pantheism.	Humans are partly god-like themselves, since man is part god. Humans are basically good, with one nature divided into two parts—the physical and the spiritual. Within every human lies a thetan spirit, a spirit that is eighty trillion years old, and which survives death to be reimplanted within another person. The ultimate goal is to achieve this divinity completely.	Jesus plays little role in Scientology.	Humans are caught in a web of reincarnations, which can only be ended through the process of "auditing," a kind of spiritual therapy. This therapy enables them to eliminate the accumulation of "engrams" which humans acquire through the course of each individual existence and even the aggregate of former existences. These engrams often develop as a result of maltreatment at the hands of parents and others and can only be eliminated through auditing.	When one develops "clarity" and then passes through progressive levels of development, one can achieve true knowledge of his thetan spirit, join the intergalactic thetan collective, and cease the cycle of reincarnation.
WICCA	There is no common scripture in this tradition, only intuitive convictions that characterize its various groups and forms.	The deity is a polarity, with a horned male god and a mother goddess. Wiccans claim that this brings balance, though in actuality many female Wiccans reject the male deity as inferior.	Humans have an inner divinity that connects them with god/goddess. Humans, and the world in general, are extensions of god's essence (panentheism). All the world is divine.	Jesus plays little role in most Wiccan traditions, though some co-opt him as a supporter, while others see him as an enemy.	There is no real sin in Wicca, so no real redemption. "Do what you will if it harm none" is a major theme. Joy is found in finding god in the phenomena of this life, such as food and sex. The predominantly feminine forms often see maleness as the problem of the world.	

HEBREW KINGS CHRONOLOGY

TEXT	DATE (BC)	KING	NATION	SYNCHRONIZATION	LENGTH	NOTES
1 Kg 12:1-24 1 Kg 14:21-31	930–913	Rehoboam	Judah		17 years	
1 Kg 12:25–14:20	930–909	Jeroboam I	Israel		22 years	
1 Kg 15:1-8	913–909	Abijam	Judah	18th of Jeroboam I	3 years	
1 Kg 15:9-24	910–869	Asa	Judah	20th of Jeroboam I	41 years	
1 Kg 15:25-31	909–908	Nadab	Israel	2nd of Asa	2 years	
1 Kg 15:32–16:7	908–886	Baasha	Israel	3rd of Asa	24 years	
1 Kg 16:8-14	886–885	Elah	Israel	26th of Asa	2 years	
1 Kg 16:15-20	885	Zimri	Israel	27th of Asa	7 days	
1 Kg 16:21-22	885–880	Tibni	Israel	27th of Asa	6 years	overlap with Omri
1 Kg 16:23-28	885 885–880 880–874 880	Omri	Israel	27th of Asa 31st of Asa	12 years	made king by the people overlap with Tibni official reign = 11 years beginning of sole reign
1 Kg 16:29–22:40	874–853	Ahab	Israel	38th of Asa	22 years	official reign = 21 years
1 Kg 22:41-50	872–869 872–848 869 853–848	Jehoshaphat	Judah	4th of Ahab	25 years	coregency with Asa official reign beginning of sole reign Jehoram is coregent
1 Kg 22:51—2 Kg 1:18	853–852	Ahaziah	Israel	17th of Jehoshaphat	2 years	official reign = 1 year
2 Kg 1:17 2 Kg 3:1–8:15	852 852–841	Joram	Israel	2nd of Jehoram 18th of Jehoshaphat	12 years	official reign = 11 years
2 Kg 8:16-24	848 848–841	Jehoram	Judah	5th of Joram	8 years	beginning of sole reign official reign = 7 years
2 Kg 8:25-29 2 Kg 9:29	841 841	Ahaziah	Judah	12th of Joram 11th of Joram	1 year	nonaccession-year dating accession-year dating
2 Kg 9:30–10:36	841–814	Jehu	Israel		28 years	
2 Kg 11:1-21	841–835	Athaliah	Judah		7 years	
2 Kg 12:1-21	835–796	Joash	Judah	7th of Jehu	40 years	
2 Kg 13:1-9	814–798	Jehoahaz	Israel	23rd of Joash	17 years	
2 Kg 13:10-25	798–782	Jehoash	Israel	37th of Joash	16 years	

TEXT	DATE (BC)	KING	NATION	SYNCHRONIZATION	LENGTH	NOTES
2 Kg 14:1-22	796–767 792–767 793–782	Amaziah	Judah	2nd of Jehoash	29 years	overlap with Azariah coregency with Jehoash
2 Kg 14:23-29	793–753 782	Jeroboam II	Israel	15th of Amaziah	41 years	total reign beginning of sole reign
2 Kg 15:1-7	792–767 792–740 767	Azariah	Judah	27th of Jeroboam I	52 years	overlap with Amaziah total reign beginning of sole reign
2 Kg 15:8-12	753	Zachariah	Israel	38th of Azariah	6 months	
2 Kg 15:13-15	752	Shallum	Israel	39th of Azariah	1 month	
2 Kg 15:16-22	752–742	Menahem	Israel	39th of Azariah	10 years	ruled in Samaria
2 Kg 15:23-26	742–740	Pekahiah	Israel	50th of Azariah	2 years	
2 Kg 15:27-31	752–740 752–732 740	Pekah	Israel	52nd of Azariah	20 years	in Gilead; overlapping years total reign beginning of sole reign
2 Kg 15:32-38 2 Kg 15:30	750–740 750–735 750–732 750	Jotham	Judah	2nd of Pekah	16 years	coregency with Azariah official reign reign to his 20th year beginning of coregency
2 Kg 16:1-20	735–715 735	Ahaz	Judah	17th of Pekah	16 years	total reign
2 Kg 15:30 2 Kg 17:1-41	732 732–723	Hoshea	Israel	12th of Ahaz	9 years	20th of Jotham
2 Kg 18:1–20:21	715–686	Hezekiah	Judah	3rd of Hoshea	29 years	
2 Kg 21:1-18	697–686 697–642	Manasseh	Judah		55 years	coregency with Hezekiah total reign
2 Kg 21:19-26	642–640	Amon	Judah		2 years	
2 Kg 22:1–23:30	640–609	Josiah	Judah		31 years	
2 Kg 23:31-33	609	Jehoahaz	Judah		3 months	
2 Kg 23:34–24:7	609–598	Jehoiakim	Judah		11 year	
2 Kg 24:8-17	598–597	Jehoiachin	Judah		3 months	
2 Kg 24:18–25:26	597–586	Zedekiah	Judah		11 years	

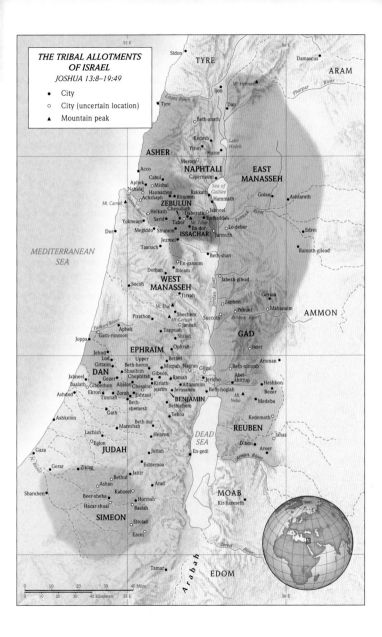

THE TRIBAL ALLOTMENTS
OF ISRAEL
JOSHUA 13:8–19:49

• City
○ City (uncertain location)
▲ Mountain peak

**THE KINGDOMS OF
ISRAEL AND JUDAH**
1 KINGS 12

- City
- ★ Capital city
- ○ City (uncertain location)
- ▲ Mountain peak

Israel
Judah
International roads
Local roads

0   10   20   30   40   50 Miles
0   10   20   30   40   50 Kilometers

34 E

Beirut

PHOENICIA

Sidon

Mt. Hermon

Damascus

Tyre

Litani River

Ijon

Abel-beth-maacah

Dan
Jeroboam built a sanctuary

ARAM

Achzib

Kedesh

Lake Huleh

Acco

Hazor

Chinnereth

Sea of Galilee

GESHUR

Mt. Carmel

Gath-hepher

Aphek

Ashtaroth

MEDITERRANEAN
SEA

Dor

Megiddo

Mt. Tabor

Jezreel

Mt. Gilboa

Edrei

Taanach

Beth-shan

Jordan River

Yarmuk River

Ramoth-gilead

Dothan

Ibleam

Pehel

Jabesh gilead

Socoh

Tirzah

Samaria
Political capital of Israel from Omri onward

Mt. Ebal

ISRAEL

Penuel

Mahanaim

Shechem

Succoth

Jabbok River

Aphek

Mt. Gerizim

Adam

Joppa

Shiloh

Jeroboam built a sanctuary

Rabbah
(Amman)

AMMON

Upper Beth-horon

Bethel

Lower Beth-horon

Mizpah

Jericho

Yarkon River

Gezer

Geba

Heshbon

Ashdod

Aijalon

Ramah

Gibeah

Mt. Nebo

Ekron

Jerusalem

Medeba

Gath

Azekah

Bethlehem

Mareshah

Beth-zur

Tekoa

Ashkelon

Lachish

Dibon

Hebron

Adoraim

Zlph

DEAD SEA

Arnon River

Gaza

Carmel

Gerar

Maon

JUDAH

King's Highway

Kir-hareseth

Beer-sheba

Arad

Negev

MOAB

International Coastal Highway

Wadi el-Arish

Zered River

Tamar

Route of the Patriarchs

Bozrah

Eastern Desert

Kadesh-barnea

EDOM

Wilderness

36 E

ISRAEL IN THE
TIME OF JESUS

- • City
- ○ City (uncertain location)
- ● Decapolis city
- ○ Decapolis city
  (uncertain location)
- ★ Administrative capital
- ▲ Mountain peak
- — Major roads
- — Other roads
- First procuratorship
- Territory of Antipas
- Territory of Philip
- Syrian territory

Coponius was named the first
prefect and established the
administrative capital at
Caesarea Maritima

ABILENE

Sidon

ITUREA

Damascus

PHOENICIA (TYRE)

Mt. Hermon

Abana R.

Pharpar R.

Tyre

Caesarea Philippi
(Panias)

GAULANITIS

Raphana

Cadasa
(Kedesh)

Gischala
(Gush Halavi)

BATANEA

Ptolemais
(Acco)

GALILEE

Capernaum

Bethsaida

Sea of
Galilee

Gergesa (Kursi)

Canatha

Jotapata

Sepphoris

Geba

Nazareth

Tiberias

Hippos

Gamala

Adraa
(Edrei)

Mt. Carmel

Xaloti (Chesulloth)

Mt. Tabor

Gadara

Abila

Legio
(Megiddo)

Jezreel Valley

Scythopolis
(Beth-shan)

AURANITIS

Dora

Kishon R.

Ginae
(Jenin)

Aenon

Pella

Dion

Bostra

Caesarea Maritima
(Strato's Tower)

SAMARIA

Salim

Gerasa
(Jerash)

DECAPOLIS

MEDITERRANEAN
SEA

Sebaste
(Samaria)

Mt. Ebal

Amathus

Apollonia

Mt. Gerizim

Neapolis
(Shechem)

Antipatris
(Aphek)

Coreae

Yarkon R.

Alexandrium

Jabbok R.

Joppa

Ephraim
(Ophrah)

Gedor (Gadara)

Philadelphia (Amman)

Lydda

Archelais

PEREA

Jamnia

Emmaus
(Nicopolis)

Jericho

Cypros

Esbus
(Heshbon)

Azotus
(Ashdod)

Jerusalem

Bethany

Mt. Nebo

Medeba

Ascalon
(Ashkelon)

Betogabris
(Beth-guvrin)

Hyrcania

Mesad Hasidim
(Qumran)

Machaerus

Gaza

Hebron

DEAD
SEA

Callirrhoe
(Zereth-shahar)

Eastern
Desert

Arnon R.

En-gedi

International Coastal Highway

IDUMEA

Masada

Route of the Patriarchs

Arad

King's Highway

Raphia

N. Besor

Beer-sheba

Malatha

NABATEA

Arabah

Zered R.

Khirbet Tannur

0   10   20   30   40   50 Miles

0 10 20 30 40 50 Kilometers

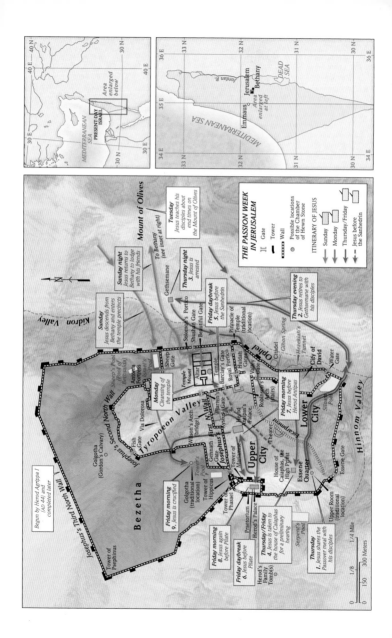

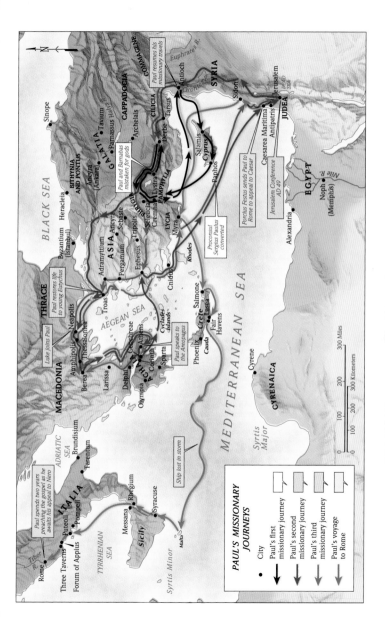

PAUL'S MISSIONARY JOURNEYS

- City
- Paul's first missionary journey
- Paul's second missionary journey
- Paul's third missionary journey
- Paul's voyage to Rome

Paul resumes his missionary travels

Paul and Barnabas mistaken for gods

Proconsul Sergius Paulus converted

Porcius Festus sends Paul to Rome to appeal to Caesar

Jerusalem Conference AD 49

Luke joins Paul

Paul restores life to young Eutychus

Paul speaks to the Areopagus

Ship lost in storm

Paul spends two years preaching the gospel as he awaits his appeal to Nero

BLACK SEA

Sinope
Heraclea
Byzantium (Istanbul)
THRACE

BITHYNIA AND PONTUS
Ancyra (Ankara)
GALATIA
Tavium
Parnassus Halys
CAPPADOCIA
Archelais
COMMAGENE
Euphrates R.

Sebaste
Tripolis
Antioch
Derbe
CILICIA
Tarsus
SYRIA
Orontes R.

Adramyttium
Pergamum
ASIA
Ephesus
PISIDIA
Cremna
PAMPHYLIA
Perga
LYCIA
Myra

Salamis
CYPRUS
Paphos
Sidon

Caesarea Maritima
Antipatris
JUDEA
Jerusalem
Dead Sea

EGYPT
Noph (Memphis)
Nile R.

Alexandria

Troas
AEGEAN SEA
Cnidus
Rhodes
Cyclade Islands

MACEDONIA
Neapolis
Amphipolis
Thessalonica
Berea
Larissa
Delphi
Olympia
ACHAIA
Corinth
Cenchreae
Athens
Sparta

Crete
Salmone
Lasea
Fair Havens
Phoenix
Cauda

MEDITERRANEAN SEA
Cyrene
CYRENAICA
Syrtis Major
Syrtis Minor

ADRIATIC SEA
Brundisium
Tarentum
ITALIA
Puteoli
Pompeii
Three Taverns
Forum of Appius
Rome
Tiber R.

Rhegium
Messana
Sicily
Syracuse
TYRRHENIAN SEA

Malta

0   100   200   300 Miles
0   100   200   300 Kilometers

N

PHOTO AND ART CREDITS

B&H Publishing Group is grateful to the following persons and institutions for use of the graphics in the *Ultimate Bible Guide to Defend Your Faith*. Where we have inadvertently failed to give proper credit for any graphic used in the guide, please contact us (bhcustomerservice@lifeway.com) and we will make the required correction on the next printing.

Photographs/Photographers

David Bjorgen: page 121

HolyLandPhotos.org: page 107, 139 (bottom), 148, 156, 157 (top right), 176 (bottom), 177 (bottom)

iStock: pages 2, 3, 5, 9, 14, 15, 16, 18, 23 (middle right), 29 (bottom right), 30, 31, 32 (bottom left), 35, 36 (middle right; bottom), 37, 40, 41 (bottom), 42, 43 (bottom right), 44, 46 (bottom left), 47, 87, 88 (bottom right), 92 (top center), 95 (center left), 96 (top center), 99 (bottom center), 103 (top left), 104, 105 (top left; bottom), 113 (center left), 115 (bottom right), 123, 127, 130, 134, 136 (center left), 140 (top right), 145, 151 (bottom left); 154 (bottom right), 158, 159, 162, 165 (top left/right), 169 (top right), 173, 175 (bottom left), 176 (top left/right), 177 (top right), 178, 181, 182

NASA: pages 13 (bottom left), 19 (top left images), 20, 25, 122, 128, 161

Wikimedia Commons: pages 59 (bottom left), 61, 63 (bottom), 64, 68, 72, 73, 75, 77, 79 (top left), 80, 81, 90 (top right), 91, 92 (bottom left), 94, 95 (top and bottom left), 96 (bottom left), 97, 98, 99 (top center), 100, 106 (bottom right), 108, 109, 111 (bottom left), 113 (top), 114, 115 (top right), 116 (bottom right), 117, 119 (bottom left), 123, 124, 125, 132 (bottom right), 135, 136 (top left), 146 (top right), 153, 157 (top left)

PAINTINGS/SCULPTURES

ARTISTS

Fra Angelico: page 161
Ashburnham Pentateuch: page 91
Caravaggio: Page 154
Carlo Crivelli: page 17
Giotto: page 155
Gustave Doré: page 167 (bottom right)
El Greco: page 112
Meister von Hohenfurth: page 141
Ingeborg Psalter: page 86
Michelangelo: page 129, 152 (bottom right), 168
Hans Memling: page 133
Don Lorenzo Monaco: page 143
Meister der Palastkapelle: page 152 (top)
Marco dal Pino: page 133
Raphael: page 171
Rembrandt: page 119
Meister der Reichenauer Schule: page 147
Tintoretto: page 160
Meister des Tucher: page 142
Diego Velasquez: page 140